International Sign

The Sociolinguistics in Deaf Communities Series

Ceil Lucas, General Editor

VOLUME 1 Sociolinguistics in Deaf Communities

VOLUME 2 Multicultural Aspects of Sociolinguistics in Deaf Communities

VOLUME 3 Deaf Children in Public Schools

VOLUME 4 Pinky Extension and Eye Gaze: Language Use in Deaf Communities

VOLUME 5 Storytelling and Conversation: Discourse in Deaf Communities

VOLUME 6 Bilingualism and Identity in Deaf Communities

VOLUME 7 Sociolinguistic Variation in American Sign Language

VOLUME 8 Turn-Taking, Fingerspelling, and Contact in Signed Languages

VOLUME 9 Language and the Law in Deaf Communities

VOLUME 10 To the Lexicon and Beyond: Sociolinguistics in European Deaf Communities

VOLUME 11 The Rising of Lotus Flowers: Self-Education by Deaf Children in Thai Boarding Schools

VOLUME 12 Multilingualism and Sign Languages: From the Great Plains to Australia

VOLUME 13 Sign Languages in Contact

VOLUME 14 Hearing, Mother Father Deaf: Hearing People in Deaf Families

VOLUME 15 Extraordinary from the Ordinary: Personal Experience Narratives in American Sign Language

VOLUME 16 Language Policy and Planning for Sign Languages

VOLUME 17 Discourse in Signed Languages

VOLUME 18 Language Attitudes in the American Deaf Community

VOLUME 19 Form, Meaning, and Focus in American Sign Language

VOLUME 20 Teaching and Learning in Bilingual Classrooms: New Scholarship

VOLUME 21 International Sign: Linguistic, Usage, and Status Issues

International Sign

Linguistic, Usage, and Status Issues

Rachel Rosenstock and Jemina Napier, Editors

GALLAUDET UNIVERSITY PRESS

Washington, DC

Sociolinguistics in Deaf Communities

Gallaudet University Press
Washington, DC 20002
http://gupress.gallaudet.edu

Printed in the United States of America

Library of Congress Cataloging-in-Publication Data
ISBN 978-1-56368-656-6; 1-56368-656-2
ISSN 1080-5494

♾ This paper meets the requirements of ANSI/NISO Z39.48-1992
(Permanence of Paper).

Contents

Editorial Advisory Board

Contributors

Brett Best
Independent Researcher
London, United Kingdom

Andy Carmichael
Freelance Interpreter
Scotland, United Kingdom

Pamela F. Collins
Department of Interpretation
Gallaudet University
Washington, DC

Martje Hansen
Department for Sign Language Pedagogy
Humboldt-Universität zu Berlin
Berlin, Germany

Jemina Napier
Department of Languages and Intercultural Studies
Heriot-Watt University
Edinburgh, Scotland, United Kingdom

Joni Oyserman
Department of Linguistics
University of Amsterdam
Amsterdam, The Netherlands

Oliver Pouliot
Overseas Interpreting
Paris, France

Rachel Rosenstock
Department of Applied Linguistics and Intercultural Communication
University of Applied Science Zwickau
Zwickau, Germany

Debra Russell
Department of Educational Psychology
University of Alberta
Calgary, Alberta, Canada

Naomi Sheneman
Department of Interpretation
Gallaudet University
Washington, DC

Irma Sluis
Freelance Interpreter and Independent Researcher
Den Haag, Zuid-Holland, The Netherlands

Christopher Stone
School of Social, Historical and Political Studies
University of Wolverhampton
Wolverhampton, United Kingdom

Lori Whynot
Department of Linguistics
Macquarie University
Sydney, Australia

Maya de Wit
Freelance Sign Language Interpreter and Independent Researcher
Baarn, The Netherlands

International Sign

Introduction: To International Sign or not to International Sign? That Is the Question

Rachel Rosenstock and Jemina Napier

> While thinking of signed languages as a collective "international language" is wrong, this misconception contains a grain of truth: Signed languages seem to allow communication across language boundaries to a degree that is inconceivable in spoken languages. Not surprisingly, this unique linguistic fact has long been part of the heritage of Deaf people, who take pride in being an international community. Transnational communication, as practiced by Deaf people, has come to be known as International Sign (IS). While IS lacks the differentiation and efficiency of well-established national sign languages, it is uniquely successful in allowing Deaf people to overcome linguistic borders, allowing for the development of a sense of connectedness between Deaf people of different origins.
>
> —Signs2Cross, retrieved from http://www.acm5.com/signs2cross/international-sign/

The opening quotation is taken from an introduction to the Signs2Cross project, an online resource to learn International Sign (IS) through the use of natural signed languages (NSLs) that was developed by several European institutions. The project is just one of many resources pointing to increased use of a linguistic phenomenon referred to as *International Sign* in the international Deaf community. A brief webometric analysis of the prevalence of webpages that use this term reveals 450,000 results in Google; "International Sign Language" resulted in another 80,900 hits. A search for "International Sign" on YouTube results in links to 735,000 videos. Other resources and instances of usage include, but are not limited to the following:

- Online IS dictionaries (http://www.sematos.eu/isl.html, http://www.handspeak.com/world/isl/)
- Information presented in IS on webpages (e.g., World Federation of the Deaf webpage, http://wfdeaf.org; 2010 FIFA world cup match results and summaries; announcements about Deaf community events, such as DeafFest in the United Kingdom, https://www.youtube.com/watch?v=RyEfty_LhXw)
- World and current affairs information presented in IS (e.g., H3 TV, http://h3world.tv)
- IS interpretation of cultural events (e.g., 2015 Eurovision Song Contest, https://www.youtube.com/watch?v=H-wJXREikYo)
- Information translated into IS (e.g., United Nations Convention on the Rights of Persons with Disabilities, http://wfdeaf.org/human-rights/crpd)
- Conferences held completely in IS (e.g., the Deaf Academics conference, http://deafacademics2015.com)
- General assemblies, committee meetings, and conferences organized by international Deaf associations (e.g., the European Union of the Deaf, the World Federation of the Deaf, and the Comité International des Sports des Sourdes, CISS)
- IS interpreting at conferences and seminars (e.g., http://www.lesico2-conference-paris.com, WFD, World Association of Sign Language Interpreters)
- Research projects (e.g., http://www.ecml.at/F5/tabid/867/Default.aspx) and training programs (e.g., Frontrunners Deaf Leadership program, http://frontrunners.dk/portfolio/3493/, and the European Masters in Sign Language Interpreting, http://www.eumasli.eu)
- Research projects that directly involve IS (e.g., Signs2Cross, http://signs2cross.signwiki.org/index.php/Main_Page; Insign, http://www.eu-insign.eu)

Increased usage goes hand in hand with the growing recognition of IS in more formal contexts: for example, in 2014, the Association International des Interprètes de Conférence (AIIC) admitted its first sign language interpreter as a member, who provides IS interpreting in European Commission and European Union (EU) parliament meetings (http://aiic.net/page/6866/aiic-s-first-sign-language-member-maya-de-wit/lang/1). Guidelines for remuneration of IS interpreters for World Federation of the Deaf (WFD) and United Nations (UN) events have been implemented (see www.wfdeaf.org/databank/guidelines), and the WFD and the World Association of Sign Language Interpreters (WASLI) established a working group to develop a new joint system for officially recognizing and accrediting IS interpreters to work at the United Nations (UN), in official EU meetings and for official WFD and WASLI business (Turner & Napier, 2014).

Despite these developments, after conducting a survey of self-identified experts, the WFD asserted that it does not recognize IS as a language (Mesch, 2010),[1] and the EUD has also issued a disclaimer to the same effect.[2] Historically, publications on IS are concerned with its evolution, linguistic status, nomenclature, or anecdotal reports on interpretation and functionality of the system. The small number of empirical studies published to date variously call IS a pidgin (Moody, 1994, 2002; McKee & Napier, 2002), a *koine* (Webb & Supalla, 1995), and a contact language (Adam, 2012), or a lingua franca (Rosenstock, 2004), functional terms pointing to the widespread use in the international Deaf community but not defining a linguistic status. Ceil Lucas (personal communication, December 18, 2013) puts it aptly:

> Look at what human beings are willing to do: do some kind of signing, probably different in every venue, and label it IS. . . . [A]s sign linguists, we are used to being told that what we are studying is not a "real language", even though we have ample evidence from description and use that it is; with IS, we now have the opposite: we don't know what it is, really, but people are obviously quite happy to slap a label on it, for a variety of reasons—the need in the community for this variety is probably the main reason—a very interesting turn of sociolinguistic events.

DEFINING INTERNATIONAL SIGN

In the case of IS, practice is ahead of theory, and researchers are struggling to capture the nature of the subject of investigation. Nevertheless,

1. http://wfdeaf.org/wp-content/uploads/2015/03/International-Sign-Fee-Guidelines-for-WFD-Events-Approved-March-2015.pdf

2. http://www.eud.eu/International_Sign_Disclaimer-i-206.html

defining and differentiating factors are starting to be identified. What follows is an overview of key issues in relation to what we *do* know about IS in terms of its history, linguistic structures, function and application, and policy.

History

> Through the language of gestures, which they practice and keep alive, deaf people are able to establish friendly relations across any frontier (British Deaf Association, 1975, p. 1)

Deaf people in the Western and Middle Eastern worlds have gathered together using sign language for 2,000 years (Woll & Ladd, 2003). Stone (2012, p. 981) quotes Michael Miles, who describes the function of deaf-mutes as language brokers in the court system of the Ottoman empire. According to Miles, the Deaf interpreters were brought together from throughout the empire, and thus we can assume that a version of IS was used. Adam (2012, p. 915) refers to Pierre Desloges, who described gatherings of Deaf people from all over Europe in the context of the establishment of the Paris School for the Deaf toward the end of the 18th century, where participants reportedly communicated without difficulties.

The need to standardize an international sign system arose in the context of the founding of institutions and was discussed at the first World Deaf Congress in 1951, when the WFD was formed (McKee & Napier, 2002). In the following years, a form of international signed communication that was mutually intelligible developed as the delegates from different language backgrounds communicated with each other, and in 1973, a WFD committee ("The Commission of Unification of Signs") was established, which sought to create an international language for Deaf people to use (Moody, n.d.). This was done by selecting "naturally spontaneous and easy signs in common use by deaf people of different countries" (British Deaf Association, 1975, p. 2), which were then compiled into a photographic dictionary and published under the title *Gestuno: International Sign Language of the Deaf*. The dictionary contains a vocabulary list of about 1500 signs. The name *Gestuno* was chosen, referencing to gesture and a sense of oneness.

However, when Gestuno was first used at the WFD congress in Bulgaria in 1976, it was incomprehensible to deaf participants (Moody, 2002). The term *Gestuno* fell out of use, and so the book also fell out of favor. Although the Gestuno dictionary has influenced IS lexicon in some contexts (e.g., at the Intenational Committee of Sports for the Deaf (ICSD) and WFD business meetings), it did not standardize the improvised nature of cross-signing as used informally by Deaf people.

Although a form of IS has been used as the political language of Deaf people (for example, in meetings of the WFD) since the 1960s (Moody, n.d.), the use of some kind of internationally understood gestural communication system has existed for much longer. Moody (n.d.) and Scott Gibson and Ojala (1994) have all described international communication amongst Deaf people as early as the beginnings of the 19th century. Initially, this would have been for sporting or cultural events, but as time moved on and Deaf people became more politically organized on a global scale, the use of this communication mode has moved into the Deaf political arena.

After IS interpretation was provided for the first time at a WFD-organized conference in 1976, it was followed by later controversial attempts that were ineffective because Deaf audiences did not understand them (Scott Gibson & Ojala, 1994).

Nonetheless, perseverance has led to the regular provision of IS interpreting at conferences, using a pool of interpreters who are able to interpret effectively using this sign system mixed with gesture and other resources. Since the 1990s, it is rare to attend international Deaf conferences without IS interpretation being provided.

Linguistic Structures

Webb and Supalla (1994) and Supalla and Webb (1995) described the grammatical structures of IS in an attempt to understand its linguistic status. They analyzed presentations given by Deaf people in IS and concentrated their analysis on five types of negation markers, each of which "is used with remarkable consistency and structural regularity" (Webb & Supalla, 1994, p. 181). As a consequence, they surmise that IS is "more grammatically complex than a typical pidgin" (p. 182). They also found that verb agreement and word order are used systematically, in much the same way as natural sign languages. In further research, Supalla and Webb (1995) identified the grammatical use of space as a structure of IS, which is consistent with other sign languages.

Allsop, Woll, and Brauti (1995) identified some lexical and grammatical features of IS in an experimental study of the production of IS by Deaf people of different countries. They found that the duration of a narrative in IS is longer than its equivalent in native sign languages. They also noted that the lexical content varies according to the content of a narrative and whether there is an established IS sign that can be used. If not, signers have to decide whether to use a sign from a natural sign language, mime, or use classifiers. An important conclusion of this study is that users of IS "combine a relatively rich and structured grammar with a severely impoverished lexicon" (1995, p. 187).

McKee and Napier (2002) and Rosenstock (2004, 2008) investigated the features of IS as used by interpreters at international events and found a number of structures drawn from natural signed languages (depiction, use of surrogate and token space, nonmanual adverbials, negation, use of facial expressions for grammatical purposes, etc.) as well as features specific to interpretations of IS (larger signing space, slower production rate, clusters of different signs denoting the same concept).

The source of the IS lexicon has been controversial. Woll (1990) found that 70% of all signs in her IS data (collected exclusively in the United Kingdom) were identical to British Sign Language (BSL) signs. Rosenstock (2004) found a substantial number of signs that were considered common and found in sign languages from both Western and Eastern origins (p. 85ff.). Whynot (2015) based her investigation of the origins of IS on American Sign Language (ASL) and Auslan, as well as the Gestuno dictionary (British Deaf Association, 1975) and compilations of IS signs. Results are reported in this volume.

More recently, Zeshan et al. (2013) and Zeshan (2015) introduce the term *cross-signing* to describe the ad hoc "meaning making" between signers of different linguistic and cultural backgrounds (p. 212). The majority of the 2015 article focuses on the co-construction of meaning; however, the iconic nature of the lexical choices by the participants is discussed in detail.

One of the main issues with discussing linguistic properties of IS (or cross-signing, in the cases of Zeshan et al. 2013 and Zeshan 2015) is the variability of it. While analyses of particular data captured at a particular event of particular presenters or interpreters can provide insights into the idiosyncratic usage of IS and certainly some of the general cognitive processes at work, it is impossible to infer from case studies any generalized properties of a system that might not even be stable enough to be called such, let alone be labeled a pidgin or a language. On the other hand, the instances of IS studied so far reveal a great degree of similarity, something that Newport and Supalla (2000, p. 109) explain: "[C]ross-linguistic research on sign languages does not yet include any languages that are radically different in typology from ASL. In short, whereas each sign language looks like some spoken language of the world, different sign languages thus far look unexpectedly like each other." Studies of IS can thus contribute to a better understanding of cross-linguistic differences and similarities in the visual-gestural modality.

Function and Application

Until the work of McKee and Napier (2002) and Rosenstock (2004), there were no empirical analyses of IS interpreting. Earlier publications by experienced IS interpreters (e.g., Scott Gibson & Ojala 1994; Moody 1994, 2002) reported on necessary skills and strategies used in IS interpretation. In particular, Scott Gibson and Ojala (1994) stated that to interpret competently into IS, knowledge of the linguistic properties of sign languages is essential. In their view, IS interpreters must draw upon these universal sign language constructs, such as localization, verb modification, question forms, facial expression, negation, borrowed signs, and pantomime, and they need to be flexible and creative in their use of IS.

McKee and Napier (2002) confirmed that interpreting into IS requires a free interpretation, in particular reducing lexical density, adding examples or making abstract ideas more concrete, highlighting salient information, and using local contextual knowledge. They conclude:

> The notion of the interpreter as "conduit" thus does not adequately capture the role of IS interpreters, who clearly engage in a complex decision making process as they filter incoming messages with a higher than normal sensitivity to relevance and comprehensibility in relation to the target audience. Given the unusual communication situation of a linguistically heterogeneous audience and the constraints of a pidgin language, free interpretation is certainly the only method by which this task could be approached. (p. 52)

This mentioned comprehensibility of IS has been analyzed empirically in only three studies so far. Rosenstock (2004) and Whynot (2015) attempt to capture the comprehension of interpreted and signed IS respectively. Both reflect that methodologically this is not easy to achieve (see also Rosenstock, this volume). Zeshan (2015) analyzes in detail the meaning making in cross-signing, where comprehension depends on the co-construction and negotiation of meaning. Given that many settings where IS is used are unidirectional, this process of meaning making is essentially relegated to the presenter or interpreter and is based on assumptions of what might or might not be understood by the given audience. The relatively weak scores on comprehension measures (Rosenstock, 2004; Whynot, 2015) strongly suggest the need to rethink the quality and usefulness of IS provision in some contexts (but see Best et al., this volume).

Enhancing both interpreter quality and comprehension of IS can be achieved through teaching the basic principles (in the case of the receiver) or complexities of the linguistic properties (in the case of potential interpreters) of IS. Sources for autodidactic acquisition of IS lexicon or structures are now emerging (see the previous list of IS resources). However, formal training courses or a curriculum for teaching IS are not yet established. There are, however, skilled users of IS who offer classes or workshops (see Oyserman, this volume).

Policy

To date there has been very little exploration of policies in relation to the use of IS. The WFD position paper published in 2010 (Mesch, 2010) and the EUD disclaimer (http://www.eud.eu/International_Sign_Disclaimer-i-206.html) are examples of such policies. Green (2014, p. 445) discusses in more detail the opposing interests of the WFD in regard to language policy and IS. On the one hand, usage of IS is pervasive at WFD events and was determined to be the only means of communication (e.g., at the General Assembly in 2007), practically excluding usage of interpreters into national sign languages. On the other hand, the WFD promotes and supports the recognition of NSLs as part of their mission. Recognizing IS as anything more than a helpful tool in the absence of funds to supply NSL interpreters will endanger the larger goal to promote recognition of NSLs and secure funding for interpreter provision. In fact, Ceil Lucas (personal communication, June 12, 2015) states:

> The apparent need for IS is something that definitely should be explored in more depth—what need do community members, conference organizers, and interpreters think they are meeting and how does this compare to the actual intelligibility and practicality of this entity called IS. In the current climate of the emergence and description of many natural sign languages around the world and in the spirit of diversity and inclusiveness in both hearing and deaf communities, the need may simply be a desire to make sure that everyone is included, that everyone can understand. This is an admirable need, of course, but the studies are showing that IS may not be meeting it. It may be that, for example,

financial support for interpreters of the natural languages at conferences and workshops, for their work and their travel expenses, may be the simplest and best way to ensure that everyone is included and that every language is properly recognized. It may be that that's where conference and workshop resources should go, instead of for the support of IS interpreters. IS may have outlived whatever usefulness it had.

This provocative statement certainly reflects the need to advocate for financial support of NSL interpretation at international events, both as a policy decision and in recognition of the better comprehension of NSLs. Until such time that NSL interpretation is ensured, however, IS is viewed as a solution for inclusion and seems to provide at least a modicum of access. Further exploring the rhetoric around language policies at conferences and in institutions would be a fruitful endeavor to determine attitudes and perceptions of IS.

ORGANIZATION OF THIS VOLUME

This volume brings together a group of contributors who in some capacity are involved in using or investigating IS. A range of Deaf and hearing authors explore a variety of issues with respect to the status, linguistics, and use of IS. To contextualize each of the contributions, the authors were asked to put forth their own definition of IS. In recognition of the many different views, we did not edit the terminology used to denote the phenomena investigated here, and all the authors introduce their own terms. In part 1, we explore the status of IS with a chapter from Martje Hansen, who problematizes the notion of IS and what we mean by it. Part 2 features chapters that focus on linguistic analyses of IS: Lori Whynot analyzes IS lexicon in expository text; Christopher Stone and Debra Russell provide a comparative analysis of depicting signs in IS and NSL interpreting; and Rachel Rosenstock discusses Deaf users' comprehension of expository and interpreted IS. Part 3 includes chapters from contributors who explore how IS is used in context by interpreters and how it can be taught to IS interpreters: Maya de Wit and Irma Sluis focus on the preparation considered necessary by IS interpreters; Brett Best, Jemina Napier, Andy Carmichael, and Oliver Pouliot present a linguistic case study of interpretation from IS into spoken English; Naomi Sheneman and Pamela Collins critically evaluate interpreting at international events; and, finally, Joni Oyserman provides an overview of considerations for teaching IS to interpreters.

A FINAL WORD

There are topics and people missing from this book: policies around IS usage are touched upon in various chapters (most notably de Wit & Sluis, this volume) but there is no comprehensive analysis included. This is due, in part, to the fact that IS policies are just emerging and are as yet mostly limited to the provision of IS as a means of communication at particular events. We also would have liked to include perspectives from researchers, users, and interpreting practitioners from countries in Africa, Asia, the Middle East, or South Africa. While the participation of signers from these regions is increasing at international Deaf events (Mori, 2011), research has yet to emerge. Whynot (this volume) has analyzed data from signers and users of IS from these regions, and we hope more studies focusing on multilingual and multicultural events outside Europe, North America, and Australia will follow.

REFERENCES

Adam, R. (2012). Language contact and borrowing. In R. Pfau, M. Steinbach, & B. Woll (Eds.), *Sign language: An international handbook* (pp. 841–861). Berlin, Germany: De Gruyter Mouton.

Allsop, L., Woll, B., & Brauti, J. M. (1995). International sign: The creation of an international Deaf community and sign language. In *Sign language research 1994: Proceedings of the Fourth European Congress on Sign Language Research, Munich, September 1–3, 1994*. Hamburg, Germany: Signum.

British Deaf Association (BDA). (1975). *Gestuno: International sign language of the Deaf*. Carlisle, UK: British Deaf Association.

Green, E. M. (2014). Building the tower of Babel: International Sign, linguistic commensuration, and moral orientation. *Language in Society, 43*(4), 445–465.

McKee, R., & Napier, J. (2002). Interpreting into international sign pidgin: An analysis. *Journal of Sign Language and Linguistics, 5*(1), 27–54.

Mesch, J. (2010). *Perspectives on the concept and definition of International Sign*. Retrieved from the World Federation of the Deaf website: http://www

.wfdeaf.org/wp-content/uploads/2012/03/Perspectives-on-the-Concept-and-Definition-of-IS_Mesch-FINAL.pdf
Moody, B. (n.d.). [International communication among Deaf people]. Unpublished paper.
Moody, B. (1994, April). International Sign: Language, pidgin, or charades? In *Issues in Interpreting* 2. Conference conducted at the University of Durham, Durham.
Moody, W. (2002). International Sign: A practitioner's perspective. *Journal of Interpretation*, 1–47.
Mori, S. (2011). *IS Interpreter in Asia and Pacific region: From experience as IS Interpreter for JICA-JFD Deaf leadership training programme*. Retrieved from http://efsli.blogspot.de/2011/07/is-interpreter-in-asia-and-pacific.html
Newport, E. L., & Supalla, T. (2000). Sign language research at the millennium. In K. Emmorey & H. Lane (Eds.), *The signs of language revisited: An anthology in Honor of Ursula Bellugi and Edward Klima* (pp. 103–113). Mahwah, NJ: Lawrence Erlbaum.
Rosenstock, R. (2004). *An investigation of international sign: Analyzing structure and comprehension* (Unpublished doctoral dissertation). Gallaudet University, Washington, DC.
Rosenstock, R. (2008). The role of iconicity in international sign. *Sign Language Studies*, *8*(2), 131–159.
Scott Gibson, L., & Ojala, R. (1994, August). *"International Sign" interpreting*. Paper presented at the Fourth East and South African Sign Language Seminar, Uganda.
Stone, C. (2012). Interpreting. In R. Pfau, M. Steinbach, & B. Woll (Eds.), *Sign language: An international handbook* (pp. 980–998). Berlin, Germany: De Gruyter Mouton.
Supalla, T., & Webb, R. (1995). The grammar of international sign: A new look at pidgin languages. In K. Emmorey & J. S. Reilly (Eds.), *Language, Gesture, and Space: International Conference on Theoretical Issues in Sign Language Research* (pp. 333–352). Hillsdale, NJ: Erlbaum.
Turner, G. H., & Napier, J. (2014). On the importance of professional sign language interpreting to political participation. In A. Pabsch (Ed.), *UNCRPD implementation in Europe: A deaf perspective. Article 29: Participation in political and public life* (pp. 54–71). Brussels, Belgium: EUD.
Webb, R., & Supalla, T. (1994). Negation in international sign. In I. Ahlgren, B. Bergman, & M. Brennan (Eds.), *Perspectives on sign language structure: Papers from the Fifth International Symposium on Sign Language Research* (pp. 173–185). Durham: ISLA.
Whynot, L. A. (2015). *Assessing comprehension of international sign lectures: Linguistic and sociolinguistic factors* (Unpublished doctoral dissertation). Macquarie University, Sydney.

Woll, B. 1990. International perspectives on sign language communication. *International Journal of Sign Linguistics, 1*(2), 107–120.

Woll, B., & Ladd, P. (2003). Deaf communities. In M. Marschark and P. Spencer (Eds.), *The handbook of Deaf studies, language, and education* (pp. 151–163). Oxford, UK: Oxford University Press.

Zeshan, U. (2015). "Making meaning": Communication between sign language users without a shared language. *Cognitive Linguistics, 26*(2), 211–260.

Zeshan, U., Sagara, K., & Bradford, A. (2013, July). *Multilingual and multimodal aspects of "cross-signing": A study of emerging communication in the domain of numerals*. Poster presentation at TISLR 11, DCAL, London. Retrieved from http://www.ucl.ac.uk/dcal/tislr/tislr-programme

Part I **Status**

What Is International Sign?

The Linguistic Status of a Visual

Transborder Communication Mode

Martje Hansen

When discussing the linguistic status of International Sign (IS), first I have to specify what *language* means. Many linguists feel uneasy when talking about IS as a language, because it displays conflicting characteristics. Is IS a language system comparable to American Sign Language (ASL) or German Sign Language (DGS)? Probably not. With the use of different unconventional iconic elements, IS is quite different from national sign languages that possess a standardized lexicon and grammar. Nevertheless, IS is surely not a kind of universal language understood in the same way and to the same extent by signers all over the world. Sign languages have been grouped into families,[1] and the Eastern sign language family (Japanese Sign Language, Korean Sign language, etc.) shows quite different features than Western sign languages, for example, in relation to the use and forms of classifiers or facial expressions (cf. Fischer & Gong, 2010, p. 516ff.), and IS used during conferences in Europe or the United States is difficult to understand for nonwestern signers (cf. Mori, 2011).

Looking at essential characteristics of language, I find many features that apply to IS as well as to national sign languages. In the conference about language universals in 1961, C. F. Hockett listed a set of criteria for language—that is, if a communicative system has all features of the set, "it is proposed we call it a language" (Hockett, 1963, p. 2). I find that most of his criteria are valid for IS communications:

1. See, for example, Fischer and Gong (2010) and other articles in Brentari (2010), wherein sign languages are grouped by single linguistic features and geographical criteria. A thorough discussion about sign languages in a typological perspective is given by Zeshan (2006) and Zeshan et al. (2013).

We can consider the following *defining set for language*: openness (2.11), displacement (2.10), duality (2.13), arbitrariness (2.8), discreteness (2.9), interchangeability (2.4), complete feedback (2.5), specialization (2.6), rapid fading (2.3), and broadcast transmission with directional reception (2.2). Any system that has these ten properties will here be called a language; any language manifested by our own species will be called a human language. Every language also has semanticity (2.7), since the contrast between arbitrariness (2.8, included in the defining set) and iconicity is meaningless without it. Presumably, but not so clearly, every language has prevarication (2.14) and reflexiveness (2.15); at least, every human language does. (Hockett, 1963 p. 12; emphasis added).

Hockett explains in detail the relationship among semanticity, arbitrariness, and discreteness, criteria that are particularly relevant for IS:

2.7. Semanticity: Linguistic signals function in correlating and organizing the life of a community because there are associative ties between signal elements and features in the world; in short, some linguistic forms have denotations. The distension by roe of the belly of the female stickleback, is part of an effective signal, but does not "stand for" something else.

2.8. Arbitrariness: The relation between a meaningful element in language and its denotation is independent of any physical or geometrical resemblance between the two. Or, as we say, the semantic relation is *arbitrary* rather than *iconic*. There are marginal exceptions, including traces of onomatopoeia. In bee dancing, the way in which the direction towards the target site is mapped into a direction of dancing is iconic. The relation between a landscape painting and a landscape is iconic; the relation between the word *landscape* and a landscape is arbitrary.

2.9. Discreteness: The possible messages in any language constitute a discrete repertory rather than a continuous one. Any utterance in a language must differ from any other utterance of the same length by at least a whole phonological feature. Utterances cannot be indefinitely similar to one another. Bee-dances can be: the repertory of possible dances constitutes a twofold continuum. In a continuous semantic system (one with property 2.7 but with the converse of 2.9), the semantics must be iconic rather than arbitrary. But in a discrete semantic system, there is no necessary implication as to iconicity or arbitrariness;

therefore, for language, 2.8 is independent of 2.7 and 2.9. (Hockett, 1963, pp. 8f.; emphasis in the text)

Hockett considered only spoken languages in contrast to animal communication systems when defining this set of criteria for human language, and therefore some features such as arbitrariness (Hockett did not consider the possibility of a mixture of arbitrary and iconic elements, apart from some onomatopoeia in spoken languages; cf. ibid., p. 8) or broadcast transmission (due to the nature of sound waves) have to be modified in relation to signed languages. On a theoretical level, he did not exclude languages using other channels than the vocal-auditory one, thus admitting implicitly the status of language also to sign languages (cf. ibid., p. 15, where he excludes explicitly the criterion "Every human language has the vocal-auditory channel" from the list of defining set). The duality (of patterning) applies only partially to IS and a little more to national sign languages, where we find an interplay of dually constructed semiotic signs and gestural components. Nevertheless, IS conforms to most of these criteria, and thus it might be possible to conclude that IS is a language.

On the other hand, I consider a language to be a relatively stable object, at least stable in relation to a specific regional, historical, and social area (i.e., a signing community in a geographically definable area at a certain point in time). IS does not fit into this concept: It is not the native language of a Deaf community, transmitted from parents to children and peers to peers. It is used only in specific moments and in varying locations, when Deaf people with different native sign languages gather; every participant switches to his or her native sign language when conversing with members of his own sign language community or leaving the meeting. Furthermore, we may have to differentiate between the IS used during international meetings and conferences and the IS used during informal encounters of Deaf people while traveling. The former IS has been the object of most of the literature about IS and especially the research of Rosenstock (2004) and Whynot (this volume). The IS created and used during informal meetings while traveling (called "cross-signing" by Zeshan, Keiko, & Bradford, 2013; Zeshan, 2015) is much more difficult to capture and related research has just started.

So we may consider IS a mixed language, arising between signers of different sign language communities. For spoken languages, this phenomenon has been widely discussed in relation to pidgin and creole languages. Spoken pidgins display relatively simple linguistic structures in order to facilitate the communication in particular situations such as trading: they display simple phonological, morphological, and syntactic structures and a reduced lexicon, and they use a lot of paraphrases and metaphors (cf., e.g., Holm, 1988/1989). Often, pidgins based on spoken languages came into being as a result of colonialism, when the European language of colonialists was imposed on indigenous speakers; the particular lexicon and grammar mirrored power relations, with "the more powerful language becoming the primary lexifier language of a power pidgin" (Mühläusler, 1996, p. 642); when contact due to trade was the base of cross-linguistic communication, the resulting forms may be labeled "egalitarian pidgins" that "come close to the common core or fifty-fifty languages" (p. 644). Pidgins may differ structurally according to linguistic, social, and historic factors, but generally speaking, scholars distinguish an initial form based on individual strategies (*jargon*), which can develop into a *stable pidgin*, giving way to *expanded pidgins*, which are very close to first language creoles (p. 643). Pidgin and creole studies have developed strongly during the past two decades; while the original studies on pidgins were focused on those with a lexicon related to a European language, today, we find descriptions of pidgins and creoles based on non-European languages, such as Pidgin Hindustani (see APiCS online for further information and examples).[2]

Some linguists (e.g., Moody, 2002, p. 37; McKee & Napier, 2002; with some reservations, Supalla & Webb, 1995) adopted the term *pidgin* to characterize IS, making reference to the traditional concept of mixed languages that developed due to the contact between two or more spoken languages.[3]

However, the label *pidgin* does not apply very well to IS. Especially when IS is used during informal encounters, it does not display a stable lexicon; apart from a very small conventionalized number of lexemes used in formal international meetings (cf. Adam, 2012, p. 853), we find signs borrowed from the various native sign languages of the participants, ad hoc signs, paraphrases, depicting classifier constructions, pointing, and constructed action (cf. Rosenstock, 2004; Whynot, 2013). Thus, the existence of a fixed IS lexicon is questionable. Contrary to the morphosyntactical structures of spoken pidgins, the morphosyntactical structures

2. http://apics-online.info, accessed July 15, 2015.

3. I do not consider bimodal forms of contact signing like the one arising between ASL and English, which was described and discussed by Lucas and Valli (1992).

of IS communications are quite complex, especially the use of space to convey grammatical information, which is found to be as in national sign languages. Nevertheless, complex sentences are rare, and the grammatical use of facial expressions seems to be reduced (cf. Rosenstock, 2004).

The first systematic use of IS during an international meeting took place in 1975. The British Deaf Association and the World Federation of the Deaf (WFD) collected a list of basic signs and edited a photographic lexicon called *Gestuno: The International Sign Language of the Deaf*. Many Deaf signers criticized the signs because they were "not iconic enough to be readily understood" (Moody, 2002, p. 16). The use of Gestuno during a congress of the WFD in Bulgaria in 1979 resulted in a communicative disaster because the interpreters did not make use of the signing space, constructed action, or facial expression.

Hiddinga and Crasborn (2011, p. 492ff.) point to the fact that the use of IS is strongly dependent on the situation and the signers (their national sign language, their cultural and social background), resulting in very heterogeneous forms, which cannot be compared to the relatively fixed pidgins based on spoken languages. Furthermore, we do not know of any Deaf group using IS as its main means of communication, by which IS would have potential to develop into a kind of creole language.

Supalla and Webb (1995) considered the similarities between the European and the North American sign languages on the morphosyntactic level and discussed the possibility that IS might be a kind of *koiné*. In their view (this is also discussed by Moody [2002, p. 26] and Adam [2012, p. 854]), morphological constructions of European sign languages could have transferred to IS because of their similarities:

> International Sign was influenced very little by contact with South American, Asian, or African sign languages at the time that we collected our data. We therefore assume in this chapter that it has developed within the European community, with some contact with North Americans. (Supalla & Webb, 1995, p. 348)

The authors considered the historical relations between these sign languages in combination with the iconic resources of the visual modality to be the basis of the communicative power of IS, but a *koiné* is defined as an originally regional variant in a linguistic area with several interrelated dialects. One of these regional variants loses its specific, regional features due to language contact and becomes the generally accepted mode of communication in this area. This was the case for the dialect of Athens in the fourth century BC. At first sight, ASL may be a possible candidate for a *koiné* within the Western sign languages: Rosenstock (2004) found that 53% of all signs originated from the Western sign language family and many of these were (also) ASL signs[4]; Whynot (2013) found a share of 34% of ASL signs. In other IS communications with signers from other countries, other shares of national signs can be assumed to be used, so stating that IS is based on an originally national sign language used more by signers of other sign languages is problematic, and thus the term *koiné* does not fit its characteristics.

Notwithstanding all arguments against the classification of IS as a pidgin, creole, or *koiné,* we find some striking structural similarities between national sign languages and spoken pidgins and creole languages, even when these are used in the territory of different national spoken languages. Adone (2012) discusses the hypothesis that national sign languages are creole languages based on pidgins that are rooted in home-sign systems. Home signing starts when deaf children communicate with their hearing parents and becomes a more complex system when used constantly with deaf siblings or peers, constituting a signed pidgin.[5] This form of pidgin becomes the native language of the following generations, giving rise to fully developed sign languages. This idea was discussed in the 1970s and 1980s with regard to national signed languages (cf. Fischer, 1978; Woodward, 1978; Gee & Goodheart, 1988). On the one hand, this approach may explain the relatively similar grammatical systems among Western sign languages (and consequently the adoption of many morphological features in IS communication) and their similarities with spoken pidgins and creoles.

Relating this concept to the debate about IS, Supalla and Webb (1995) discuss the classification of national sign languages as creoles and the reasoning that IS may constitute a hybrid language based on signed creoles:

4. "The relative high score of the LATE group in this study (59% correct answers) suggests that the advantage of knowing ASL vocabulary and structure outweighs the lack of native competence. In a future study, an inclusion of late learners of a SL unrelated to European SLs or ASL would provide more insights into the comprehension of late learners in general" (Rosenstock, 2004, p. 248ff.)

5. It is quite evident that the use of the term *pidgin* for any kind of signed language rooted in home signing can refer only to structural similarities with spoken pidgins. Signed languages are native languages of the signers, which is not the case for speakers of pidgins.

> First, most sign language users are first generation users of the language, and therefore, their native signing children often acquire it as a creole. . . . Sign languages are thus never many generations away from their pidgin /creole origins, and this may account for their similarity in structure to creoles. (Supalla & Webb, 1995, p. 348)

However, the authors do not exclude the possibility that either the historical relatedness of the European and North American signed languages or the constraints of the visual modality may be an explanation for these similarities (cf. ibid.).

Considering all these findings and arguments, IS can be termed as a kind of lingua franca used to overcome linguistic barriers. This functional term is uncontroversial, but at the same time noncommittal. It grasps the communicative function of IS without saying anything about its linguistic status.

IS AS A DYNAMIC PROCESS

A definition of the linguistic status of IS seems to be difficult, when we think only in terms of the Saussurian concept of *langue*, i.e., a language system of elements and rules derived from the utterances of its users (cf. Saussure, 1916/1975, pp. 104ff.). A fixed set of lexemes and a set of rules how to combine them are difficult to extract from the acts of signed communication we encounter in bi- and multilateral encounters of Deaf people. We can isolate some signs, which are found often in IS communication, and we find some regularities and constructions similar to the ones used in several national sign languages, but it seems impossible to derive from these observations a set of rules valid for all occasions when IS is used. All the same, IS communication is functional. IS is being used at international meetings such as WFD Congresses and events such as the Deaflympics (see http://wfdeaf.org/our-work/focus-areas/sign-language). Furthermore, many international conferences involving sign language issues offer two conference languages: English and IS (e.g., the International Gesture Conference, 2016, in Paris, retrieved from http://isgs7.sciencesconf.org/?lang=en). Other conferences offer IS in addition to national sign languages interpreting.

Moody (2002) discusses several issues, which may explain the regularities found in IS communication. Apart from the historical relations between the Western sign languages, which might be responsible for many similarities, he classifies sign languages as "young languages," still close to their "mimetic/iconic roots of languages in the visual/gestural modality" (ibid., p. 27). He closes his overview with some advice for professional interpreters when working with IS. These suggestions indicate that IS is a communicative resource, heavily based on situational and cultural contexts, and used by people who are familiar with communication in the visual modality (cf. ibid., pp. 33ff.).

Stressing the context dependency, Adam (2012, p. 854) labels IS "situational pidgin." Zeshan (2015, p. 212) uses "jargon," stressing the fact that IS or "cross-signing" may give new insights into the development of (pre)pidgins. Hiddinga and Crasborn (2011, p. 484) describe IS not as "an established contact language, but a mode of communication that arises on the spot, which combines elements of the sign languages of the people involved, elements of shared spoken languages, and the intensified use of iconic or pantomimic structures that are already inherent to various extents in any sign language."

The authors summarize comments of IS users that IS does not achieve the same communicative function as national sign languages, but they stress the point that it demonstrates the visual and communicative creativity of signers.

So, even if we cannot determine the language system of IS, IS demonstrates surely the properties of *langage*, the human language capacity. The human capacity to communicate by symbolic means (even if some elements are iconic and gradient) is not restricted to the actualization/realization (*parole*) of a language system (*langue*, cf. Saussure, 1916/1975, p. 27ff.). When we start to think on the level of *langage*, keeping in mind Humboldt, who was the first to distinguish between language as a process and language as a product (he introduced the terms *ergon*, language as a product, and *energeia*, the activity of communicating via linguistic means),[6] we may elaborate an understanding of human communication

6. Cf. Mueller-Vollmer (2011): "It is not identical with the distinction introduced by Saussure between *langue* and *parole*, since Humboldt's distinction cuts across both *langue* and *parole* and both can be seen from the angle of either process or product. . . . Thus he distinguished sharply (as did his contemporary Schleiermacher) before Saussure and twentieth-century linguistics, between language (*Sprache*) and speech (*Rede*). In his French essay of 1811 he also uses Saussure's third term, *langage*, in a similar manner as pertaining to language in a general sense."

as a dynamic process. This perspective requires a broader understanding of language and linguistics.[7]

As linguists, we think mainly on the level of *langues*, language systems. But these language systems are based ontogenetically as well as phylogenetically on our *langage*, human language capacity. Adopting a broader perspective including *langage*, we may discuss IS as a linguistic activity (and its resulting forms) situated between the human language capacity and a language system: it is a communicative resource and it results in highly adaptive forms in relation to very different situations and users. Something similar may occur when pidgins or other contact forms between hearing people arise. The acoustic mode is much less adaptable to new communicative situations, but even there, something similar happens.

A specific form of language contact is discussed by Klein and Perdue (1997) and Klein (2001). In a large project, the learner varieties of 40 adult hearing learners were analyzed. The source languages consisted of Punjabi, Italian, Turkish, Moroccan, Arabic, and Spanish. The target languages were English, German, Swedish, Dutch, and French. The adults did not receive any language lessons, but learned the target languages in daily life communication. The authors found that

> all 40 learners investigated developed a relatively stable system to express themselves which:
>
> - seemed to be determined by the interaction of a small number of organizational principles,
> - was largely (though not totally) independent of the specifics of source and target language organization,
> - was simple, versatile, and highly efficient for most communicative purposes. This system we call the Basic Variety (henceforth BV). (Klein & Perdue, 1997, p. 303)

Notwithstanding the differences between the source and target languages of these 40 learners, the authors find structural similarities: some basic constraints determining the utterance structure, such as, a phrasal constraint, which results in three constructions, NP_1-V-(NP_2), NP_1-COP-NP_2/PP, and V/COP-NP_2; a semantic constraint, which results in the first position for NP with the highest control (the controller of source state outweighs controller of target state); and a pragmatic constraint, which

7. Cf. the monograph of Oesterreicher (1979) or the (brief) introduction to the different meanings of *langage, langue,* and *parole* by Klein (2001).

puts a topical referent in the first position. If the referent is in focus, we find a V-NP construction.

Klein and Perdue find quite a lot of temporal adverbials, such as these:

> (a) the calendric-type adverbials (Sunday, in the evening); (b) anaphoric adverbials expressing the relation AFTER (then, after), and also typically an adverbial which expresses the relation BEFORE; (c) some deictic adverbials such as yesterday, now; (d) a few frequency adverbials, notably always, often, two time, etc.; (e) a few durational adverbials, normally as bare nouns, such as two hour, etc. Temporal adverbials involving two reference points such as again, still, already do not belong to the standard repertoire of the BV. (Klein & Perdue, 1997, p. 320ff.)

Furthermore, they find signals for indicating the beginning or the end of a situation talked about like "work finish" and "after work is / was / will be over" (ibid., p. 321). Temporal adverbials are located at the beginning of an utterance; if the utterance is without a temporal indication, the current time of speech is intended (ibid.).

> Under this perspective, learner varieties are not imperfect imitations of a "real language"—the target language—but systems in their own right, error-free by definition, and characterized by a particular lexical repertoire and by a particular interaction of organizational principles. Fully developed languages, such as English, German, French, are simply borderline cases of learner varieties. They represent a relatively stable state of language acquisition. (Klein & Perdue, 1997, p. 307ff.)

The learner varieties are not simply transitional forms between a first and a second language but constitute also a resort to basic principles of language constructions that results in a simple and efficient linguistic form. The lexicon and the composition rules of this basic variety (BV) display many similarities to pidgin and creole languages and the authors ask

> Is the BV a "real language", or is it just a kind of more or less rudimentary protoform? Stated in this way, the question is hardly answerable, because the notion of "real language" is anything but clearly defined. The BV is a highly efficient system of communication, and in this sense, it is surely a real language; at the same time, it lacks some of the structural characteristics which we typically find in fully-fledged languages. (Klein & Perdue 1997, p. 333)

The authors suppose some similarities between the basic variety and pidgins, such as the lack of inflectional morphology, but they stress that "pidgins have hardly ever been systematically investigated with respect to organising principles of the type discussed . . . above. Therefore, all we can say at this point is that there are certainly similarities, but it is quite unclear how deep-reaching these are" (Klein & Perdue, 1997, p. 340). In relation to the basic variety, the morphological structure of IS communication seems to be more complex; many findings especially in relation to the lexicon seem to relate more to national sign languages like ASL or DGS (which supports the claims of Supalla & Webb, 1995, or Adone, 2012). However, the basic semantic and pragmatic constraints found in the rules of composition of the basic variety might probably be found in IS too.

Because of its iconic resources, the visual mode is more apt than the acoustic mode to create linguistic forms that may overcome linguistic barriers—a very interesting example of hearing people[8] creating a system of visual communication is the sign language of the Plains Indians. Moody (2002, p. 13ff.) refers to reports that Garrick Mallery brought some Ute Indians to Gallaudet, who communicated with Deaf people relatively easily. By reading Mallery thoroughly, however, it becomes quite clear that we cannot speak of one sign language of the North American Indians:

> But it happened that there was a delegation of Absaroka (Crows) at the same hotel, and the two parties from such widely separated regions, not knowing a word of each other's language, immediately began to converse in signs, resulting in a decided sensation. One of the Crows asked the Apaches whether they ate horses, and it happening that the sign for eating was misapprehended for that known by the Apaches for many, the question was supposed to be whether the latter had many horses, which was answered in the affirmative. Thence ensued a misunderstanding on the subject of hippophagy, which was curious both as showing the general use of signs as a practice and the diversity in special signs for particular meanings. (1881, p. 328)

Mallery shows quite clearly that the sign language of the Indians was not so much one language but the capacity to communicate in the visual mode:

8. Other secondary sign languages used by Aboriginals in Australia or monks in certain cloisters are not used to communicate with members of other language communities (cf. Pfau, 2012).

> An Indian skilled in signs, as also a deaf-mute, at the sight of a new object, or at the first experience of some new feeling or mental relation, will devise some mode of expressing it in pantomimic gesture or by a combination of previously understood signs, which will be intelligible to others, similarly skilled, provided that they have seen the same objects or have felt the same emotions. (1881, p. 388)

His reflections about the way visual communication between the Indian tribes is functioning, are quite clear sighted:[9]

> An argument for the uniformity of the signs of our Indians is derived from the fact that those used by any of them are generally understood by others. But signs may be understood without being identical with any before seen. The entribal as well as intertribal exercise of Indians for generations in gesture language has naturally produced great skill both in expression and reception, so as to render them measurably independent of any prior mutual understanding. (p. 332)

IS is not comparable to a language system; its versatility hinders the fixing of a lexicon and a grammar. But when we look at IS not as a static object but as a dynamic process based on our human language capacity, new questions arise that transcend the traditional borders of linguistics. The classical approach of language analysis may be useful to a limited extent when we focus on the IS forms used during formal international meetings for monologues such as addresses of welcome or lectures and the related interpretations, which after some days tend to be partially conventionalized, and which constitute the basis for further conventionalization in following meetings when the same people meet again. During informal meetings on a private basis, an even more versatile form of IS arises. In ongoing friendships, the IS forms used will likely also become more negotiated, but every newcomer with another national sign language refuels the process of lexical negotiations and trial-and-error processes for iconic and arbitrary communication. Both forms of IS contain basically the same or at least similar mechanisms to secure the communicative process.

When Deaf signers with different language backgrounds meet for the first time, the communicative negotiation process starts immediately,

9. We may speculate that the ability of hearing Indians to communicate with signs might have been rooted in the existence of home-sign systems in the different tribes due to deafness of some tribe members, maybe giving rise to some kind of village sign language.

making use of all resources available to create an intersubjective cognitive space:

> the communicative situation in cross-signing may best be viewed as a process of dynamic interaction between three multilingual-multimodal spaces: each signer's own space, and an intersubjective space that is shared between the two participants. At the beginning of data collection for cross-signing, each participant comes to the table with his or her own multilingual-multimodal space, which includes all the gestural, written, spoken and signed languages, and modes that the individuals have experienced in their lifetime. . . . During the interaction, a shared multi-lingual-multimodal space is created and successively enriched with linguistic structures and other strategies. As participants become increasingly familiar with each other, the shared space expands and includes more and more communicative resources, while discarding failed communicative attempts. (Zeshan, 2015, p. 236)

Zeshan (2015) analyzes first meetings of Deaf signers from different countries and cultures without any common language. Because of methodological considerations, the study focuses on numerals. Apart from the resources used during these encounters, she also analyzes the interactional mechanisms used to introduce new lexemes, back-channeling signals to communicate understanding or misunderstanding, the function of repetition of lexemes, and constructions and variation within these repetitions. Post hoc introspective interviews give evidence that

> all participants continuously entertain multiple simultaneous hypotheses, both about what their interlocutor is likely to understand (which then, in turn, influences the choices in their own signed output), and about the likely meaning of what their interlocutor is signing to them. (Zeshan, 2015, p. 248)

This study shows in a very convincing way what we may gain when we undertake more than the collection and analysis of lexical and morphological relevant IS elements and their rules of combination (without denying the necessity to do also this kind of research). An analysis of IS communication that comprises cognitive interactional issues can be related to studies about the origin of human communication; for example, Tomasello (2008), who claimed that the human capacity to communicate is based first of all on the ability to create a joint or shared intentionality:

> And what about language? The current hypothesis is that it is only within the context of collaborative activities in which participants share intentions and attention, coordinated by natural forms of gestural communication, that arbitrary linguistic conventions could have come into existence evolutionarily. Conventional languages (first signed and then vocal) thus arose by piggybacking on these already understood gestures, substituting for the naturalness of pointing and pantomiming a shared (and mutually known to be shared) social learning history (p. 9f).

This base of shared intentionality is not only necessary in first (and second) language acquisition, it is (inter alia) also the base of IS. Another fruitful perspective might arise from considering current gesture studies, even if the tackling with methodological problems concerning the border between gestural and linguistic elements in signed communication is still at its very beginning.

CONCLUSION

The visual mode is more apt than the acoustic mode to convey information iconically, thus functioning even between hearing nonsigners, who retreat to gestural communication and pantomime, if necessary. To understand this kind of basic human communication, it is useful to keep in mind the distinction between language as a product (*ergon*) and an activity (*energeia*) introduced by Humboldt. Both concepts rely on our human language capacity, termed later by Saussure as *langage*. Like the spoken basic variety, analyzed by Klein and Perdue (2001), I propose seeing IS as an outcome of our language capacity, to be situated somewhere on the line of development between *langage* and *langue*. Obviously, IS as a visual communication mode is much more functional from its very beginning than a spoken communication.

When IS is used repeatedly in the same meetings or conferences by the same people, IS as an outcome/product will be closer to *langue*; on the other end of the spectrum, it will be relatively close to *langage* when used for the first time and/or for varying topics. The process of developing into a partially conventionalized system or the return to the very base of human communication including the use of all available individual, cultural, and situational resources are based on, and fueled by, the Humboldtian energeia.

ACKNOWLEDGMENT

I sincerely thank Jens Hessmann for many rich discussions about IS and valuable comments on this text.

REFERENCES

Adam, R. (2012). Language contact and borrowing. In R. Pfau, M. Steinbach, & B. Woll (Eds.), *Sign language: An international handbook* (pp. 841–862). Berlin, Germany: Mouton de Gruyter.

Adone, D. (2012). Language emergence and creolisation. In R. Pfau, M. Steinbach, & B. Woll (Eds.), *Sign language: An international handbook* (pp. 862–889). Berlin, Germany: Mouton de Gruyter.

Brentari, D. (2010). *Sign languages.* Cambridge, UK: Cambridge University Press.

Fischer, S. (1978). Sign languages and creoles. In P. Siple (Ed.), *Understanding language through sign language research* (pp. 309–331). New York, NY: Academic Press.

Fischer, S., & Gong, Q. (2010). Variation in East Asian sign language structures. In D. Brentari (Ed.), *Sign languages* (pp. 499–518). Cambridge, UK: Cambridge University Press.

Gee, J. P., & Goodheart, W. (1988). American Sign Language and the human biological capacity for language. In M. Strong (Ed.), *Language learning and deafness* (pp. 49–74). Cambridge, UK: Cambridge University Press.

Hiddinga, A., & Crasborn, O. (2011). Signed languages and globalization. In *Language in Society, 40*, 483–505.

Hockett, C. F. (1963). The problems of universals in language. In J. H. Greenberg (Ed.), *Universals of language: Report of a conference held at Dobbs Ferry, New York, April 13–15, 1961* (pp. 1–22). Cambridge, MA: MIT Press. Retrieved from https://ia600603.us.archive.org/18/items/universalsoflangoounse/universalsoflangoounse.pdf

Holm, J. (1988/1989). *Pidgins and creoles.* Cambridge, UK: Cambridge University Press.

Humboldt, W. von. (1963). *Schriften zur Sprachphilosophie: Werke in fünf Bänden.* Darmstadt, Germany: Wissenschaftliche Buchgesellschaft.

Klein, W., & Perdue, C. (1997). The basic variety; Or, couldn't natural languages be much simpler? In *Second Language Research, 13*, 301–347.

Klein, W. (2001). Elementary forms of linguistic organization. In S. Ward & J. Trabant (Eds.), *New essays on the origins of language* (pp. 81–102). Berlin, Germany: Mouton de Gruyter.

Lucas, C., & Valli, C. (1992). *Sociolinguistic variation in American Sign Language.* New York, NY: Academic Press.

Mallery, G. (1881). Sign language among North American Indians compared with that among other peoples and deaf-mutes. In J. W. Powell (Ed.), *First annual report of the Bureau of Ethnology to the Secretary to the Smithsonian Institution 1879–1889* (pp. 263–552). Washington, DC: US Government Printing Office. Retrieved from http://www.gutenberg.org/files/17451/17451-h/17451-h.htm

McKee, R., & Napier, J. (2002). Interpreting into international sign pidgin: An analysis. *Journal of Sign Language and Linguistics, 5*(1), 27–54.

Moody, B. (2002). International Sign: A practitioner's perspective. *Journal of Interpretation*, 1–47.

Mori, S. (2011). IS interpreter in Asia and Pacific region: From experience as IS interpreter for JICA-JFD Deaf leadership training programme. Retrieved from http://efsli.blogspot.de/2011/07/is-interpreter-in-asia-and-pacific.html

Mühlhäusler, P. (1996). Pidginization. In H. Goebl, P. H. Nelde, & Z. Starý (Eds.), *Kontaktlinguistik* (pp. 642–649). Berlin, Germany: Mouton de Gruyter.

Mueller-Vollmer, K. (2011). Wilhelm von Humboldt. In E. N. Zalta (Ed.), *The Stanford encyclopedia of philosophy*. Retrieved from http://plato.stanford.edu/archives/fall2011/entries/wilhelm-humboldt/

Oesterreicher, W. (1979). *Sprachtheorie und Theorie der Sprachwissenschaft.* Heidelberg, Germany: Carl Winter Universitätsverlag.

Pfau, R. (2012). Manual communication systems: Evolution and variation. In R. Pfau, M. Steinbach, & B. Woll (Eds.), *Sign language: An international handbook* (pp. 513–551). Berlin, Germany: Mouton de Gruyter.

Rosenstock, R. (2004). *An investigation of international sign: Analyzing structure and comprehension* (Unpublished doctoral dissertation). Gallaudet University, Washington, DC.

Saussure, F. de. (1916/1975). *Cours de linguistique générale*, T. de Mauro (Ed.). Paris, France: Payot.

Supalla, T., & Webb, R. (1995). The grammar of International Sign: A new look at pidgin languages. In K. Emmorey & J. S. Reilly (Eds.), *Language, gesture, and space* (pp. 333–352). Hillsdale, NJ: Lawrence Erlbaum.

Tomasello, M. (2008). *Origins of human communication.* Cambridge, MA: MIT Press.

Whynot, L. (2013). *International Sign lexical frequency and distribution by sign type* (Working Paper). Sydney, Australia: Department of Linguistics, Macquarie University.

Woodward, J. (1978). Historical bases of ASL. In P. Siple (Ed.), *Understanding language through sign language research* (pp. 333–348). New York, NY: Academic Press.

Zeshan, U. (2006). Roots, leaves, and branches—The typology of sign languages. In R. M. de Quadros (Ed.), *Sign languages: Spinning and unraveling the past, present, and future: Theoretical Issues in Sign Language Research Conference, Florianopolis, Brazil, December 2006*. Petrópolis, Brazil: Editora Arara Azul. Retrieved from http://www.editora-arara-azul.com.br/ebooks/catalogo/48.pdf

Zeshan, U. (2013). Sign languages. In M. S. Dryer & M. Haspelmath (Eds.), *The world atlas of language structures online*. Leipzig, Germany: Max Planck Institute for Evolutionary Anthropology. Retrieved from http://wals.info/chapter/s9

Zeshan, U. (2015). Making meaning: Communication between sign language users without a shared language. In *Cognitive Linguistics, 26* (2), 211–260.

Zeshan, U., Keiko, S., & Bradford, A. (2013, July). *Multilingual and multimodal aspects of "cross-signing"—A study of emerging communication in the domain of numerals*. Poster session presented at TISLR 11, London, UK. Retrieved from http://www.ucl.ac.uk/dcal/tislr/tislr-programme

Part II **Linguistics**

Telling, Showing, and Representing: Conventions of the Lexicon in International Sign Expository Text

Lori Whynot

"International Sign" (IS) is an underresearched form of sign language contact that serves as a de facto lingua franca for globalizing deaf communities. In recent years, it is increasingly recruited and promoted as an official "language" at international conferences pertaining to Deaf communities, interpreting, sign language academia, and sports. Notably, there is a lack of consensus about the linguistic status of IS (Mesch, 2010) and there is no standard definition to discuss IS phenomena in the small amount of literature, or in public discourse about it. The term *International Sign* is used broadly to refer to semiotic strategies employed by deaf people to communicate with other deaf people who do not share the same conventional, natively occurring signed language. *International* may very well describe the contexts of such signed language contact, but a singular standard IS form may not exist, although the nomenclature may lead to such an assumption.

Mesch (2010) makes a distinction between two types of IS communication; the first is an informal ad-hoc signing method between people who do not necessarily know each other's signed languages (SLs). The second is a conventionalized form of IS by groups of signers in somewhat regular contact. This paper discusses the latter type and specifically focuses on a genre I identify as *expository IS*. Expository IS is defined as group communications that take the form of uni-directional address by presenters and interpreters at global deaf conferences and meetings, aimed at communicating with a diverse SL-using audience rather than

This research would not have been possible without the generous willingness of my study participants, and several deaf leaders including Markuu Jokinen and Colin Allen of the World Federation of the Deaf, and the research support of Macquarie University, Research Excellence Scholarship iMQRES– No. 2010086 communicating with an established, mutually understood native sign language (NSL).

This chapter presents a lexical frequency study and describes types of signs used by deaf presenters at an international conference of the World Federation of the Deaf (WFD). It is part of a larger doctoral research project I recently completed on factors for IS comprehension (Whynot, 2015). Findings are reported from a collection of IS conference presentations by Deaf community leaders from 14 different countries and uncover quantitative and qualitative information about meaning-making in multilingual, international settings.

Multilingual signed language contact is a new subject of inquiry. Recent study of "cross-signing" (Zeshan, 2015) describes how shared multilingual, multimodal communication between unrelated signed language users involves the creation of agreed upon form-meaning symbols through accommodation, persistence, and blending of shared communicative resources. However, face-to-face negotiated cross-signing is quite different from uni-directional conference platform address. Conference lectures are expository texts with very little opportunity to negotiate meaning, therefore IS presenters (and interpreters) using it must aim for meaning-making that reaches any number of different signed language users in the audience. An IS presenter makes assumptions about what may be recognizable to the audience from what are thought to be shared linguistic or gestural conventions.

Other issues arise from the study and application of IS in real-world settings. Several proposed glossaries (or "dictionaries")[1] about IS are basic, word list suggestions with typically no information about methods of collection, nor adequate description about IS sign meanings and usage constraints. Therefore, empirical evidence for training or teaching about IS is lacking, and evidence is limited about semiotic strategies, patterns, and linguistic characteristics of expository IS—especially compared to patterns in natively occurring signed languages.

Information is needed about recurrent lexical forms in lecture-style IS and meaning-making strategies used by signers in contact with each other. Conference lecture IS needs improved description if interpreters and presenters are expected to use it effectively, as if it were a language. Finally, descriptive distinctions need to be made between expository and other

1. For a discussion on sign language dictionaries and standardization, see Johnston (2003b).

types of international signing contact, such as 1:1 interaction between two individuals and examples of small group SL contact that involve different goals of interaction.

The existing, small collection of literature on IS discusses the presence of grammatical, iconic, and gestural elements in IS that also are observed in natively occurring signed languages (Allsop, Woll, & Brauti, 1994; Woll, 1990; Supalla & Webb, 1995; Rosenstock, 2004, 2008; Whynot, 2015), interpreting strategies and challenges (Moody, 2002; McKee & Napier, 2002; de Wit, 2010), IS emergence and globalized Deaf communities (Hiddinga & Crasborn, 2011; Green, 2014) and critical evaluations about IS comprehension (Rosenstock, 2004; Whynot, 2015). There is a need for additional quantitative research on the composition of linguistic and gestural forms in IS lecture material and how this distribution compares to lectures given in NSLs.

By definition, language involves the conventional patterning of linguistic symbols, with core and non-core lexicon conveying consistent meaning between interlocutors. Gestures, which are generally nonconventional, flexible, and context-dependent, play an important part alongside linguistic information in discourse (Kendon, 2004; Liddell, 2003; Wilcox, 2004; Schembri, Jones, & Burnham, 2005). Of interest here is the interplay between conventional linguistic and nonconventional gestural elements employed by deaf presenters, the lexical distribution and patterns in IS lectures, all of which have implications for IS meaning-making, audience comprehension, and effectiveness of conference IS interpreting. To this end, the following research questions will be addressed:

1. What types of and how much linguistic and gestural material do deaf people recruit when they create expository, lecture-type IS to convey ideas at international conferences?
2. What comparisons can be made about the IS lexicon and the lexical composition of NSLs?
3. What can be reported about the communicative strategies—telling, showing, and representing—employed to convey ideas in this type of sign language contact?

TELLING, SHOWING, AND REPRESENTING

Language is the faculty by which we make sense of our experiences. As a result, language—as it resides in the mind—cannot be studied in isolation from human embodiment (Evans & Green, 2006, p. 44). We live and think in our bodies and understand our surroundings through our physical interaction with them. Regular usage of form-meaning symbols within a language community shapes the use of those symbols. In recent decades, cognitive approaches to the description of SLs have emerged (for ASL: Liddell, 2003; for Auslan: Ferrara, 2012; Johnston & Ferrara, 2014), with emphasis on the idea that language is a human cognitive faculty that relies on mental representations or schemas. When we communicate a message our intention is to prompt meaning in the mind of the receiver of our message. Meaning is prompted by linguistic symbols (such as conventional words or signs) as well as nonlinguistic symbols (gestures, contextual clues, or iconic representations). Enfield (2009, p. 2) points out that language is merely a subset of the resources necessary for recognizing the intentions of others.

When attempting to communicate in a contact situation with users of one or more distinctly different SLs, signers bring their own set of "full resources"—material from their own NSLs that is both linguistic and gestural, which is informed by their linguistic and cultural backgrounds. Additional external factors that shape a contact situation also must be considered, such as the demographic profile of the community of users, cultural traditions, settings where a contact variety is used, and the sociopolitical systems of deaf people.

When people communicate in face-to-face interaction, they utilize any combination of three strategies: the use of description, pointing (to referents–real or imagined), and demonstration (Clark & Gerrig, 1990). Ferrara (2012) established relevance of Clark and Gerrig's ideas to clauses and composite utterances in Australian Sign Language, Auslan. It was noted that signers are able to describe, or *tell* meaning, and demonstrate, or *show* meaning (Ferrara, p. 102). Telling meaning aligns with giving *specific* description with established signs that are fully lexical, whereas showing aligns with demonstration through the use of gestures, and to some extent pointing signs and depicting signs. Depicting signs are considered to be simultaneously linguistic and gestural (following Liddell, 2003; Schembri, 2001; Schembri, et al., 2005), and are characterized as partly lexical (Johnston & Schembri, 1999).

In cognitive linguistics, the term *representation* is often aligned with mental representations or construals that arise in the mind of interlocutors. In this study of IS lexicon, the use of depiction blends and exploitation of common embodied metaphor are also considered as a way that IS represents meaning. This is because metaphors are types of blends, where the elements of one domain are used to represent elements of another domain. In blending, through conceptual integration (Fauconnier & Turner, 1996), structure from two input spaces is projected to a third space, which then has its own unique semantic structure. In the blend, elements of one conceptual domain are mapped onto those of another (e.g., in the metaphor LIFE-IS-A-JOURNEY, *bumps in the road* meaningfully represents *difficult challenges*, such as *financial hardship* or *relationship trouble).*

In SLs, metaphoric blending means that iconic images are extended and their meanings can reference abstract ideas (Brennan, 1990; Taub, 2001; Wilcox, 2000). Often, metaphors derived from human-embodied experience become ingrained in everyday language; our human conceptual system is by nature metaphoric (Lakoff & Johnson, 1980). One of the common spatial metaphors used in some spoken and SLs is the UP-IS-GOOD metaphor.

Varied linguistic and gestural forms from a person's NSL provide strategies for signers to communicate information. They do so with specific "telling" symbols (conventional lexical signs), iconically "showing" (through points, enactment, and gestures), and "representing" (through depicting signs, blending, and metaphor). When IS presenters communicate information to a multilingual audience, how do they tell, show, and represent?

Fully Lexical Signs

When people think about any particular language, what comes to mind is the basic unit of individual words, or the lexicon. Knowing minimal units of meaning in a language means that a person has the ability at some basic level to compose and to understand messages using these meaningful elements. The next degree of complexity is grammatical relations between meaningful elements. In this study, a distinction is made between "lexicalized" signs and those that are partly lexical or nonlexical as outlined by Johnston and Schembri (2007) and Johnston (2012).

Lexicalization in SLs essentially occurs when a signed unit acquires a clearly identifiable and replicable citation form that is regularly and strongly associated with a meaning that is more specific than the sign's componential meaning potential, even when cited out of context; cannot be predicted based on these components alone; or is quite unrelated to its componential meaning potential; that is, it may be arbitrary (Johnston, 2012, p. 166).

Fully lexical signs are those that are defined as conventional in their form and meaning, such as signs listed in a dictionary. Johnston and Schembri (1999) distinguish fully lexical signs from partly lexical stating that a lexeme (word/sign) is "a linguistic unit with a 'given' rather than a 'generated' meaning" (p. 2). A sign may also be lexicalized instantaneously when a linguistic community establishes and accepts any form/meaning connection (Johnston & Ferrara, 2014, p. 236). Lexicalized signs are therefore linguistic symbols that *tell* specific meaning and in this study include high frequency signs used by IS presenters, whether from their own NSL or ones that have become typically borrowed into the IS contact strategy.

The ability for sub-lexical components (handshape, orientation, etc.) to become engaged in a new form and usage is one of the aspects of productivity seen in SLs that enable creation of new sign forms. This productivity is thought to enable ease of understanding across signed language users. Some of these productive, created forms are partly lexical depicting signs, which are outlined in the next section.

Partly Lexical Signs

Many NSLs exhibit complex forms that can be characterized as partly lexical. These complex signs have properties of gradation and category, rely on discourse context for meaning, and are not specified for usage in a conventional way. The specified aspects of these signs typically come from their handshape and orientation, and their movements are mapped in the signing space in any variety of constructions and discourse contexts to create gradations of meaning (Schembri, 2001). Parts of these complexes—handshape, orientation, location, and movement—often have their own meaning, although there is no consensus about their status as morphemes (Johnston & Schembri, 2007; Okrent, 2002, p. 176). Two kinds of partly lexical signs are points and depicting signs (Johnston & Schembri, 2007).

Pointing signs are a type of deictic gesture that are meaningful. They have several functions in SLs, one of the most important of which is reference tracking. They also serve an adverbial locating function, a determiner function, and a discourse cohesive function (buoys). Pointing signs indicate physical referents in space as well as imagined entities in the form of tokens or buoys in the signing space. Referents are established through deixis in signing space in front of the signer, and used when referring back (anaphora) to previously established referents (Lillo-Martin & Klima, 1990; McBurney, 2002). The imagined entities that points refer to are placeholders for conceptual real-space referents in the signed discourse (Liddell, 2003, p. 192). Some researchers also analyze them with grammatical distinction between pronominal first person and non-first person (Engberg Pederson, 1993). The pronominal status of points in SLs is questioned and it has been defended that points participate in discourse as independent signs or blends to direct and indicate verbs (Johnston, 2013b; Liddell, 1995). Pointing signs are complex elements in SLs and they have been characterized as hybrid (partly conventional, partly nonconventional) forms, and it is suggested that points are gestural, much like co-speech gestural pointing that occurs with spoken languages (Johnston, 2013a). It appears that these sign types are common among all SLs to (at the very least) indicate and locate, and are context-dependent for their meaning. In this way pointing signs both *tell* and *show* meaning in the discourse.

Depicting signs are another type of partly lexical signs that are often engaged in real space blends in signed languages. They depict a shape, location, or movement of a referent with sometimes iconic portrayal of the referent through productive, sub-lexical sign parameters of handshape, orientation, location, movement, and nonmanual signals. For example, the flat B-hand held palm down generally refers to a flat, horizontally oriented entity like a table top. The handshape parameter is particularly salient, so it has been credited with prompting meaning (Brennan, 1992) mainly because it is easy to isolate this sub-lexical component of a sign (Johnston & Schembri, 1999).

There is ongoing discussion in the literature about the status of location and movement components of signs. It is debated whether they are nonlinguistic gestural components (Liddell, 1995) or linguistic types of agreement marking (Supalla, 1982). The productive aspects of what are referred to here as depicting signs are discussed in the IS literature under these different assumptions, just as they are in the general SL linguistic literature. In the SL literature, these are morphemic analyzes (e.g. Supalla, 1978; Schick, 1990) or nonlinguistic, analogue analyzes (e.g., DeMatteo, 1977). Recent works identify both linguistic and gestural elements in depicting signs (polycomponential verbs, Schembri, 2001). Some of the many references to these sign types in IS are "verbs of motion and location" (e.g. Supalla & Webb, 1995), "classifiers" (Allsop et al., 1994; McKee & Napier, 2002), "spatial verbs" and "classifier morphology" (Woll, 1990), and "depicting verbs" (Rosenstock, 2004). As noted earlier, the term "depicting signs" is used throughout this paper and can be analyzed (as well as pointing signs) as comprising a combination of both linguistic and gestural components, following Liddell (2003), Schembri (2001), and Schembri et al. (2005).

Nonlexical Signs

The third category of sign types is nonlexical signs. Nonlexical signs (gestures), are important to include in the comparisons of sign type distribution in NSLs and IS lectures, particularly given that they are assumed to be prevalent and important to meaning making in IS discourses, according to prior claims (Moody, 1987; McKee & Napier, 2002). Nonlexical signs are intentional bodily actions that convey meaning but they are not conventional in terms of their form or meaning. They are dependent upon context for their interpretation and situated in context, they demonstrate or *show* meaning. In this study, two types are categorized: the first type are signs that appear to be gesture-like manual movements that do not have established, conventional meaning, but depend on context to convey meaning. In the analysis, gesture also includes the elaborate pantomime and enacting behaviors known as constructed action (CA) and constructed dialogue (CD) (Roy, 1989; Winston 1991; Metzger 1995; following Tannen, 1986). Enactments were observed in instances of nonlinguistic behavior, facial expressions, and bodily movements that are mimed emotions and actions. Some nonlexical signs provide a discourse pragmatic function such as the hand waving HEY gestural form, which is not just for getting attention but is used to express surprise or to mark a change in topic (Hoza, 2010). Another function of some gestures is to mark prosodic boundaries between utterances in SLs (e.g., the form annotated as G(5-UP):WELL in this study and in work on the Auslan corpus) In this way, nonlexical signs can also prompt new mental spaces in the build-up of discourse.

Gestures are types of signs or symbolic bodily movements that are seen commonly across all SLs (Wilcox, 2004). Through a lexical analysis of sign types in expository IS, identification of nonlexical forms such as gesture and enactment leads to an understanding about how prevalent they are in meaning construction in IS.

DATA COLLECTION AND ANALYSIS

This investigation captured authentic expository IS in a typical usage setting and included deaf people from varied countries. Situated use of IS lectures by deaf presenters was collected at the 2011 congress of the WFD and the 2011 World Association of Sign Language Interpreters (WASLI) conference. The live, expository lectures were given to large, diverse audiences in South Africa. Audiences were composed of 300 to 2,000 mixed deaf and hearing attendees, representing as many as 25 different countries. The historical longevity of WFD conferences provides a consistent, stable forum for expository IS use.

The methods of lexical frequency analysis were applied to the dataset, so that observed linguistic and gestural forms could be compared to findings in the few published NSL frequency studies (Johnston, 2012; Morford & MacFarlane, 2003; Cormier, Fenlon, Rentelis, & Schembri, 2011). Lexicological analysis in this research aims (1) to test intuitions that IS elements are more "gestural" and less linguistic than native SLs and (2) to identify conventions of lexicon and depicting structures in the IS used by deaf presenters. The goal is to provide a quantitative description about varied sign types, gestural enactment (constructed action), and spoken language mouthings that IS signers use to convey meaning. Further, an analysis of influential origins of lexicalized signs was made, with fully lexical signs being tagged as citation ASL signs, citation Auslan (BANZL)[2] signs, signs listed in the Gestuno glossary, and signs presented in WFD International Sign video materials.[3]

Participants

Fourteen lecturers gave permission to be filmed for this study. Ten of them have used their native SL since birth or before age 6, the other four

2. Auslan is very closely related to BSL and together with New Zealand Sign Language, the three have been described as dialects of a larger language group, named BANZSL (Johnston, 2003a). In this chapter references to Auslan also imply BSL. When BSL alone is intended, "BSL" will be used. When there is a need to reinforce reference to the whole language family, "BANZSL" will be used.

3. World Federation of the Deaf (WFD). (2008). *Suggested International Signs for use at the World Federation of the Deaf (WFD) General Assembly*. A 25-minute digital media production by the WFD, Norwegian Association of the Deaf and Ål Experiential College and Conference Center for Deaf People, and Døves Media.

used home signs and learned their local SL during their teenage or young adult school years. Twelve of the fourteen read and write English in addition to communicating fluently in their first sign language. All presenters are well traveled, having met other deaf people in their travels, and most had some knowledge of (an)other sign language(s). Notably, for those whose first language is not ASL, most report knowing some amount of ASL and/or BSL.

Data Collection

A total of 283 minutes of IS video samples was collected and available for analysis. Mori (2011) points out that much of the research on IS has not included signers of Asian or other non-Western SL backgrounds. In an effort to balance the heavy percentage of Western samples, the data was refined to 212 minutes of source IS in the collection. One hundred and one (101) minutes of source IS were analyzed for this study, roughly half of the balanced collection of IS data.

Categorizing and Naming Lexical Elements of IS

In this study, the corpus is monologic, expository IS source video, which is taken as a snapshot in time, and which may be expanded later or enriched further for additional types of analysis. This research project creates a basic machine-readable corpus (Johnston, 2014, p. 11) with two foundational tiers (dominant and nondominant hand), translation tier, and a few other, study-specific tiers in order to answer some of the research questions posed.

The taxonomy of sign types applied in the analysis of the IS source data includes the above described categories: (1) fully lexical, (2) partly lexical, and (3) nonlexical. Examples of each sign type in the IS dataset are shown in Table 1, with a description and example of how each type was named with a gloss. Fully lexical signs were glossed with an English word and a tag denoting its citation form origin (e.g., NOW[ASL]; HAVE[AUS], COUNTRY[WFD]).

Partly lexical depicting signs were glossed with DS (depicting sign), and a letter denoting sub-type of depicting sign (S for size and shape specifier; H, for handling of entity; M for movement of entity; L for location of entity; and G, often for nondominant hand that backgrounds the entity). Depicting signs were glossed in the following manner: DSS/H/L/M/G(HANDSHAPE):BRIEF-DESCRIPTION-OF-MEANING-OF-SIGN.

TABLE 1. *Examples of Sign Types in IS*

Lexical category	Example of type	Note
Fully lexical sign		Used regularly in expository IS to mean "ratify, or approve a document, a policy, or law." Seen here listed as an entry in the 1975 BDA Gestuno glossary (reprinted with permission). Glossed as APPROVE (GEST).
Partly lexical sign, depicting sign		A depicting sign glossed here as DSM (BENT5): ENTITY-EXPANDS-INCREASE-IN-NUMBER-OF-MEMBERS.
Partly lexical sign, pointing sign		A pointing sign that aids in referencing in IS discourse. This example is glossed as PT:DET (determiner).
Nonlexical sign, gesture		A gesture, fully depending on context, movement, and facial features, which is glossed here as G(5-UP): WELL, OR G(5-UP):HUH, G(5-UP): SO (other glosses are also possible).

Partly lexical points were glossed with PT and the apparent type of point — PRO1 for first person, PRO2 for second person, etc. or POSS, if it appeared to be a point indicating possession. Some points were directed at entities, such as list buoys or fragments, and were noted as PT:LBUOY(4) for example.

Nonlexical signs glossed with "G" and additional information about the handshape if it was a manual gesture and also glossed with meaning information. Other gestures that were nonmanual, bodily enactments or facial expressions were glossed with G and the tag CA (for constructed action), (e.g., G[CA]: CROSS-ARMS). Additional information about periods of constructed action and constructed dialogue were noted on the separate CA tier as well. Table 1 provides examples of these three sign types analyzed in the dataset.

In summary, the expository IS lexical frequency dataset was annotated on several tiers during several passes of lexical analysis for the following: (1) presence of fully lexical forms; (2) presence of depicting, pointing, and gestural signs; (3) periods of constructed action; (4) presence of spoken language (English) mouthing; (5) selected depicting sign segments and their meanings and blended domains.

RESULTS

High Frequency Signs in IS

A frequency count of the annotated IS data yielded 7,033 tokens comprising 1,751 different sign forms. The top 50 most frequent signs are shown in Table 2. These account for 42.5% of all tokens in the annotated collection, with pointing signs figuring prominently.

The top four most frequent sign types are pointing signs, which in total comprise 14.5% of the signs in expository IS. Lexical frequency studies of Auslan, ASL, BSL, and NZSL also report points are the highest frequency signs.

After separating out lexical signs from partly lexical and nonlexical signs, the distribution of lexical signs from the rest (n = 4,383) comprise 62.3% of all tokens. The first 10 of the 50 most frequent lexical signs (n = 4,383) are DEAF-H(AUSLAN), WHAT(ASL), DEAF1(ASL), SAME(AUSLAN), HAVE(AUSLAN), PERSON (AUSLAN), SIGN (AUSLAN), GOOD (AUSLAN), DIFFERENT(ASL), TEACH (ASL). It is not surprising that the most frequent lexical signs used by IS presenters are DEAF, SIGN (language), TEACH, WORK, IMPORTANT, ASSOCIATION, INTERPRETER, HELP, PROGRESS, COUNTRY, and WORLD. There are also many signs that are easily understood as ASL citation forms and Auslan citation forms (and they may be citation forms in other SLs, but this would require further study to compare).

TABLE 2. *Fifty Most Frequent Signs in Expository IS* (n = 7,033)

Rank	ID gloss	Total	% of n	% Cumul
1	PT:PRO3	193	2.7	2.7
2	PT:PRO1	182	2.6	5.3
3	PT:DET	163	2.3	7.7
4	PT:LOC	141	2.0	9.7
5	DEAF(AUS)	126	1.8	11.5
6	G(5-UP):WELL	110	1.6	13.0
7	WHAT(ASL)	99	1.4	14.4
8	DEAF1(ASL)	98	1.4	15.8
9	SAME(AUS)	96	1.4	17.2
10	HAVE(AUS)	94	1.3	18.5
11	PERSON(GEST)	85	1.2	19.7
12	SIGN(AUS)	87	1.2	21.0
13	PT:PRO2PL	75	1.1	22.0
14	G(6-UP):GOOD	62	0.9	22.9
15	TEACH(ASL)	61	0.9	23.8
16	WORK(GEST)	59	0.8	24.6
17	DIFFERENT(ASL)	56	0.8	25.4
18	G(5-UP):HUH	56	0.8	26.2
19	ONE(ASL)	56	0.8	27.0
20	IMPORTANT(ASL)	55	0.8	27.8
21	ASSOCIATION(GEST)	54	0.8	28.6
22	G(5-UP):SO	51	0.7	29.3
23	INTERPRETER(WFD)	50	0.7	30.0
24	HELP(ASL)	49	0.7	30.7
25	WORLD(GEST)	47	0.7	31.4
26	CONNECT(ASL)	42	0.6	32.0
27	CAN(ASL)	41	0.6	32.5
28	PT:PRO3PL	39	0.6	33.1
29	NOW(GEST)	38	0.5	33.6
30	KNOW(ASL)	37	0.5	34.2
31	GOVERNMENT(GEST)	35	0.5	34.7
32	PT:POSS3	33	0.5	35.1
33	ANALYZE(ASL)	32	0.5	35.6
34	FINISH(ASL)	32	0.5	36.0
35	NS:JAPAN	32	0.5	36.5
36	THINK(ASL)	32	0.5	37.0
37	COUNTRY(WFD)	31	0.4	37.4
38	EXPLAIN(WFD)	31	0.4	37.8
39	GROUP TOGETHER(ASL)	30	0.4	38.3
40	PROGRESS(ASL)	30	0.4	38.7
41	YEAR(ASL)	29	0.4	39.1
42	DISABLED(WFD)	28	0.4	39.5
43	NINE(WFD)	27	0.4	39.9
44	TWO(ASL)	27	0.4	40.3
45	WRITE(ASL)	27	0.4	40.7
46	GIVE(ASL)	26	0.4	41.0
47	HOW(ASL)	26	0.4	41.4
48	WANT(AUS)	26	0.4	41.8
49	WOMANB(WFD)	26	0.4	42.1
50	HEARING(WFD)	25	0.4	42.5

The 100 most frequent signs (all types) comprise 55.6% (3,910) of all of the sign tokens (7,033) in the dataset, with a large variety of different sign forms appearing. In addition, 1,162 signs occur only once in the corpus. More than half of these are depicting signs (n = 462) and gestures (n = 230). The other half are varied singly occurring forms from presenters' NSLs, variations of these, as well as numbers, fingerspelled words, or low incidence signs that are listed in the Gestuno glossary or the WFD video materials. With this large number of varied sign forms and the relatively small number of highly occurring signs, the data empirically supports intuitions about the "limited" conventional lexicon in this international sign contact system.

Distribution of Sign Types

The analysis of sign types in expository IS indicates lexical signs comprise 63.6% of the lexicon, with partly lexical pointing signs and depicting signs constituting the next largest type at 14.5% and 10.2% respectively (see Table 3). Gesture signs and the embodied enactment of constructed action (CA) and constructed dialogue (CD) make up the nonlexical material in expository IS, although only a few instances of CD occurred in the IS dataset. Gesture signs make up 8.8% of the tokens. Constructed action dialogue enactments were annotated on a separate CA tier in ELAN and was therefore tallied separately from gesture signs. There were 572 periods of CA in the dataset, which means that for every 12 signs (on average), a period of CA occurs. Many gestures occurred within a period of CA (206 out of 645). Lastly, there are equal amounts of fingerspelling and name signs, at 1.7% each.

Lexical Signs in IS and Their Origins

Findings indicate that 63.6% of sign types in expository IS created by deaf presenters are lexical forms with some degree of conventional use in the international conference setting. A majority of lexical signs, 58%, in IS are recognized citation forms in ASL, with the second most prevalent forms, 20.7%, recognizable as citation Auslan signs, a BANZSL sign language. Because lexical forms in IS have been shown previously to belong to more than one SL or SL group (Rosenstock, 2004), one cannot say for certain that the sign forms observed in this dataset are *only* ASL or BANZSL signs. The amounts of fully lexical signs by SL origin is therefore limited by only these viewpoints. Many signs listed in WFD resources or known IS forms from conferences and activities of the WFD

TABLE 3. *Comparing IS Sign Type Distribution to NSL Sign Type Distribution*

Sign type	IS lectures (n = 7,033)	Auslan lectures (n = 1,137)	Auslan corpus formal (n = 22,100)[a]	ASL formal (n = 1,363)[b]	BSL[c] (n = 24,864)
Fully lexical	63.6%	71.3%	69.4%	80.2%	62.0%
Fingerspelling	1.7%	8.3%	4.7%	4.8%	2.5%
Name signs	1.7%	0.1%	0.5%	0.7%	1.1%
Depicting	10.2%	3.9%	1.6%	0.9%	2.3%
Pointing	14.5%	15.0%	15.0%	13.4%	22.9%
Gesture	9.0%	2.8%	8.8%	0.1%	8.7%

[a]From Johnston, 2012 .
[b]From Morford and MacFarlane, 2003.
[c]Data from Cormier et al., 2011; depicting signs are called classifier signs in Cormier et al., 2011, and Morford and MacFarlane, 2003.

are also frequent, comprising 10.7% of the lexical signs in the dataset. Signs that are listed in the Gestuno glossary comprise 7.9% of tokens. The remaining 2.3% sign forms are unknown, likely sourced from other SLs.

Comparing IS to NSL Frequency Studies

Results from quantitative analysis of the 7,033 tokens indicate similarities as well as differences in the type of signs distributed in the lexicon of expository IS compared to NSLs (see Table 3). The distribution of IS sign types is compared to what is reported in Auslan, ASL, and BSL to ascertain any unique type characteristics of IS expository discourses. The differences in distribution of sign types shown in Table 3 likely is due to the varying text types genres in the different corpora as well as coding differences between researchers (Cormier et al., 2011), which impacts comparability of data (Johnston, 2012). In order to make genre-specific comparisons between international contact signing and a NSL, two 5-minute Auslan lecture segments (publicly available) were also analyzed using the same methods as the IS source dataset. Although limited by sample size (n = 1,137), two samples of Auslan expository presentations were included to augment the comparison to Auslan formal texts (interviews).

The amount of fully lexical signs are lower in IS than in other sign language frequency results. Lexicalized signs comprise a lower percentage of the total in IS, at 63.6% when compared to ASL formal texts (80.2%), Auslan lectures (71.3%), and the more formal texts in the Auslan corpus. IS exhibits much less fingerspelling than the NSLs, but overall much more depiction and gesture than ASL and BSL. These differences are more pronounced when comparing data from similar text genre and register.[4]

Turning to other potential meaning-making elements in IS, one can see differences in the distribution of partly lexical and nonlexical components in expository IS when compared to comparable text genres in NSLs, except for pointing signs. It is notable that the frequency distribution of pointing sign types is remarkably similar to their distribution in NSLs; in particular, prototypical indexing types are the most frequent sign types in IS as they are in Auslan, ASL, and NZSL (Johnston, 2012a). However, it cannot be assumed that points function with any universality in NSLs (and therefore in IS) as pronominal linguistic types or deictic gestural types (Johnston, 2013b) without further study of their form and function in a variety of NSLs (and in IS).

The largest difference is that expository IS exhibits a higher amount of both depiction and gesture than Auslan (formal and lecture) and ASL formal texts. Depicting signs are productive signs with categorical and gradient properties and in NSLs combine meaningful units (handshapes, movements, locations, etc.) to create new forms (Brennan, 1992; Johnston & Schembri, 2007). In IS the need to create nonce forms to supplement limited established signs is more pronounced, given that lack of conventional fully lexical forms available for discourse.

The differences in gesture distributions are not easily compared. The ASL study does not elaborate on coding of gesture, and the Auslan data was based on formal interviews, not monologic lecture. Johnston notes that in the interview texts, there appeared to be many gestures due to the interactive nature of the data, such as cues for turn-taking. Neither the ASL nor the Auslan study reports on the amount of the gesture that is constructed action (Johnston, 2012, p. 14). Yet, a recent study on depicting signs in Auslan grammar showed that CA is exploited in narrative text clauses (37.2%) rather than in the interactive conversations (6.1%) (Ferrara, 2012). CA occurred 572 times in the IS dataset, which suggests that gestural material in IS is much higher than what is reported in other similar NSL data.

Lexical Signs Can Be Modified to Show Meaning

In the data, there are numerous examples of signs that are sufficiently highly frequent and stable in form and meaning that they can be said

4. The BSL corpus data is not easily or fully compared given that the data includes conversational data rather than expository, formal text.

FIGURE 1. *Examples of modified citation lexical signs: (a)* ASSOCIATION (GEST) *(b)* ASSOCIATION (GEST), *modified, and (c)* ACCEPT (ASL), *modified.*

to have citation, established forms. At the same time, some of these are modified to express related meanings. The sign ASSOCIATION (Figure 1a), which is listed in the Gestuno glossary, is a high frequency lexical sign in the data that conventionally tells specific information.

When this form is used, it typically refers to national or local deaf associations or organizations, yet in a few instances it was seen modified, by movement and location in space in a way that employs the form to mean TO ASSOCIATE WITH AND COLLABORATE TOGETHER (Figure 1b). In this way the sign uses movement between two locations to show that collaborative work was being done between two different country deaf associations.

Another example of a lexical sign in IS that was modified by a signer is the sign ACCEPT(ASL) (Figure 1c). He articulates it markedly slowly, with the two-handed 5 hands moving in toward the chest and simultaneously starting to close into two flat O handshapes on the upper chest, but stopping just before completing the final position of the sign. In most cases, the citation form occurs in the IS dataset (more quickly articulated start to finish, and without facial nonmanual signals to alter meaning). In this one case described above, the meaning the signer attempts to convey is JSL LEGAL RECOGNITION IS IN THE PROCESS OF BEING ACCEPTED. He does so by modifying a very specific ASL citation "telling" sign, ACCEPT, in a gestural way that both shows and represents meaning abstractly. The slowed movement demonstrates the extended time it has taken to obtain government acceptance of Japanese Sign Language (JSL), and because the sign is nearly completely articulated (but not fully!), metaphoric reference is relied upon to represent meaning. THE-BODY-IS-A-CONTAINER metaphor is seen here in the meaning intended; the flat O hands have not fully closed nor rested onto the chest to indicate bodily possession of the "thing," that is, Japanese government acceptance had not fully been completed. Another simultaneous metaphor is operating in this sign: TIME-IS-A-SPACE-WE-MOVE-THROUGH. The time line that runs behind and through to the front of the body is often used in signed languages to indicate past, present and future. The sign shows "government acceptance" approaching slowly but since it has not yet been taken possession of, it remains just in front of the signer, yet slightly out of reach.

In these examples, it is evident that conventional signs in IS tell specific semantic information and they are modified in expository IS to gesturally show and metaphorically represent meaning. Showing and representing is even more evident in partly lexical signs and nonlexical gesture in IS.

Partly Lexical Signs in IS

Signs that are partly lexical and rely to a high degree on the context of the utterance are also observed in expository IS. These two types are pointing signs and depicting signs, described earlier.

POINTING SIGNS

Noted above, the most frequent signs in IS are pointing signs, comprising 14.5% of all tokens in the data. The top four frequent sign types are points (PT:PRO3, PT:PRO1, PT:DET, and PT:LOC) respectively.

Pointing signs have several functions in SLs, one of the most important of which is for reference tracking. Others include an adverbial locating function, a determiner function, and a discourse cohesive function (via buoys). In a segment from one presentation in the data, an IS signer uses as many as nine pointing signs of varied subtype in a 12-second span, underlying their importance in the discourse.

In the segment, the signer uses points to show referential indexing to himself, and he directs points at tokenized objects of discourse or topics not physically present. He also points at fragment buoys, which are nondominant handshape holds at the end of a sign, to show the viewer what was just mentioned. Points also direct the audience to physical entities in space that are real, such as the large screen behind the presenter.

In the IS data, pointing signs may be exploiting the gestural aspect of these signs, or they may be recruited for some linguistic role that might be pronominal or contributing to argument (subjects/objects) structure. There is continued discussion in the literature about pointing signs and their function, with recent evidence suggesting some SLs (e.g., Auslan) lack pronouns (Johnston, 2013). Without additional study of the patterning of pointing signs in IS and other semiotic material that occurs with them (e.g., eye gaze)—especially in comparison to NSLs—it is difficult to make claims about them in IS, except that the data reveals a large variety of pointing signs and a similar percent distribution to what is reported in NSL lexical frequency studies (13.5–15%).

DEPICTING SIGNS

In the expository IS dataset there are 721 distinct depicting signs, most of which occur once, a few recurring 2, 3, or as many as 6 times. In depicting signs observed in the dataset, formational aspects of signs (the handshapes, orientation and movement parameters) bear iconic resemblance to figure and ground referents that components are depicting. It is clear that IS presenters exploit the components of signs to show what they mean through depicting signs in IS discourse.

In general, depicting signs were characterized in this study by five broad types and then further glossed with additional, more specific glossing for meaning. The majority of depicting signs represent movement (or displacement) of entities (DSM), and others depict size and shape (DSS), or are entity locating (DSL), and some are handling entities (DSH). In most cases, handling entity depicting signs (DSH) co-occurred with constructed action, because enactment often involves the handling and manipulation of entities. DSH signs were not easily distinguished from gesture signs, and if they had been glossed as gestures the number would increase the percentage of gestures in IS by 0.5 %. Lastly there were depicting signs that backgrounded an entity (DSG) which were represented by the dominant hand (however, in 180 instances the DSG were represented by the nondominant hand). Many of the depicting signs occurred on both hands, often in coordination, but also in a figure-ground relationship. The resulting effect was a large number of different depicting sign forms that were dependent on their utterance context for meaning, rather than prompting specific meaning (as a fully lexical sign would do). Additional evidence of the recruitment of formational elements of NSLs in IS is the fact that a majority of depicting signs occur only once in the dataset.

The productive nature of depicting structures, along with metaphor, is a potentially rich area of inquiry in crosslinguistic contact signing. Simple metaphor in SLs maps the linguistic form to a source domain, exploiting visual iconicity such that the linguistic form (i.e., handshape, movement, etc.) resembles the referent or a part of the referent in a metonymic relationship (Brennan, 1990; Wilcox, 2000; Taub, 2001). Often these metaphors are simple, orientational, and ontological, enabling an observer to estimate the meaning based on the iconic relationship between the articulator and the visual or embodied experience of the referent.

FIGURE 2. *Depicting the concept of [DECREASE]/[INCREASE] in IS.*

Another example of a depicting sign from this study that exploits iconic and gestural features of formational parts of signs is shown in Figure 2. Sign forms that involve a handshape movement from a lower position to an upper position convey a meaning of an "increase" of some kind. Rosenstock (2004) mentions this as one example of effective metaphoric reference that was observed in her IS data. If the semantic domain of "increasing entities" is effectively mapped onto the form—the articulating hands and arms—as long as the lexical argument is understood, the observer will know what "thing" is increasing as well as the manner of the increase. The signer in Figure 2 refers to the increased interest and number of attendees at HIV training, after previous ones were not conducted in the local SL. The image created is one of a declining then increasing slope, as if a line on a chart, quantifying a numerical increase. The second half of the sign also resembles the ASL sign DEVELOP, however the presenter delexicalized the sign by initially constructing a downward sloping movement that pivoted at the lowest point and then sloped upward.

Given that 10.2% of the signs in expository IS are depicting types, the use of depiction is evidently a strategy used to convey complex meanings in expository IS. The depicting signs from an IS utterance in Figure 3 below exploit the metaphor of UP-IS-GOOD and LOCATIONS-ARE-STATES-OF-COMPARISON. The signer indicates meaning by representing an idea that is not as explicitly specific as a fully lexical sign might tell, such as

FIGURE 3. *Depicting sign: DSM(BC):RAISE-UP-TO-EQUAL-POINT.*

the Auslan or ASL sign meaning COMPARE. Meaning is created in the blended space established by the signer articulating the first depicting sign Figure 3, where she represents two comparative things—one being lower (worse) than the other, higher (better) one. The viewer doesn't know specifically what is being told, but meaning is represented by the depicting sign sequence DSM(BC):RAISE-UP-TO-EQUAL-POINT.

Nonlexical Signs: Gesture and Constructed Action

The amount of gesture incorporated into the studied IS presentations ranged between 5% to as high as 20% by some IS signers. Gesture tokens (n = 645) comprised 9% of signs in the IS data and the most frequent seven comprise 50% of all gesture signs in the dataset. There were 399 different forms of manual gestures, most occurring once and 34 occurring twice. The three most common gestures—G(5-UP): WELL/SO/HUH—are typically seen in NSLs as cohesive, discourse-marking devices and they appear to be functioning similarly in IS (see Figure 4).

Presenters used gestures to create meaningful symbols in IS utterances, such as a hand waving gesture, G:HEY-YOU, or in the expression of enactment and emotional responses via nonmanual markers and torso movements, e.g., G(5-2H):FIGURE-IT-OUT.

Gestures that serve to negate utterances such as G(1-SHAKE):NO-NO were frequent and support other studies' reports of manual negation in IS (Supalla & Webb, 1995; Woll, 1990). One of the more common forms that most IS signers incorporated into their lectures was the gesture glossed as G(5-SHAKE):WOW. It occurred 23 times in the dataset and operates as a modifying form and in many cases means [VERY] or intensifies some aspect of what is being discussed.

In total, there were 572 periods of CA enactment. These enactments were coded separately on the CA tier and overlapped (were time-aligned) with gestures, depicting signs, and/or fully lexical signs on the dominant

FIGURE 4. *Examples of gestures in expository IS. (a)* SO/WELL, *(b)* FIGURE-IT-OUT, *and (c)* SHAKE:WOW.

and nondominant ID gloss tiers. Because of these concurrences and separate treatment of the two, the amount of CA is discussed as a separate finding and is not reported in terms of percentages of the total 7,033 sign tokens. The frequency of CA enactment ranged on average from one enactment every 33 signs, to as high as one enactment every seven signs, depending on the presenter.

McNeill (2005) describes gestural viewpoints of "observer" and "character" for co-speech gestures, with gestures often acting as a "material carrier" (p. 98). The "material" in CA in IS enacts a visual story and shows a referent's described activity. CA occurs not only simultaneously with gesture signs, but also with other types of signs. A clausal analysis was not made here; however, Ferrara (2012) showed that in Auslan, CA overlaps in clauses with sole depicting signs and in most cases CA serves as the argument in the clause. Varied frequencies of CA occurrence is suggested to be a narrative device (Ferrara & Johnston, 2014) as opposed to obligatory (Quinto-Pozos, 2008). The prevalent occurrence of periods of CA in the IS data suggests that this form of semantically coordinated gestural material aids depicting signs and lexical signs to convey meaningful utterances, similar to the way it is in NSLs, e.g., Auslan.

In the IS data, CA co-occurred with manual, fully lexical signs with a single sign to as many as 11 signs in a period of CA. Lexical signs were at times aligned 1:1 with CA and thus offered additional gestural material to fully lexical signs. Often examples of CA in the IS dataset constructed complex utterances that resembled what Dudis (2004) describes as partitioned blends. With partitioned blends, the signer uses a two-handed depicting sign to represent material from the observer point of view, and shows a second blend from the point of view of the character.

Depicting signs co-occurred with CA 152 times, gestures co-occurred with CA 206 times, and fully lexical signs were fully aligned to CA 182 times. A follow up clausal analysis of this IS data would enable one to draw more conclusions about how CA and gesture (as two kinds of gestural material in IS utterances) are distributed and participate with depicting signs and fully lexical signs. Nonetheless, some intuitions can be proposed from some of the findings.

Telling, Showing and Representing: Putting It All Together to Make Meaning

A selected discourse segment from the IS data is shown in Figure 5. The presenter describes how collaboration from Deaf associations from

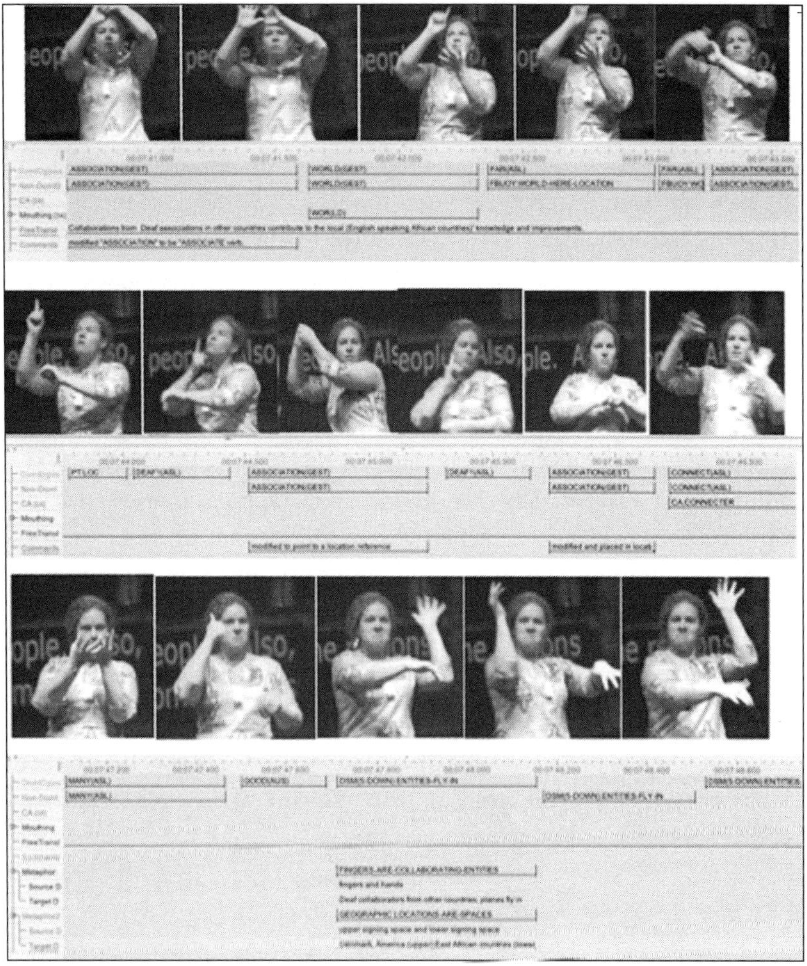

FIGURE 5. *Depicting segment DSB5. "Collaboration from Deaf associations in other countries contribute to the local (English-speaking African countries') knowledge and improvements" (translation by researcher, using a free rather than a literal approach; Napier, 2000).*

other countries has influenced improved access for deaf people in English-speaking East African countries, yet those in French-speaking West African countries experience great disparity in access to education and civic life.

The presenter uses a depicting sign, DSM(5-DOWN):ENTITIES-FLY-IN, at the end of this utterance to indicate the varied collaborators who have flown in to the area to aid in their development. She establishes discourse referents in the signing space via token blends |foreign associations| and |local association|. The discourse referents of overseas deaf associations and their geographic distance are given with fully lexical signs, ASSOCIATION(GEST) WORLD(GEST) FAR(ASL) FAR(ASL). A pointing sign PT:LOC DEAF1(ASL) ASSOCIATION(GEST) establishes the token |foreign (English-speaking community) associations| and a lexical sign articulated in a lowered, different space establishes the second token |local (English-speaking community) association|. In the utterance, the IS signer even articulates the sign ASSOCIATION (GEST) in each token location to show their different geographic location. The utterance is a good example of a complex construction that includes varied sign types (lexical signs, points, and depicting signs) and one instance of constructed action and uses signing space to map out references and build up the discourse main point.

In another example from the dataset, the IS presenter incorporates multiple, rich space blends that are highly metaphoric on several levels, and incorporates iconic elements. The signer presents abstract concepts about the struggles and progress deaf people continually experience in the aim to have SLs recognized, respected, and, in this context, integrated into appropriate and accessible education. The signed utterance is glossed as: TEACH(ASL) DEAF DSM(5-SHAKE):ENTITIES-SIGNLANGUAGES-RAISE-UP DSM(5-2H):ENTITIES-REPEATEDLY MOW-OVER (Figure 6).

The articulation of the upwardly moving 5 hands conveys the image of "signing," resembling the forms in many SLs for sign language, and also is a metaphor for achieving improvements in Deaf education. Nonmanual markers on the face and his torso movements begin the constructed ac-

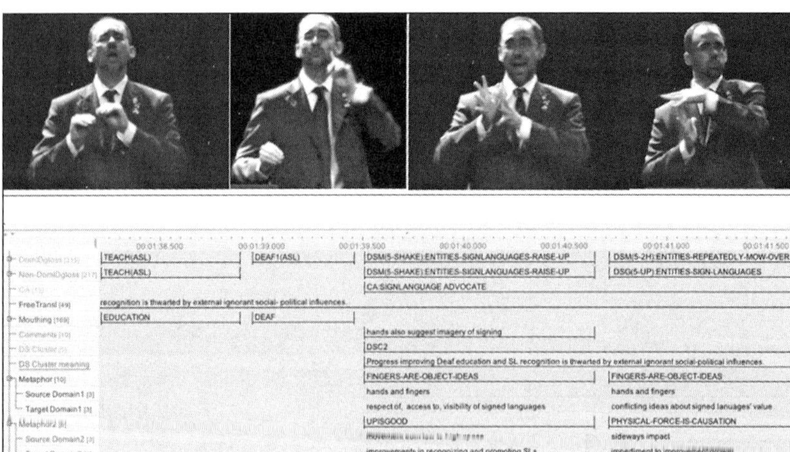

FIGURE 6. *Telling, showing, and representing with multiple sign types.*

tion, and the first depicting sign employs the 5 handshape to iconically map and represent multiple SLs (not just one SL or one group of people) in all countries on the individual fingers. The next depicting sign conveys the idea of something being mowed over, or cut off. Again, the 5 handshape depicts (and iconically maps) multiple entities approaching sideways at the nondominant hand. The nondominant hand is a fragment buoy that grounds and depicts the concept from the previous sign, RAISING-UP. The dominant downward-oriented, 5 handshape repeatedly (three times) cuts across the grounded sign. This conveys the idea that sociopolitical forces from outside of Deaf communities negatively impact the goals and aims toward SL recognition, respect, and inclusion in Deaf education programs. In this example, the signer constructs meaning by using a lexical sign to tell the topic, then depicting signs and CA to show his points.

CONCLUSIONS

It is evident that in conference contexts where IS presentation is used, a small number of highly occurring signs, and a large amount of depicting signs, points, and gestures contribute to the construction of meaning in these discourses.

In this study, the reported high frequency lexical signs in IS indicate that presenters have a small set of regular, specific signs with which they construct meaning for a multilingual audience. However the observed increased distribution of depicting signs, gesture, and enactment (CA) compared to what is reported in frequency studies of natively occurring signed languages suggests that deaf IS presenters incorporate other strategies to demonstrate what they mean. These frequency results provide insight into unique characteristics of expository IS that enrich the description of IS and supplement what has been observed in other studies.

Because of this fact, and given what I have shown regarding the reduced distribution of fully lexical signs in expository IS, presenters have less material to *tell* their specific information and resourcefully rely on demonstration to *show* meaning and *represent* meaning through pointing and gestural forms and metaphoric blending.

According to the data, there are at least 10% less established, lexical material in IS than in the same genre NSL texts. Even if only approximate, these numbers support prior claims that there is a smaller number of lexicalized forms in IS than in NSLs. While not unexpected, what this implies for expository IS discourse is that limited conventional, fully lexical signs used in IS presentations potentially impact the information gleaned. The semantic economy and specificity provided by conventional lexical forms would therefore be lacking and the presenter's messages would need to be grounded in additional meaning-making elements in the discourse through depiction and gesture. Fully lexical signs in expository IS may resemble lexicalized sign in the viewer's native SL that tell the same meaning or a completely different meaning, hence either helping or hindering comprehension. How this impacts comprehension needs closer examination and is addressed in Rosenstock (this volume) and Whynot (2015).

This chapter uncovers meaning-making strategies employed by deaf conference presenters, but leaves open other questions about the effectiveness of the forms created and whether they are understood by different audience members. At the very least, it offers empirical data that can help inform others about the creative resources that signed language users recruit to communicate across language barriers and it contributes to the small amount of information about a specific genre of International Sign contact.

REFERENCES

Allsop, L., Woll, B., & Brauti, J. M. (1994). International Sign: The creation of an international deaf community and sign language. In H. Bos & G. Schermer (Eds.), *Sign language research* (pp. 171–188). Hamburg, Germany: Signum Press.

Brennan, M. (1990). Productive morphology in British Sign Language: Focus on the role of metaphors. In S. Prillwitz & T. Vollhaber (Eds.), *Current trends in European sign language research: Proceedings of the Third European Congress on Sign Language Research, Hamburg July 26–29, 1989* (pp. 205–228). Hamburg, Germany: Signum Press.

Brennan, M. (1992). The visual world of BSL: An introduction. In D. Brien (Ed.), *Dictionary of British Sign Language/English* (pp. 1–133). London, UK: Faber and Faber.

Clark, H. H., & Gerrig, R. J. (1990). Quotations as demonstrations. *Language, 66*(4), 764–805.

Cormier, K., Fenlon, J., Rentelis, R., & Schembri, A. (2011). Lexical frequency in British Sign Language conversation: A corpus-based approach. In P. K. Austin, O. Bond, L. Marten, & D. Nathan (Eds.), *Proceedings of the Conference on Language Documentation and Linguistic Theory 3*. London,

UK: School of Oriental and African Studies. Retrieved from http://kearsy.macmate.me/web/Publications_files/Lexical%20frequency%20in%20British%20Sign%20Language%20LDLT3.pdf

De Matteo, A. (1977). Visual imagery and visual analogies in American Sign Language. In L. Friedman (Ed.), *On the other hand—New perspectives on American Sign Language* (pp. 109–136). New York, NY: Academic Press.

Dudis, P. (2004). Body partitioning and real-space blends. *Cognitive Linguistics, 15*(2), 223–238.

Enfield, N. J. (2009). *The anatomy of meaning: Speech, gesture, and composite utterances.* Cambridge, UK: Cambridge University Press.

Engberg-Pedersen, E. (1993). *Space in Danish Sign Language: The semantics and morphosyntax of the use of space in a visual language.* Hamburg: Signum Press.

Evans, V., & Green, M. (2006). *Cognitive linguistics: An introduction.* Edinburgh, UK: Edinburgh University Press.

Fauconnier, G., & Turner, M. (1996). Blending as a central process of grammar. In A. Goldberg (Ed.), *Conceptual structure, discourse, and language* (pp. 113–130). Stanford, CA: CSLI Publications.

Ferrara, L. (2012). *The grammar of depiction: Exploring gesture and language in Australian Sign Language (Auslan)* (Doctoral dissertation, Macquarie University, Sydney, Australia).

Ferrara, L. & Johnston, T. (2014). Elaborating who's what: A study of constructed action and clause structure in Auslan (Australian Sign Language). *Australian Journal of Linguistics, 34*(2), 193–215.

Green, E. M. (2014). Building the tower of Babel: International Sign, linguistic commensuration, and moral orientation. *Language in Society, 43*(4), 445–465.

Hiddinga, A., & Crasborn, O. (2011). Sign languages and globalization. *Language in Society, 40*(4), 483–505.

Hoza, J. (2011). The discourse and politeness functions of HEY and WELL in American Sign Language. In C. B. Roy (Ed.), *Discourse in Signed Languages.* (pp. 69–95). Washington DC: Gallaudet University Press.

Johnston, T. (2003a). BSL, Auslan and NZSL: Three signed languages or one? In A. Baker, B. van den Bogaerde, & O. Crasborn (Eds.), *Cross linguistic perspectives in sign language research: Selected papers from TISLR 2000* (pp. 47–69). Hamburg, Germany: Signum Verlag.

Johnston, T. (2003b). Language standardization and signed language dictionaries. *Sign Language Studies, 3*(4), 431–468.

Johnston, T. (2012). Lexical frequency in sign languages. *Journal of Deaf Studies and Deaf Education, 17*(2), 163–193.

Johnston, T. (2013a). Towards a comparative semiotics of pointing actions in signed and spoken languages. *Gesture, 13*(2), 109–142.

Johnston, T. (2013b). Formational and functional characteristics of pointing signs in a corpus of Auslan (Australian sign language): Are the data sufficient to posit a grammatical class of "pronouns" in Auslan? *Corpus Linguistics and Linguistic Theory*, 9(1), 109–159.

Johnston, T. (2014). *Auslan corpus annotation guidelines*. Retrieved from http://media.auslan.org.au/attachments/Johnston_AuslanCorpusAnnotationGuidelines_14June2014.pdf

Johnston, T., & Schembri, A. (1999). On defining lexeme in a sign language. *Sign Language and Linguistics*, 2(2), 115–185.

Johnston, T., & Schembri, A. (2007). *Australian sign language (Auslan): An introduction to sign language linguistics*. Cambridge, UK: Cambridge University Press.

Kendon, A. (2004). *Gesture: Visible action as utterance*. Cambridge, UK: Cambridge University Press.

Lakoff, G., & Johnson, M. (1980). *Metaphors we live by*. Chicago: University of Chicago Press.

Liddell, S. K. (1995). Real, surrogate, and token space: Grammatical consequences in ASL. In K. Emmorey & J. Reilly (Eds.), *Language, gesture, and space* (pp. 19–41). Hillsdale, NJ: Lawrence Erlbaum.

Liddell, S. K. (2003). *Grammar, gesture, and meaning in American Sign Language*. Cambridge, UK: Cambridge University Press.

Lillo-Martin, D., & Klima, E. S. (1990). Pointing out differences: ASL pronouns in syntactic theory. In S. Fischer & P. Siple (Eds.), *Theoretical issues in sign language research: Vol. 1. Linguistics* (pp. 191–210). Chicago, IL: University of Chicago Press.

McBurney, S. L. (2002). Pronominal reference in signed and spoken language: Are grammatical categories modality-dependent? In R. P. Meier, K. Cormier, & D. Quinto-Pozos (Eds.), *Modality and structure in signed and spoken languages* (pp. 329–369). Cambridge, UK: Cambridge University Press.

McKee, R., & Napier, J. (2002). Interpreting into International Sign pidgin: An analysis. *Sign Language and Linguistics, 5*(1), 27–54.

McNeill, D. (2005). *Gesture and thought*. Chicago, IL: University of Chicago Press.

Mesch, J. (2010). *Perspectives on the concept and definition of International Sign*. Helsinki, Finland: World Federation of the Deaf. Retrieved from http://www.wfdeaf.org/wp-content/uploads/2012/03/Perspectives-on-the-Concept-and-Definition-of-IS_Mesch-FINAL.pdf

Metzger, M. (1995). Constructed action and constructed dialogue in American Sign Language. In C. Lucas (Ed.), *Sociolinguistics of deaf communities* (pp. 255–271). Washington DC: Gallaudet University Press.

Moody, B. (1987). Sign language: International gestures. In J. V. van Cleve (Ed.). *Gallaudet encyclopedia on deaf people and deafness: Vol 3* (pp. 81–82). New York, NY: McGraw-Hill.

Moody, B. (2002). International Sign: A practitioner's perspective. *Journal of Interpretation* (pp. 1–47). Silver Spring, MD: RID Publications.

Morford, J. P., & Macfarlane, J. (2003). Frequency characteristics of American Sign Language. *Sign Language Studies, 3*(2), 213–223.

Mori, S. (2011). *IS interpreter in Asia and Pacific region: From experience as IS interpreter for JICA-JFD Deaf leadership training programme.* Retrieved from http://efsli.blogspot.de/2011/07/is-interpreter-in-asia-and-pacific.html

Napier, J. (2000). Free interpretation: What is it and does it translate into training? In A. Schembri, J. Napier, R. Beattie, & G. Leigh (Eds.), *Deaf Studies, Sydney 1998: Selected papers from the Australasian Deaf Studies Research Symposium* (pp. 21–33). Sydney, Australia: North Rocks Press.

Okrent, A. (2002). A modality-free notion of gesture and how it can help us with the morpheme vs. gesture questions in sign language linguistics (or at least give us some criteria to work with). In R. Meier, K. Cormier, & D. Quinto-Pozos (Eds.), *Modality and structure in signed and spoken languages* (pp. 175–198). New York, NY: Cambridge University Press.

Quinto-Pozos, D. (2008). Sign language contact and interference: ASL and LSM. *Language in Society, 37,* 161–189.

Rosenstock, R. (2004). *An investigation of International Sign: Analyzing structure and comprehension* (Doctoral dissertation, Gallaudet University, Washington, DC).

Rosenstock, R. (2008). International Sign: Surprising sources of the lexicon. In R. M. de Quadros (Ed.), *Spinning and unraveling the past, present, and future, TISLR 9: Forty-five papers and three posters from the Ninth Theoretical Issues in Sign Language Research Conference Sign Languages.* Petrópolis, Brazil: Editora Arara Azul.

Roy, C. (1989). Features of discourse in an American Sign Language lecture. In C. Lucas (Ed.), *The sociolinguistics of the deaf community* (pp. 231–251). San Diego, CA: Academic Press.

Schembri, A. (2001). *Issues in the analysis of polycomponential verbs in Australian Sign Language (Auslan)* (Doctoral dissertation, University of Sydney, Sydney, Australia).

Schembri, A., C., Jones, C., & Burnham, D. (2005). Comparing action gestures and classifier verbs of motion: Evidence from Australian Sign Language, Taiwan Sign Language, and nonsigners' gestures without speech. *Journal of Deaf Studies and Deaf Education, 10*(3), 272–290.

Schick, B. S. (1990). Classifier predicates in American Sign Language. *International Journal of Sign Linguistics, 1*(1), 15–40.

Supalla, T. (1978). Morphology of verbs of motion and location in American Sign Language. In F. Caccamise & D. Hicks (Eds.), *Proceedings of the Second National Symposium on Sign Language Research and Teaching,* (p.27-45). Silver Spring, MD: National Association of the Deaf.

Supalla, T. (1982). *Structure and acquisition of verbs of motion and location in SL* (Doctoral dissertation, University of California, San Diego, CA).

Supalla, T., & Webb R. (1995). The grammar of International Sign: A new look at pidgin languages. In K. Emmorey and J. S. Reilly (Eds.), *Language, gesture, and space* (pp. 333–352). Hillsdale, NJ: Lawrence Erlbaum.

Tannen, D. (1986). *That's not what I meant! How conversational style makes or breaks your relations with others.* London, UK: J. M. Dent & Sons.

Taub, S. F. (2001). *Language from the body: Iconicity and metaphor in American Sign Language.* Cambridge, UK: Cambridge University Press.

Whynot, L. A. (2014). *Assessing comprehension of international sign lectures: Linguistic and sociolinguistic factors* (Doctoral dissertation, Macquarie University, Sydney, Australia).

Wilcox, P. (2000). *Metaphor in American Sign Language.* Washington, DC: Gallaudet University Press.

Wilcox, S. (2004). Gesture and language: Cross-linguistic and historical data from signed languages. *Gesture* 4(1), 43–73.

Winston, E. (1991). Spatial referencing and cohesion in an American Sign Language text. *Sign Language Studies*, 73, 397–409.

Wit, M. de. (2010). EUMASLI module 3.1—Linguistic coping strategies from international sign to English. European Master in Sign Language Interpreting. Research report.

Woll, B. (1990). International perspectives on sign language communication. *International Journal of Sign Linguistics,* 1(2), 107–120.

Zeshan, U. (2015). "Making meaning": Communication between sign language users without a shared language. *Cognitive Linguistics,* 26(2), 211–260.

Comparative Analysis of Depicting Signs in International Sign and Natural Sign Language Interpreting

Christopher Stone and Debra Russell

Across the globe, there are increased opportunities for Deaf interpreters to provide interpreting services in a range of settings, from one-to-one interactions between Deaf and nondeaf participants in medical, legal, and/or employment settings, to working with larger audiences in educational and conference settings. While frequently the work of Deaf interpreters and their co-interpreters occurs in the national signed language of the country (for example, into British Sign Language [BSL] or Langue des Signes Québécoise), there are other occasions when Deaf interpreters provide interpreting services into what is known as International Sign (IS). Recently, research attention has turned to the work of interpreters providing IS, with the goal of increasing our understanding of this unique language contact between users of different signed languages.

In this study, we examined the work of IS teams providing interpretation at an international conference. Previous research emphasized clear, communicative IS as being visually motivated, without further descriptions of the embodied nature of experience and its role in motivating IS production (Allsop, Woll, & Brauti, 1995; Suppalla & Webb, 1995; Rosenstock, 2008). The term *visual* could mean iconic language use, although iconicity is complex and may be further categorized (Taub, 2001). Depiction is one type of iconicity where, in addition to their usual function, verbs also depict the event they encode (Dudis, 2007) and usefully describes experientially motivated decisions in IS interpreting. Using a

We thank Keith Gamache, the research assistant who worked on this project at Gallaudet University. We also thank the ESRC and SSRC for funding through the Collaborative Visiting Fellow program, which supported the collection of these data.

depiction framework from the work of Dudis (2007), we broadened our analysis of previously reported findings (Stone & Russell, 2014) and analyzed verbs that depict action and verbs that depict process within the pivot languages (Kaiser, 1999) of the co-interpreter (CI) and IS of the Deaf interpreter (DI). Finally we examined the nonmanual markers used to depict the experience of self within the interpretation by observing the similarities and differences among the DIs, CIs (American Sign Language [ASL] and BSL were the pivot languages), and ASL interpreters. The results showed that the manifestations of depiction in the signing of the deaf interpreters is more evident than in that of the nondeaf CIs. Across all interpreters, the highest ranked categories were indicating verbs and depicting verbs, and the lowest ranked were *life size I* (i.e., the depiction of life-sized objects and events in front of the signer), *hand/entity/self D* (i.e., the hand represents an entity associated with the "experiencing self" being depicted that does not occupy a location in the life-sized depiction), and *space as entity* (i.e., a two-dimensional plane in front of the signer that cannot be manipulated such as a calendar or map). The results hold implications for interpreters working in teams to provide IS interpretation and interpreter educators who are preparing Deaf and nondeaf teams to work between a natural signed language and IS. The results may also be of interest to organizations tasked with developing the early accreditation processes for IS interpreters.

WHAT IS INTERNATIONAL SIGN?

International Sign has been described as a contact phenomenon and situational pidgin (McKee & Napier, 2002), although its features do not match those of a pidgin (see Lucas & Valli, 1992). It is ostensibly an extension of foreigner talk; that is, it incorporates the same types of language modification native signers use to interact with nonnative signers. Foreigner talk includes "slower rate of speech, louder speech, longer pauses, common vocabulary, few idioms, greater use of gesture, more repetition, more summaries of preceding utterances, shorter utterances and more deliberate articulation" (Gass & Madden, 1985, p. 4).

International Sign has no single, globally established form, although there does exist some organizationally established lexicon (Supalla & Webb, 1995). The organizational use of an established lexicon and international signing strategies differs from the gesture-rich interaction one might see in an ad hoc situation where two Deaf people engage in communicative "translanguaging" (Creese & Blackledge, 2010). This is where Deaf people from different cultures communicate by drawing upon their knowledge of the iconicity of signs and other foreign sign languages. Organizational lexicons are situational in nature and thus are not able to easily convey rich meanings to Deaf people who have had no exposure to or practice with the organization's established lexicon. Greater mobility of Deaf people within some transnational regions (e.g., Europe) results in greater frequency of exposure to Deaf people from other countries within those regions, greater knowledge of the lexicon of other signed languages, and more frequent use of "international" signing strategies. This is by no means a new phenomenon; Laffon de Ladébat (1815) describes Clerc's meeting with the deaf children at the Braidwood school:

> As soon as Clerc beheld this sight [the children at dinner] his face became animated; he was as agitated as a traveller of sensibility would be on meeting all of a sudden in distant regions, a colony of his own countrymen. . . . Clerc approached them. He made signs and they answered him by signs. This unexpected communication caused a most delicious sensation in them and for us was a scene of expression and sensibility that gave us the most heartfelt satisfaction. (pp. 170–173)

This gives us an example of a situational pidgin between a Deaf person who used langue des signes française (LSF) and Deaf children who used BSL. This type of contact was not uncommon within Europe. The Paris banquets for deaf-mutes (*sic*) in the 19th century are another example of the coming together of Deaf people in a transnational context, although it is not clear whether a situational pidgin was used in Paris:

> There were always foreign deaf-mutes in attendance, right from the first banquet. At the third, there were deaf-mutes from Italy, England, and Germany. . . . It seems that many of these foreign visitors . . . were painters drawn to Paris to learn or to perfect their art, and even to stay on as residents. Several decades later, deaf American artists . . . and the painter J. A. Terry (father of the Argentinean deaf movement) probably all participated in the banquets. (Mottez, 1993, p. 147)

Mottez continues:

> Deaf-mute foreigners, in their toasts, never missed a chance to emphasize the universal nature of signs, claiming that "it easily wins out over

all the separate limiting languages of speaking humanity, packed into a more or less limited territory. Our language encompasses all nations, the entire globe." (p. 149)

It is not clear whether another signed language served as a matrix language (the pattern) for less fluent LSF users with LSF vocabulary brought in, thus creating a situational pidgin, or whether the length of stay of the banqueters meant that LSF was the language of interaction.

Deaf people traveling is not the only form of transnational contact within the Deaf community. The education of teachers of the Deaf has often resulted in some signed languages having similarities. As McCagg (1993) notes, teachers of the Deaf for the Hapsburg Empire were trained in Germany. In Ireland, the education system and Irish Sign Language (ISL) were originally influenced by BSL and then later by LSF (Burns, 1998). All three of these languages (BSL, ISL, and LSF) have influenced or become the progenitor of other signed languages that have become dialects or independent signed languages (Aarons & Akach, 1998; Johnston, 2001). As with spoken languages, sign language labels often depend on politics rather than linguistic description. These influences spread throughout the globe from across Europe to the Americas to the Antipodes.

The colonial influence on sign languages via institutional education is something that has likely influenced the comprehensibility of "international" signs. European sign languages were brought to many countries; BSL has directly influenced many signed languages and in turn some of its dialects have been influenced by LSF, particularly those also influenced by ISL (Woll, Sutton-Spence, & Elton, 2001). LSF has had a profound influence on many signed languages, including ASL (Lane, 1984) and Russian Sign Language (Mathur, Rathmann, & Mirus, cited in Woll, Sutton-Spence, & Elton, 2001, p. 29), and its footprint spread across central Asia into the area of the old Soviet empire (Ojala-Signell & Komarova, 2006). The sign languages of other colonial powers in Europe influenced the education systems of the Americas (such as Italian Sign Language [LIS] and Spanish Sign Language [LSE], which influenced Argentina's languages), and German Sign Language (DGS) has had an influence on Israeli Sign Language (Namir, Sela, Rimor, & Schlesinger, 1979). ISL and ASL have been brought to many countries in the southern hemisphere through education and religious missionary work (Hiddinga & Crasborn, 2011; Nyst, 2010).

These linguistic influences could also affect the types of linguistic structures that we see in IS, including the use of timelines, topographic space, and the metaphoric use of space (with the future in front, the past behind, and hierarchies of more powerful higher and less powerful lower, etc.). Although the use of family trees to document the influence of one sign language on another has not been that successful, it is clear that many urban signed languages (Jepson, 1991) have complex relationships with each other. It is not clear how useful and effective IS would be for users of rural signed languages (Jepson, 1991).

International Sign is, however, an effective mode of communication for many Deaf people in transnational contexts and has been used as a lingua franca at international events, including all the Deaflympics and the first Silent Games in 1924, in which nine European countries took part. International signing was also used in a global political movement, the World Federation of the Deaf (WFD), established in Rome in 1951. Interpretation into IS has been provided since 1977 (Scott Gibson & Ojala, 1994).

Thompson, Vinson, and Vigliocco (2009) have shown a processing advantage for Deaf people in language-based tasks of iconicity. This heightened awareness may be attributed to daily gestural interactions with hearing nonsigners with no exposure to a visual language, where iconic signs influence the signer's gesture repertoire and signs found to be frequently effective inform signer notions of iconicity. Some parameters of some signs may be more transparent to other Deaf individuals (metaphoric path movement, metaphoric location, mouth gestures) than others (handshape). Furthermore, visual motivations for iconicity may well be more transparent in much the same way that Japanese *giseigo* (words mimicking voices) are more transparent for English speakers with no exposure to spoken Japanese (Iwasaki, Vinson, & Vigliocco, 2007), due to the direct resemblance.

When two Deaf individuals come together, both having similar experiences of interacting with hearing nonsigners with no exposure to a visual language and both having experience of using a visual language, iconic signs can be used effectively to generate a situational pidgin. The more experience one has in trying to communicate with Deaf people who use different languages, the greater the exposure to different visually motivated lexicons and the greater number of strategies and resources an individual signer will have for situational translanguaging. This also coincides with the tolerance of the Deaf community for low frequency or atypical grammar, due to the low incidence of native signers with typical language acquisition (Neidle, MacLaughin, Lee, Bahan, & Kegel, 1998, p. 34).

This communication also heavily relies on the inferential processes of the watcher to understand the lexical narrowing or broadening of the sign presented. Strings of actions and descriptions are presented from an experiential perspective for interlocutors to understand context-specific meanings.

THEORETICAL FRAMEWORK: WHAT IS DEPICTION?

Dudis (2007), building on the work of Liddell (2003), uses the term *depiction* to describe the iconic mapping terms that visually represent semantic components in signed languages.[1] Further, Dudis suggests that there are additional components within these iconic representations, namely the subject (or the self), vantage point, and temporal progression. Distinguishing between depicting and nondepicting verbs, Dudis stresses that depicting verbs depict the event they encode (2007) and that signers can depict an experiencing self, through constructed dialogue, constructed action, or handling classifiers. Such depictions can be represented within the life-sized depiction or be physically associated with the self but not occupy a life-sized location. In addition, Dudis suggests that an event can be depicted without any representation of self, using devices for describing an event or scene or concrete object, exploiting generic space, event space, real space, or blended space (see Dudis, 2007, for a complete discussion of this topic).

Dudis provides compelling evidence for the depiction of settings, objects, and events as core features of ASL discourse, where iconicity is demonstrated and explicated. Thus, this cognitive linguistic framework led us to question whether the interpreters working in IS might demonstrate similar approaches in representing depicting verbs. Further, we wondered whether the co-interpreter acting as the feed interpreter to the Deaf IS interpreter might use specific forms of depicting verbs and whether these verbs would be retained or changed in the IS interpretation. If they were changed, in what ways were they different? Would there be a difference in the occurrences of each depiction type in each language? How might individual preferences or team strategies differ? By examining our dataset

1. For many years depiction was the study of classifiers (see Zwiterslood, 2012, for a comprehensive discussion of classifiers).

through this linguistic framework, we sought to explore the potential significance for understanding the nature of experientially motivated linguistic decisions in IS interpreting.

DESCRIPTION OF STUDY AND DATASET

This study is an examination of a team of Deaf interpreters and nondeaf[2] co-interpreters working as interpreting teams at an international academic conference. We also have data of a team of nondeaf interpreters working from spoken English to ASL at the conference, although that dataset is not analyzed here. We explore the strategies utilized by Deaf-nondeaf (DI-CI) interpreting teams to provide renderings into IS (see Stone & Russell, 2014). The nondeaf co-interpreters provided the pivot language (Kaiser, 1999) in a natural signed language (ASL or BSL) and the Deaf interpreters worked from natural signed languages into IS.

For the purposes of this chapter, we have drawn data addressing the following three research questions:

1. Will verbs that depict action and verbs that depict process within the pivot language of the CI be retained or changed in the IS interpretation of the DI?
2. Will we see differences in the use of depiction within the interpretation between the DIs and CIs?
3. In what ways might individual interpreter preferences or team preferences impact the use of depiction in the target IS?

At a large international conference, we recruited experienced interpreters to participate in the study. The University of Alberta granted ethics approval for the study. A total of four interpreters participated, and each had at least 10 years of experience as sign language interpreters. All participants had extensive experience working in multilingual, international settings, where teams of interpreters work concurrently. The interpreters working from English BSL IS had previous experience as a team; the English-ASL-IS team members had not worked with each other before.

All four interpreters had been involved in interpreter education, both as recipients and as instructors. All of the interpreters possessed professional certification in their own countries, were active members of their

2. We use the term *nondeaf* rather than *hearing* to ensure the discussion is Deaf-focused.

national interpreter professional associations, and were involved in transnational interpreter organizations. The DIs have been actively involved as interpreter leaders, promoting the use of Deaf interpreters in all aspects of community, conference, and multilingual settings.

The two Deaf interpreters have been sign language users since birth, born to sign-language-using families. Both CIs are nonnative sign language users with more than 25 years of experience using their signed language; both were working in their principal language combination (ASL-English or BSL-English) and had experience working with DIs in both community and conference settings. The two English-ASL interpreters are also nonnative sign language users and both have used ASL for more than 25 years. During rest periods and when communicating among the wider interpreting team (DIs, CIs, and English-ASL interpreters), all of the interpreters used ASL.

Data Collection

The interpreting data were collected during a single session. During that presentation session, several interpreting teams were working alongside each other. These included a team that was providing an IS interpretation from the English source message; a team that was providing an ASL interpretation; an English-French interpreter; and several other teams of sign language interpreters working in languages other than the conference's official languages.

The video footage of the interpreters' work was imported into ELAN (a video annotation software developed by MPI). Time-coded annotations were added to the footage to explore depiction strategies within and between the DI-CI teams. Different tiers were used to identify the depiction features used in structure of the pivot language and the target language.

DATA ANALYSIS

Three individuals analyzed the data: a Deaf doctoral student, who is a native signer of ASL with more than 5 years of signed language annotation experience, and the two researchers. The Deaf doctoral student had limited exposure to IS, and despite several experiences interacting with non-American Deaf people, he was not familiar with using IS within academic conferences or other institutional settings. The goal of having an IS-naïve coder was to ensure that any depiction identified by the coder was transparent to an IS-naïve Deaf viewer. As he said,

> It is part of the project to see me, as a native ASL user, how I see depiction in international sign. It is outside my norm, and sometimes I struggle to understand if it is actually a depiction.

Thus part of the project's design is profiting from the intuitions of our ASL-native data coder during the first and subsequent viewings of the natural sign language and IS interpreted language product.

Using the coding descriptions created by Dudis in a depiction flowchart,[3] separate tiers were created for each of the categories. The linguistic types included in the analysis were metonymy, indicating verb, depicting verb, partitioning, constructed dialogue, contrasted action, temporal compression, diagrammatic setting, diagrammatic event, multiple life size, psychological experience, life-sized scene no self, life-sized hand entity and self, space as entity, buoy, timeline, and token. The data were coded, contrasting the interpreting work of the Deaf interpreter and nondeaf co-interpreter within the teams and across the teams.

RESULTS AND DISCUSSION

In Table 1 we show the total number of depicting signs used by the DIs and CIs, arranged from the most frequently used numerically to the least frequently used numerically. When considering the differences between Deaf and nondeaf interpreters, two (nonsignificant) differences indicated a larger sample size might provide us with a significant difference for the following: the *total use of depiction* for Deaf interpreters ($M = 253.33$, $SD = 33.08$) and nondeaf interpreters ($M - 174.67$, $SD = 41.48$); $t(4) = 2.57$, $p = 0.062$; and the *use of depicting verbs* for Deaf interpreters ($M = 33.00$, $SD = 7.81$) and nondeaf interpreters ($M = 19.33$, $SD = 8.39$); $t(4) = 2.07$, $p = 0.108$. This would appear to confirm anecdotal discussions of the visual nature of IS. Depicting verbs that "depict the event they encode" such that "the verb's iconicity constrains its usage" (Dudis, 2007, p. 3), and this specific type of iconic encoding motivated from a visual-tactile experience of the world, aptly identify this visual nature of "good" sign language production.

3. See http://www.sign-lang.uni-hamburg.de/lrec2008/pdf/lrec2008_dudis.pdf.

TABLE 1. *Use of Depiction.*

Depiction type	DI1	DI1(2)	CI1	CI1(2)	DI2	CI2	Total
Indicating verb	51	94	30	61	75	45	356
Depicting verb	29	42	15	29	28	14	157
Constructed dialogue	13	36	10	19	28	18	124
Constructed action	25	25	19	40	7	6	122
Token: N	8	11	5	1	52	21	98
Life-sized scene no self: G	25	11	17	11	7	7	78
Diagrammatic setting	11	21	12	9	9	5	67
Buoy: L	7	16	2	12	7	11	55
Temporal compression	10	14	13	5	10	1	53
Diagrammatic event	19	4	5	7	12	5	52
Metonymy	3	5	8	13	8	3	40
Psychological experience	4	7	10	6	5	1	33
Multiple life-size: C	1	1	7	1	7	3	20
Partitioning	2	2	3	2	7	0	16
Timeline: M	5	1	4	5	0	0	15
Space as entity: K	2	1	2	0	3	1	9
Hand entity and self: D	1	0	0	0	0	0	1
Life size: I	0	0	0	0	0	0	0
Total	216	291	162	221	265	141	1296

Note. See Dudis's flowchart for a description of the depiction types with letter, such as Token: N.

The use of indicating verbs, the most frequent type of depicting signs used by all of the interpreters, showed no significant difference between Deaf interpreters ($M = 73.33$, $SD = 21.55$) and nondeaf interpreters ($M = 45.33$, $SD = 15.50$); $t(4) = 1.83$, $p = 0.142$. Further analysis of natural sign languages and IS would be needed to ascertain whether indicating verbs are more frequently used in natural sign language use or if this is specific to interpreted sign language.

These data suggest that when CIs are providing the pivot language for DIs there is a desire to ensure that patient and agent roles are clearly identifiable—hence the use of verbs that indicate who is doing what to whom. The DIs then produce the target language (IS), which has a greater number of indicating verbs than the pivot language. This could be an example of "foreigner talk" with its greater use of gestures, in that indicating verbs are often discussed as being a fusion between morphemes and pointing gestures (Liddell, 2000). As such, this greater use of gestures by employing indicating verbs could be a strategy to ensure that semantic

TABLE 2. *Indicating and Depicting Verb Frequency.*

Depiction Type	DI1	DI1(2)	CI1	CI1(2)	DI2	CI2
Indicating verb	51	94	30	61	75	45
Depicting verb	29	42	15	29	28	14
Ratio	1.76	2.24	2.00	2.10	2.68	3.21

relationships are more transparent to the audience. Indicating verbs appear to be a feature of most sign languages described to date and as such this seems a reasonable strategy to be employed as part of foreigner talk.

As described by de Beuzville, Johnston & Schembri (2009), 18% of the tokens in a corpus of Auslan narratives were indicating verbs and a further 8% of the tokens in the corpus were depicting verbs. When compared with other text types, narratives have a greater incidence of depiction than other text types (see Fenlon, Schembri, Rentelis, Vinson & Cormier, 2014). We did not undertake a token count but we can compare the relative ratio of 2.25 indicating verbs to depicting verbs. In Table 2 we show some interaction between teams and the frequency of some depiction features. Please note that a lower ratio means that the number of indicating verbs is similar to the number of depicting verbs (i.e., a greater number of depicting verbs than one would expect in a narrative), and it is worth noting that the sources in English are presentations and lectures rather than narratives.

It is difficult to ascertain from these data whether the text type (presentation versus narrative) influences the relative ratios. During this session there were several speakers, and this might have influenced the difference between the use of indicating verbs and depicting verbs. However, the ratio of depicting verbs to indicating verbs decreases in the second session of the work of team 1.

During the first session introductions were made and descriptions were given of the local community development, including specific anecdotes of individual actions (i.e., moments of narration within a presentation/lecture text type). These would appear to be more narrative in structure with more depicting verbs than indicating verbs. Team 2 was much less narrative. Team 1 showed an increase in the relative use of indicating verbs in their second session, although this was the third interpreting period.

Team 2 still had a greater ratio of indicating verbs to depicting verbs. This could be influenced by several factors, but there appears to be some interaction or convergence of the team styles. Both teams actively

TABLE 3. *Constructed Action and Timeline Frequency.*

Depiction Type	DI1	DI1(2)	CI1	CI1(2)	DI2	CI2
Constructed action	25	25	30	40	7	6
Timeline: M	5	1	4	5	0	0

supported the rendering team and witnessed each other's work. When team 1 began their second session, they employed a greater level of indicating verbs, suggesting that once the initial session established a rapport with the audience via greater use of depicting verbs, a narrative structure was used. These data support that the target language of the CI interpreters' pivot language and DIs' target language of IS shifted during the interpretation once the discourse was established.

There are other clear differences between teams 1 and 2, as seen in Table 3.

There was one significant difference for the use of *constructed action* between team 1 (M = 27.25, SD = 8.96) and team 2 (M = 6.50, SD = 0.71); t(4) = 3.09, p = 0.037. Even though there is a clear team difference, the use of these features by the CI interpreter in the pivot language does not appear to influence the production of these features within the IS target language. DI1 clearly used constructed action as a strategy to convey meaning in IS; DI2, however, did not use constructed action as frequently.

There was also one (nonsignificant) difference that appears to indicate that a larger sample size might provide us with a significant difference—the *use of timelines* by team 1 (M = 3.75, SD = 1.89) and team 2 (M = 0.00, SD = 0.00); t(4) = 2.64, p = 0.057. Timelines were used by CI1 in the pivot language as a strategy for presenting information clearly, and this was not something that DI1 relied on. This might also demonstrate that team 1 became more used to working with each other, as DI1 showed

TABLE 4. *Team 2 Top 4 Ranked Depiction Types.*

Depiction Type	DI2	%	CI2	%
Indicating Verb	75	28	45	32
Token: N	52	20	21	15
Depicting Verb	28	11	14	10
Constructed dialogue	28	11	18	13
		70		70

TABLE 5. *Team 1 Top 4 Ranked Depiction Types Sessions 1.*

Depiction Type	DI1-1	%	CI1-1	%
Indicating Verb	51	24	30	19
Depicting Verb	29	13	15	9
Constructed action	25	12	19	12
Life-sized scene no self: G	25	12	17	10
		61		50

much less use of timelines during the second session even though the level of use by CI1 appears to be consistent.

Team 2 had the same top four ranked, with use of tokens appearing in the second position (see Table 4).

This use of tokens could either be a team strategy to manage the process, the influence of CI2 on DI2's IS language construction, or the influence of their shared natural sign language. Notwithstanding token use, indicating verbs and depicting verbs rank in the top four in team 2's use (DI2 39% and CI2 42%) and in the top four in team 1's use in both session 1 (DI1 37% and CI1 28%) and session 2 (DI1 49% and CI1 41%) (see Tables 5 and 6).

Further differences can be seen between both teams that identify the different levels of experience working with each other and again the difference in the shared natural languages being used as the pivot language. Team 1 also uses "life-sized scene no self-depiction" as a strategy in both the pivot language and the IS target language. Although team 2 also uses this strategy, it is used sparsely.

There is further evidence of convergence of interpreting style across the DIs: When DI1 undertakes session 2, constructed dialogue becomes the third most frequent depiction type used.

TABLE 6. *Team 1Top 4 Ranked Depiction Types Session.*

Type (#)	DI1-2	%	CI1-2	%
Indicating Verb	94	34	61	28
Depicting Verb	42	15	29	13
Constructed dialogue	36	13	19	9
Constructed action	25	9	40	18
		71		68

It could also be because the text type changed after the initial introductions and teams 1 and 2 were interpreting similar text types. Considering indicating verbs, depicting verbs, and constructed dialogue as the principal forms of depiction in the pivot language and IS target language, this accounts for DI1 43% and CI1 34% (session 1), DI2 50% and CI2 55%, and DI1 62% and CI1 50% (session 2) of their depiction use.

There is less consistency in the use of specific depiction types across the CIs, although the CIs do rank indicating and depiction verbs within their four most frequently used depiction types. CI1 initially uses a greater number of depiction types than CI2. In fact, in these data the top four depiction types for CI2 and DI2 are the same and account for 70% of the depiction use. This further confirms that team 2 used fewer features than team 1 generally (Stone & Russell, 2014) and might be a further indication of team 2's greater experience working as a CI/DI team.

IMPLICATIONS FROM FINDINGS

In the dataset, the number of annotations using depiction is more evident with the deaf interpreters than the nondeaf co-interpreters. Across all interpreters, the highest ranked categories were indicating verbs and depicting verbs; the lowest ranked were life size I, hand/entitity/self D, and space and entity. The findings may have implications for programs and organizations providing training for IS interpreters and Deaf/nondeaf interpreting teams as they look at the linguistic foundation and strategies that contribute to IS interpretation.

As programs examine curriculum used for such training, there are opportunities to consider the level of knowledge and awareness that the interpreters have of linguistics, particularly depiction strategies. The data revealed a greater number of depicting verbs than expected for a narrative text type even though the overriding text type was presentations/lectures. This invites further exploration and research across a larger sample and in a variety of communicative events—in what ways does the discourse or text type influence the target language output?

Finally, a noticeable shift was observed in the target language and the pivot language once the discourse appeared to be established, thus inviting future investigation about the nature of team interaction and the impact on the interpretation product and process.

As part of the global discussions about the nature of IS and how best to assess whether an interpreter is qualified to provide IS interpretation, this dataset may provide some insight into the linguistic strategies that IS interpreters adopt in order to render a visual target language text. It may also foster exploration of processes of assessment that impact performance, such as the team construction and the differences when the Deaf IS interpreter is able to choose the nondeaf CI that they work with versus being assigned a nondeaf CI who may be unfamiliar to them. These aspects are crucial elements in any discussion of the competencies required by interpreters providing International Sign.

LIMITATIONS

This exploratory study contributes to our understanding of the decisions made by interpreters working in a natural sign language as a pivot language, and interpreters working from a pivot language into International Sign. The results show the frequent use of depicting verbs in both target texts; however, these data are gathered from four interpreters at an international conference that addressed educational issues. A larger study that explores interpreting across a range of international settings, for example, political or sporting events, would broaden the dataset and may suggest different patterns of depicting verbs and representation of self.

In this study, the interpreters working in International Sign did not know the Deaf audience participants; had the interpreters and the Deaf participants known each other, it may have resulted in different linguistic motivations and decisions for structuring the iconicity with the target text.

CONCLUSIONS

Based on the results of this study, it would be useful for future research to examine a larger dataset that captures data across a range of settings and a variety of text types in order to determine if there would be significant differences in the use of depicting verbs between deaf and nondeaf interpreters.

The results showed that DIs employ a greater number of constructions using depiction than the nondeaf CIs. Across all interpreters, the highest ranked categories were *indicating verbs* and *depicting verbs,* and the lowest ranked were *life size I, hand/entity/self D,* and *space and entity.*

The results hold implications for interpreters working in teams to provide IS interpretation and interpreter educators who are preparing Deaf and nondeaf teams to work between a natural signed language and IS. The results may also be of interest to organizations tasked with developing the early accreditation processes for IS interpreters.

REFERENCES

Aarons, D., & Akach, P. (1998). South African Sign Language—One language or many? A sociolinguistic question. *Stellenbosch Papers in Linguistics, 31,* 1–28.

Allsop, L., Woll, B., & Brauti, J. (1995). International Sign: The creation of an international Deaf community and sign language. In H. F. Bos & G. M. Schermer (Eds.), *Sign language research 1994: Proceedings of the Fourth European Congress on Sign Language Research* (pp. 171–188). Hamburg, Germany: Signum.

de Beuzville, L., Johnston, T., & Schembri, A. (2009). The use of space with indicating verbs in Auslan: A corpus-based investigation. *Sign language and Linguistics, 12*(1), 53–82.

Boudreault, P. (2005). Deaf interpreters. In T. Janzen (Ed.), *Topics in signed language interpretation* (pp. 323–353). Philadelphia, PA: Benjamins.

Burns, S. E. (1998). Irish Sign Language: Ireland's second minority language. In C. Lucas (Ed.), *Pinky extension and eye gaze: Language use in deaf communities* (pp. 233–274). Washington, DC: Gallaudet University Press.

Creese, A., & Blackledge, A. (2010). Towards a sociolinguistics of superdiversity. *Zeitschrift für Erziehungswissenschaft, 13*(4), 549–572.

Dudis, P. (2007). *Types of depiction in ASL.* Retrieved from http://www.gallaudet.edu/documents/academic/drl-dudis2007.pdf

Fenlon, J., Schembri, A., Rentelis, R., Vinson, D., & Cormier, K. (2014). Using conversational data to determine lexical frequency in British Sign Language: The influence of text type. *Lingua, 143,* 187–202.

Gass, S., & Madden, C. (Eds.). (1985). *Input in second language acquisition.* Rowley, MA: Newbury House.

Hiddinga, A., & Crasborn, O. (2011). Signed languages and globalization. *Language in Society, 40,* 483–505.

Iwasaki, N., Vinson, D. P., & Vigliocco, G. (2007). What do English speakers know about *gera-gera* and *yota-yota*? A cross-linguistic investigation of mimetic words for laughing and walking. *Japanese-Language Education Around the Globe, 17*, 53–78.

Jepson, J. (1991). Urban and rural sign language in India. *Language in Society, 20*, 37–57.

Johnston, T. (2001). The lexical database of Auslan (Australian Sign Language). *Sign Language and Linguistics, 4*(1/2), 145–169.

Kaiser, W. (1999). L'Histoire de l'Association Internationale des Interprètes de Conférence (AIIC). *Interpreting, 4*(1), 81–95.

Laffon de Ladébat, M. (1815). Recueil des définitions et réponses les plus remarquables de Massieu et Clerc, sourds-muets, aux diverses questions qui leur ont été faites dans les séances publiques de M. l'Abbé Sicard, à Londres: auquel on a joint l'alphabet manuel des sourds-muets, le discours d'ouverture de M. l'Abbé Sicard, et une lettre explicative de sa méthode. [Reports of the most remarkable definitions and answers of Massieu and Clerc, deaf and dumb, the various questions that have been made to them in the public meetings of the Abbé Sicard, in London to which are added the manual alphabet deaf - mute, the opening speech of the Abbé Sicard, and a letter explaining his method.] Retrieved from https://books.google.ca/books/about/Recueil_des_définitions_et_réponses_le.html?id=hv8SAAAAIAAJ&redir_esc=y

Lane, H. (1984). *When the mind hears.* New York: Random House.

Liddell, S. K. (2000). Indicating verbs and pronouns: Pointing away from agreement. In K. Emmorey & H. Lane (Eds.), *The signs of language revisited: An anthology to honor Ursula Bellugi and Edward Klima* (pp. 303–320). Mahwah, NJ: Lawrence Erlbaum.

Liddell, S. K. (2003). *Grammar, gesture, and meaning in American Sign Language.* Cambridge, UK: Cambridge University Press.

Lucas, C., & Valli, C. (1992). *Language contact in the American Deaf community.* New York, NY: Academic Press.

McCagg, W. O. (1993). Some problems in the history of deaf Hungarians. In J. V. Van Cleve (Ed.), *Deaf history unveiled: Interpretation from the new scholarship* (pp. 252–271). Washington, DC: Gallaudet University Press.

McKee, R. L., & Napier, J. (2002). Interpreting into International Sign pidgin: An analysis. *Sign Language and Linguistics, 5*(1), 27–54.

Mottez, B. (1993). The deaf-mute banquets and the birth of the deaf movement. In R. Fischer & H. Lane (Eds.), *Looking back: A reader on the history of Deaf communities and their sign languages* (pp. 143–155). Hamburg, Germany: Signum Press.

Namir, L., Sela, I., Rimor, M., & Schlesinger, I. M. (1979). *Dictionary of Sign Language of the Deaf in Israel.* Jerusalem, Israel: Ministry of Social Welfare.

Neidle, C., MacLaughlin, D., Lee, R., Bahan, B., & Kegl, J. (1998). *American Sign Language linguistic research project* (Report No. 6). Retrieved from http://www.bu.edu/asllrp/rpt6/rpt6.html.

Nyst, V. (2010). Sign languages in West Africa. In D. Brentari (Ed.), *Sign languages* (pp. 405–432). Cambridge, UK: Cambridge University Press.

Ojala-Signell, R., & Komarova, A. (2006). International development co-operation work with sign language interpreters. In R. Locker-McKee (Ed.), *Proceedings of the Inaugural Conference of the World Association of Sign Language Interpreters* (pp. 115–122). Coleford, UK: Douglas McLean.

Ressler, C. I. (1999). A comparative analysis of a direct interpretation and intermediary interpretation in American Sign Language. *Journal of Interpreting*, 71–97.

Rosenstock, R. (2008). The role of iconicity in international sign. *Sign Language Studies, 8*(2), 131–159.

Scott Gibson, L., & Ojala, R. (1994, August). *International Sign interpreting.* Paper presented at the Fourth East and South African Sign Language Seminar, Kampala, Uganda.

Stone, C. (2009). *Toward a Deaf translation norm.* Washington, DC: Gallaudet University Press.

Stone, C., & Russell, D. (2013). Interpreting in International Sign: Decisions of Deaf and non-Deaf interpreters. In B. Costello, R. Shaw, & M. Thumann (Eds.), *Proceedings of the Conference of the World Association of Sign Language Interpreters* (pp. 100–118). Coleford, UK: Douglas McLean.

Stone, C., & Russell, D. (2014). Conference interpreting and interpreting teams. In R. Adam, C. Stone, S. Collins, & M. Metzger (Eds.), *Deaf interpreters at work: International insights* (pp. 140–165). Washington, DC: Gallaudet University Press.

Supalla, T., & Webb, R. (1994). Negation in International Sign. In I. Ahlgren, B. Bergman, & M. Brennan (Eds.), *Perspectives on sign language structure: Papers from the Fifth International Symposium on Sign Language Research, Salamanca, Spain, 25–30 May 1992* (vol. 1, pp. 173–186). Durham, UK: ISLA.

Supalla, T., & Webb, R. (1995). The grammar of International Sign: A new look at pidgin languages. In K. Emmory & J. Reilly (Eds.), *Language, gesture, and space* (pp. 333–352). Mahwah, NJ: Lawrence Erlbaum

Takeda, K. (2008). Interpreting at the Tokyo War Crimes Tribunal. *Interpreting, 10*(1), 65–83.

Taub, S. F. (2001). *Language from the body: Iconicity and metaphor in American Sign Language.* Cambridge, UK: Cambridge University Press.

Thompson, R. L., Vinson, D. P., & Vigliocco, G. (2009). The link between form and meaning in American Sign Language: Lexical processing effects. *Journal*

of Experimental Psychology: Learning, Memory, and Cognition, 35(2), 550–557.
Woll, B., Sutton-Spence, R., & Elton, F. (2001). Multilingualism: The global approach to sign languages. In C. Lucas (Ed.), *The sociolinguistics of sign languages* (pp. 8–32). Cambridge, UK: Cambridge University Press.
Zwiterslood, I. (2012). Classifiers. In R. Pfau, M. Steinbach, & B. Woll (Eds.), *Sign language: An international handbook* (pp. 158–186). Boston, MA: de Gruyter Mouton.

Comprehension of Expository

International Sign

Rachel Rosenstock

Fusillier-Souza (2006) describes a typical and central feature of urban sign language (SL) communities, namely the lack of geographic unity for Deaf communities. This holds even more true for the multilingual international Deaf community. However, Hiddinga and Crasborn (2011) contend that there is a "global, cultural community of Deaf people" (p. 489). In recent years, the body of research on cross-linguistic communication has been growing. However, discussion is often focused on nomenclature, emergence, linguistic features, and interpretation (see Woll, 1990; Supalla & Webb, 1995; McKee & Napier, 2002; Moody, 2002; Rosenstock, 2008; Hiddinga & Crasborn, 2011; Green, 2014; Whynot, 2015; inter alia).

This essay aims to expand the debate to the comprehension of cross-linguistic communication. Here, I distinguish between two forms of cross-linguistic communication within the Deaf community: On one end of a continuum of degrees of conventionalization stands *cross-signing*, a term recently coined by Zeshan, Keiko, & Bradford (2013) and described in more detail in Zeshan (2015). This denotes the ad hoc "communication between sign language users with divergent linguistic backgrounds who have no language in common and minimal experience of international contact" (Zeshan et al., 2013). As the definition states, cross-signing requires face-to-face dialogical contexts, since much of the meaning making happens cooperatively between the interlocutors (Zeshan, 2015). On the other end of the spectrum is a partially conventionalized communication system functioning as a lingua franca in the international Deaf community, in particular in the context of World Federation of the Deaf (WFD) board meetings and conferences, Deaflympics, Deaf Way, and other large gatherings (see McKee & Napier, 2002; Rosenstock, 2004; and Whynot, 2015, for detailed descriptions). Hiddinga and Crasborn (2011), as others, use the term *international sign* (IS), but in contrast to most use lowercase letters to emphasize the fact that even if partially conventionalized, "[international sign] is not a name for a specific variant, but a term that refers to a highly variable phenomenon, defined by its use rather than its structure" (p. 494). Whynot (2015) specifies IS in the context of lecture settings as *expository IS*, a term used in this chapter as well, and further distinguishes between interpreted IS and signed IS (i.e., produced directly by a presenter).

While a discussion of meaning making (a term used with regard to cross-signing by Zeshan, 2015) has been part of most studies and reports on IS, comprehension by audience members has been the focus of only two empirical studies to date, namely Rosenstock (2004) and Whynot (2015). Zeshan's (2015) article describes and discusses at length the negotiation of meaning between the participants cross-signing with each other. However, in expository IS, the strategies described for cross-signing cannot be applied (easily). Regarding IS, a part of my 2004 study compared comprehension of interpreted expository IS, directly produced IS, and American Sign Language (ASL) by nonsigners and signers of different linguistic backgrounds using a computerized nonverbal multiple-choice test as well as free summaries of the clips. It was a first attempt at capturing something that had been previously only anecdotally discussed (see Coppock, 1990a, 1990b; Bergmann, 1990; Moody, 2002; inter alia). Whynot (2015) focused her study of IS comprehension on sequences of expository IS, highly frequent lexicalized signs, and depiction sequences (p. 130). Signers' comprehension in five different countries were tested using four quantitative and one qualitative measure. To what degree and under which circumstances a communication system is comprehensible has or should have bearing on teaching international sign to new users (interpreters or not) and assessing interpreting services? Suggestions for practical applications are discussed here.

FEATURES OF EXPOSITORY INTERNATIONAL SIGN DISCOURSE

As mentioned previously, IS is used both in direct communication between individuals (e.g., the WFD General Assembly [see Green, 2014] or board meetings of the WFD or International Committee of Sports for the Deaf (ICSD) [see Mesch, 2010]). In addition, IS is used by presenters or interpreters in lecture settings (McKee & Napier, 2002; Rosenstock, 2004; Whynot, 2015). Stone (2012, p. 991) observes an increase in usage: "Besides IS serving as a direct form of communication between users of different sign languages, IS interpretation (both into and from IS) is now also increasingly provided."

Adam (2012) summarizes features of expository IS as follows: iconicity, visual-spatial expression, mime, gesture, subject-verb-object word order, five types of negation, verb agreement, referents in the environment, and signs recognized as conventional in IS. This list is certainly not exhaustive, but it shows the broad range of linguistic means available to users of expository IS. In terms of discourse structure and usage, IS texts are described as longer in duration and slower in production (McKee & Napier, 2002; Rosenstock, 2004). Hiddinga and Crasborn (2011, p. 499) point out that "while international sign is a flexible medium that can be very efficient if the interlocutors share a lot of general cultural and situation-specific background knowledge, it is not likely that the same communication speed can be obtained as when using a shared sign language."

General features of the genre apply as well and are described for ASL and Auslan by Roy (1989), Zimmer (1989), McKee (1992, in Napier, 2007, p. 410), and Napier (2006). Eye gaze, body shifts, and mouthings have been identified as playing a significant role in structuring and marking lectures in signed languages (see Napier, 2007, for a literature review). Co-construction opportunities are reported to be minimal in these settings; however, Napier (2007) describes several strategies employed by interpreters to ensure comprehension of a deaf consumer, namely eye gaze, head nod/shake, and pauses. Because of intermittent eye contact between the interlocutors, these feedback signals could be considered and, when necessary, the interpreted output adjusted. This cooperation in the creation of meaning is made much more difficult in a typical conference setting where IS might be used, because working jointly and including feedback is hardly possible for large audiences.

COMPREHENSION OF INTERNATIONAL SIGN

One of the participants in the survey by Mesch (2010) states: "It may not be necessary for IS to have a single, ideal sign for a concept. What is important is the success of communication itself" (p. 6). This immediately begs the question: what determines success? Certainly, comprehension on the part of the audience will figure prominently in the answer.

Making Meaning

Zeshan (2015) describes how in cross-signing "meaning is co-created and negotiated between sign language users from different countries who do not have any language in common" (p. 221). However, cross-signing is linked to settings where participants interactively create a "shared multilingual-multimodal space" (p. 223) in addition to their own communicative resources. This is particularly clear in Zeshan's description of communicating about dates (232ff.): the participants uniformly struggle to communicate the various formats of dates in their respective cultures to each other but succeed in the end using a variety of communicative resources: "In the absence of any shared language, the participants in the conversation are involved in a difficult 'meaning-making' task that challenges the entirety of their multilingual, multimodal, and meta-linguistic skills" (p. 228). Zeshan formulates this clearly: "the target meaning is a matter of negotiation" (p. 236) and subsequently demonstrates repeated interactional patterns ("INTRODUCTION–ACCOMMODATION–PERSISTANCE" [IAP], Zeshan et al., 2013) that reflect this meaning-making in cross-signing. Zeshan (2015, p. 251) also points out that "when [the introduction of a sign] is not immediately followed by [an accommodation] because there is a problem with comprehension, a repair sequence may intervene, sometimes repeatedly, until a form is found that is suitable for the shared multilingual-multimodal space." Zeshan describes the conversations employing cross-signing as being "full of difficulties, hesitations, misunderstandings, and repairs" (251). Through post hoc interviews, Zeshan was able to determine that despite many successful sequences, "there are many instances where attempts at communicating something are abandoned, or where signers think they have understood each other, but have actually miscommunicated" (p. 251).

Many of the described strategies employed by the participants in Zeshan's (2015) study do not apply to expository IS, although Winston and Roy (2015, p. 97) point out that "presenters frame presentations to the responses and reactions of the audience. . . . They pause for laughs or nods of agreement; they scan the audience for signs of understanding." Meaning is not negotiated in the same way between interpreter and audience as it is in instances of cross-signing (Moody, 2002). IS users will bring into a setting their respective individual "multilingual-multimodal space" consisting of "all the gestural, written, spoken and signed languages and modes that the individuals have experienced in their lifetime" (Zeshan, 2015, p. 236). While in cross-signing situations, meaning is a result of joint negotiation and the IAP process described earlier (Zeshan, 2015, pp. 236, 241); this mechanism is much more subtle or absent in expository IS. One of the participants in the WFD survey describes this: "In lectures where [there] is limited feedback available, IS is not adjusted to suit the recipient" (Mesch, 2010, p. 8).

Despite this lack of overt negotiation of meaning, the IS interpreters—like the cross-signers in Zeshan's study—arguably have a preconceived notion about what linguistic structures and lexical items will be successfully understood by the target audience: "The initial shared space would be filled not with actual linguistic structures and communicative resources, but with conjectures in terms of what each participant expects to have in common with the other participant" (Zeshan, 2015, p. 239). This notion also influences linguistic choices: "participants continuously entertain multiple simultaneous hypotheses . . . about what their interlocutor is likely to understand (which then in turn influences the choices in their own signed output)" (Zeshan, 2015, p. 248). This is described in Green (2014) as "linguistic commensuration," namely "the process whereby signers actively try to produce linguistic forms that signers of other languages can make sense of, and to understand their utterances in return" (p. 447). In the same context, she describes that it "aims at (*though does not necessarily achieve*) understanding across difference" (ibid., emphasis added).

McKee and Napier's (2002) analysis of interpreted IS identifies a number of strategies used to adjust to the multilingual audience, making the interpretation both redundant and concise, as well as "predictable in form" (p. 41). These competing motivations between being both as explicit as possible and as conventionalized as possible are also described in detail in my analysis of interpreted IS: "At times, as in the omissions or the use of tokens, the economic considerations clearly override the need for iconicity. In other contexts, such as lexical choices or explanations of basic terms, the repetitions or expansions suggest a heavier reliance on an iconic motivation" (Rosenstock, 2008, p. 154). Considering the unidirectionality of the discourse, the signer is forced to select linguistic material assumed to be understood by the diverse audience members. This is also emphasized by Moody (2002) and explained in more detail by Scott Gibson and Ojala (1994, p. 5):

The competent interpreter has developed highly refined skills in message analysis, and is able to break down the information received into its most fundamental components until the core meaning of the utterance is identified. Then, with the knowledge of Sign Languages . . . is able to produce the message in such a way that Deaf people receiving it are able to use their own knowledge and life experience to reconstruct the pared down core information for comprehension.

All these strategies, however, are limited to adjustments by the presenter or interpreter and do not reflect the actual comprehension of the target message.

Comprehension of IS

Experts seem to differ in their view on how much can successfully be transmitted using IS. Green (2014, p. 458) reports that

multiple people attending the GA [General Assembly of the WFD in 2007 in Madrid], including delegates, either told me or mentioned in my presence that they could not fully understand IS (nor could I). What is more, some people contested the very presumptions that the use of IS meant that everyone present would understand and/or that interpreters were antithetical to the GA's mission.

On the other hand, the nearly 30 years of experience with IS make another expert who participated in the WFD survey (Mesch, 2010, p. 8) much more optimistic: "It was obvious that 80% to 95% of the information is successfully transmitted now after 30 years of IS interpreter development. Very successful in international meetings when the audience is experienced with international conferences and when the interpreters are professional and experienced."

Monteillard (2001, quoted in Fusillier-Souza 2006, p. 35) discusses effective IS communication and distinguishes between discursive, cognitive, and linguistic resources. Furthermore, she describes IS as "a self-organizing linguistic strategy developed to enable *extremely efficient communication* among deaf people from all parts of the world" (quoted in Fusillier-Souza, 2006, p. 35, emphasis added). Other researchers concur: "Although deaf people report different levels of satisfaction about the efficacy and communicative depth of international sign, time and again it appears to come about spontaneously and is reasonably effective" (Hiddinga & Crasborn, 2011, p. 493). Green (2014, pp. 451ff.), however, cautions against the general assumption that comprehension of international sign is based on the selection and understanding of "individual signs (with the possible exception of signs perceived as standard) and sign combinations on the basis of a non-arbitrary form-meaning relationship, usually glossed as iconicity." In my own 2008 publication, I investigate more closely the culturally motivated nature of iconic signs and come to the conclusion that iconic signs are "iconic only to those who share the [relevant] cultural knowledge" (Rosenstock, 2008, p. 144). Green (2014) continues: "The critique of iconicity, which can be extended to metaphor, metonomy, and 'visual concepts' more broadly, makes it exceedingly clear that prior familiarity—if not with the signs then with particular social worlds—affects how and if signers understand IS" (pp. 451ff.). McKee and Napier (2002, p. 31) describe this conflict with regard to linguistic choices of IS interpreters:

> In order to judge what a translated message will mean to the target audience in relation to their experience and cultural assumptions, interpreters need a deep awareness of potentially contrasting cultural frameworks as well as fluency in the source and target languages. Familiarity with the target audience and their culture includes knowledge such as the standard of education and the kind of information and experiences that they have been exposed to, prior to and in the current context. In an international setting with a diverse deaf audience, much of this has to be assumed to be roughly in common, even though in reality there is a wide range of variation from the core commonalities.

In my own work, I analyze this aspect in the lexical composition of IS and its possible effect on comprehension: "Although the influence of European SLs on especially African SLs is widely recognized . . . , the number of cognates [of IS forms] with European SLs was significantly lower in both African and Asian SL. This suggests that despite the historic relation between European and especially African SLs, consumers of IS from Africa and Asia have a disadvantage in comparison to signers from Europe or North America" (Rosenstock, 2004, p. 67).

Both Stone (2012) and Hiddinga and Crasborn (2011, p. 494) emphasize the co-constructive role of the audience in comprehending IS: "IS interpreting can be successful as a means of communication, depending on the experience of the users of the interpreting services. . . . The conversational partner is required to make at least as much effort in understanding as the signer/speaker makes in producing understandable communication"

(Stone 2012, p. 992). This meaning construction is described in Green (2014) as drawing on two major sources. On the one hand, she describes "modality-based resources" and on the other "pragmatic strategies of sense-making" (p. 452). She explains: "Signers are aware of and capitalize on (what they assume to be) shared knowledge and experiences, such as related cultural backgrounds and being deaf in hearing-majority worlds, as well as on the more immediate context of the social setting or event" (ibid.).

Comprehension Testing in IS

To measure the efficacy of IS used by presenters and/or interpreters and identify specific linguistic and social factors influencing the efficacy, the comprehension of the target audience needs to be assessed. In order to assess both the global comprehension as well as different linguistic features of expository IS, a multiple-method approach is necessary. Finally, the audience of expository IS is typically diverse. Detailed information on their linguistic and cultural background and previous experience with IS is necessary in order to contextualize the results of comprehension tests.

In the first attempt to assess comprehension of IS empirically (Rosenstock, 2004), I recruited 51 participants who were assigned to one of five groups[1]:

1. native signers of ASL, 12 participants;
2. native signers of Western SLs, 11 participants;
3. native signers of SLs from Asia, Africa, and the Middle East, 14 participants;
4. hearing second-language (L2) users of ASL, 10 participants;
5. hearing US nonsigners, 4 participants.

Participants in groups 2 and 3 were recruited during the summer and fall from the incoming international student population at Gallaudet University and had a varying degree of exposure to IS and/or ASL and were thus deemed to be a good representation of participants at international conferences in the Deaf community. Participants were asked to complete a series of nonverbal multiple-choice questions regarding the contents of nine different video clips. Five of the clips were excerpts of interpreted IS collected at Deaf Way II, two clips were excerpts of ASL lectures from

1. For a detailed description of the classification of SLs into groups 2 and 3, see Rosenstock (2004, pp. 67ff.).

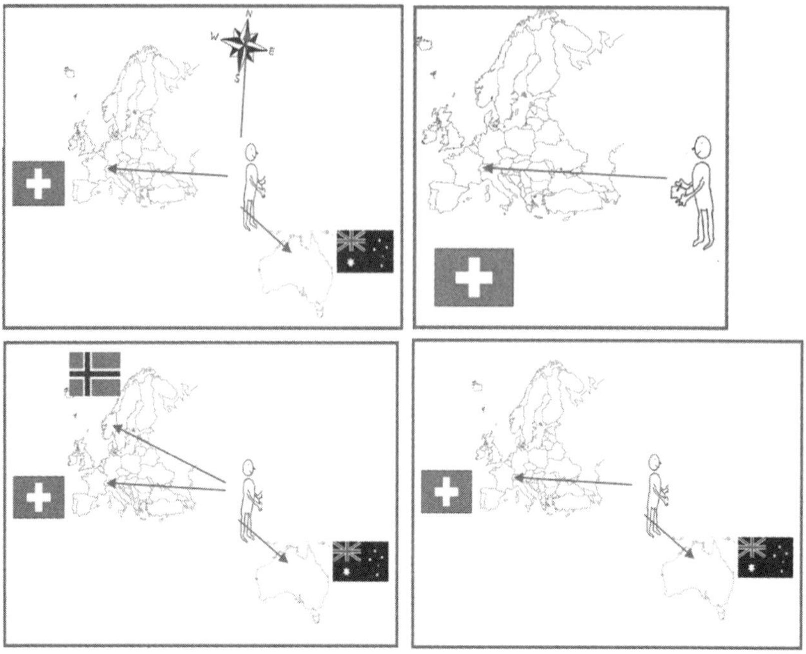

FIGURE 1. *Example of a multiple choice question for testing IS comprehension.*

the same event, and two clips of signed IS were produced for the purpose of this study by an experienced deaf IS interpreter and trainer based on contents of lectures at Deaf Way II (Rosenstock, 2004, p. 69). The clips were about 1 min long.

In a first assessment of global comprehension, participants were asked to watch each of the clips and describe the contents in free summaries, which were audio or video recorded. Deaf participants were given a choice of using their native SL or ASL; hearing participants were instructed to either use ASL or English. The free summaries were subsequently translated into English. The second approach attempted to capture comprehension of specific linguistic features of IS via a series of nonverbal multiple-choice questions (MCQs) relating to each of the video clips, presented in the program Powerlabratory (version 1.0.3). After watching each clip in turn, the participants were presented with four hand-drawn, simultaneously shown pictures, one of which accurately represented the contents and three of which were structurally or sematically similar but incorrect. This procedure was repeated for all nine clips. Figure 1 shows an example of a multiple choice question, relating to a clip on interviews with participants from different countries.

Results of the free summaries seem to indicate that signed IS (as opposed to interpreted IS and ASL) is more comprehensible across groups. This is not surprising, because without time pressures and the enormous cognitive load of the interpreting task, an IS signer is able to better plan and execute the text (Rosenstock, 2004, p. 70). Comprehension can also be differentiated according to linguistic/cultural backgroud: While not quantifiable, native ASL signers and signers of European SLs seem to grasp many of the concepts as well as the relationship between them (agens, patiens, instrument, etc.). L2 learners of ASL and signers of SLs from Asia, Africa, and the Middle East were able to understand (or reproduce) single signs, but global comprehension was low. They had "difficulties determining the relationship between the entities involved in a proposition. There were problems with both numbers and fingerspelling. While tokens were recognized as such, the concepts represented by them were not always clear. The referents for surrogate entities were often confused" (Rosenstock, 2004, p. 247). Surprisingly, nonsigners performed relatively well in the summaries, particularly when surrogates were employed. Most were able to exploit iconicity of lexical items, which confirms Pizzuto and Volterra's (2000) results on hearing nonsigners' recognition of lexical items from NSLs. Two examples of translations of summaries of clip 9 on government funding opportunites for small businesses are given:

1. "Well, deaf people, they work. Just like everyone, they need to have money. And in America, you have the SBA [Small Business Administration], that's part of the government. And deaf people can ask the SBA for a grant. So, to review: deaf people who can't find work or don't have money, there's the SBA, as a part of the government, to give out grants. So now, here in America there's this one deaf person who does have work, but he still asks the SBA for a grant. So he gets the money and continues working, all the while paying back the SBA. That's a real good system here in America and in other rich countries they have the same opportunity. But now, in poor countries, people are stuck without the SBA. They can't find any money" (European SLs, participant 8).
2. "Poor. Money. Someone is pleading and then gets money. That person works. America. Can't. Money" (other SLs, participant 5).

In the summary by participant 5, syntactic structures are mostly missing and only single concepts are listed. In contrast, the summary provided by participant 8 is (almost) complete, explains the complex sequence of events, and reflects good comprehension of lexical items.

The results of the MCQ tests confirm these qualitative results. Both linguistic background of the signers (groups 1–5) as well as type of input (signed IS, interpreted IS, ASL) yielded statistically significant results in a two-way analysis of variance (ANOVA) test (Rosenstock, 2004, pp. 228ff.), confirming that these two factors affect comprehension of IS. The tests confirm what is assumed in most papers on IS: Both signed and interpreted IS are statistically significantly easier to comprehend than ASL.

Analyses of the different groups and their comprehension of specific linguistic features is revealing in term of which strategies employed by presenters and/or interpreters are successful. Five MCQs tested comprehension of fingerspelling. Results indicate that slower production resulted in better comprehension. For number comprehension, results indicate that what Zeshan (2015) describes as representation by "digits" (number of fingers extended equals intended numeral; for numbers above ten, sequences are produced) are not always understood well. As an example, the signer in clip 7 signs TEN EIGHT to represent "18." Across groups, participants were better able to understand a sequential representation of the digits (ONE NINE NINE NINE for "1999"). Across linguistic features, the comprehension of *agens* and *patiens* in verbal constructions seemed to be most difficult. Scores for indicating verbs and surrogates are particularly low in comparison to depicting verbs or tokens, which were better understood by all the groups. Figure 2 shows the compared comprehension scores by the groups for types of linguistic structure.

Results clearly show that all signers have advantages over nonsigners in comprehending signed input. Not surprisingly, users of ASL (L1 or L2) and European SLs have an advantage when trying to comprehend IS—at least in this instance, where data was collected in the United States from IS interpreters with linguistic backgrounds in ASL and British Sign Language (BSL). More surprisingly, use of surrogates, a feature described as typical for IS and used strategically by IS interpreters (McKee & Napier, 2002), seems to be more difficult to comprehend, at least in the context of my study. The difficulty seems to lie with identifying the referents and/or understanding the generic use of the first-person reference. This is exemplified in a free summary of clip 9 by one of the nonsigning participants:

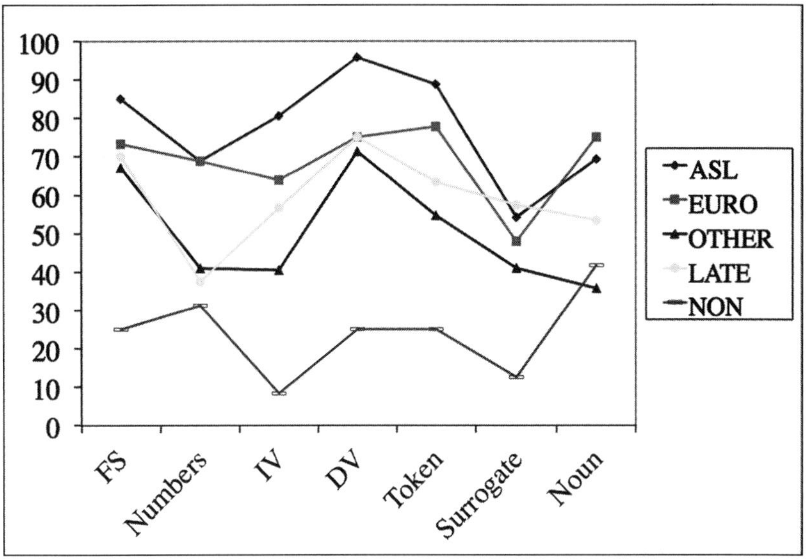

FIGURE 2. *Comprehension scores by groups and types of linguistic structure.*

3. "*I* can't find my money. *I* look everywhere, but *I* can't find it!" (nonsigner, participant 2)

Whynot (2015) focuses her analysis of IS comprehension on expository IS used directly by presenters ("signed IS") and expanded upon and improved methodology in comparison to my approach (Rosenstock, 2004). Thirty-two signers from five different countries (Japan, Czech Republic, Brasil, USA, Australia) were recruited and tested. Each was shown five segments of expository IS produced by a range of signers from different linguistic backgrounds. This was followed by a variety of comprehension tests (subjective comprehensibility ratings, structured questions, lexical identification, depicting sign clusters, and in the case of one clip a retell task). As a means of comparing comprehension of NSLs and IS, Whynot included one video segment from the IS corpus translated into the respective NSL of each participant. Whynot also developed a scoring rubrix for retold contents, creating a measurable assessment of the results.

Whynot's (2015, pp. 197ff.) results indicate that subjects believe that familiarity with the topic, use of gestural elements, and a shared cultural experience enhance comprehension. "It is suspected this is related to shared linguistic and gestural conventions, which includes recognition of familiar surrounding spoken language mouthings appearing in the IS lecture material" (p. 207). Comparisons of self-reported, subjective assessments of comprehension with the results of the structure content questions show a discrepancy: "Findings are significant here because when attendees watch an IS lecture they may think they are comprehending more than they actually are, because understanding global information and some main points may create the illusion of fuller comprehension" (p. 213). Success in comprehending the lexicon of IS "is mainly due to the observer's familiarity with the IS conventional lexical form. Otherwise, the sign may be a cognate from the observer's own NSL, or a transparent, iconic form. Unfortunately, iconicity does not always aid comprehension of a lexical sign, and there are some forms that are opaque to people who are not accustomed to using this IS contact system" (p. 226). Analyzing depicting sequences, Whynot (p. 265) emphasizes the need for context in comprehension: "Depicting signs in IS can aid comprehension of more general discourse organization, but they work in context and coordination with other symbolic material in IS discourse utterances." This confirms my own findings (Rosenstock, 2004) of participants struggling with identifying referents. Whynot's (2015, p. 238) detailed analysis of demographics linking to specific aspects of IS comprehension (lexical IS score and content questions core) identifies statistically significant factors that positively influence IS comprehension, namely, participants who had (1) any amout of travel experience; (2) are native signers of or acquired ASL before age 3; (3) know English; (4) had completed university education; and (5) had any amout of experience in using IS had an advantage over other participants (p. 242).

DISCUSSION

In her introduction to signed language interpreting, Frishberg (1986) emphasizes one of the most important aspects of SL interpreting, namely "how well the deaf viewer will understand the interpreter" (p. 41). This aspect of the interpreting process has been the focus of only a few empirical studies (Napier, 2002; Marschark et al., 2004, 2005; Rodriguez Ortiz, 2007; Rodriguez Ortiz & Mora Roche, 2008). The two studies reviewed here, Rosenstock (2004) and Whynot (2015), aim to identify factors influencing the comprehension of IS. While in both cases methodological limitations suggest the need for more research, a number of areas were identified that significantly impact the comprehension of expository IS. The studies identify several factors that influenced comprehension of IS: type of input (signed IS, interpreted IS, own NSL or ASL); linguistic/cultural background of presenter/interpreter; linguistic/cultural background of audience member; lingustic feature (lexicon, depiction strategies, fingerspelling, number system, mouthing, inter alia); type of information (pragmatic, global, detailed); and familiarity with topic. It must be assumed that there are more factors and that these interplay in complex ways. Expository IS is used in a wide variety of settings and communicative constellations. An experienced presenter using IS with an experienced audience familiar with IS will make different lexical, structural, and pragmatic choices (see Best et al., this volume) than an inexperienced user of IS in a setting with a diverse and unknown audience. In an interpretation, additional factors apply that are touched upon only briefly in this paper: multilingual international settings typically are characterized by the use of several spoken and/or signed languages, not all of which might be familiar to the interpreter, and language competency in familiar languages might vary greatly (de Wit, 2010, p. 226). Even if the interpreter knows a particular language, decoding foreign accents might complicate matters further (p. 227). As more languages are present, the process of interpreting becomes more complex, often including relay interpreting. These factors likely also have an effect on comprehension but these have not been investigated to date. de Wit points out that only two interpreting programs in Europe train students in more than one spoken/signed language. That also implies that "the interpreters currently practicing in multilingual situations do not have specialized training to do so" (p. 36). To bridge this educational gap, de Wit (2010) and de Wit and Sluis (this volume) suggest several strategies, including preparation. Most effectively, training should be provided (Scholl, 2008). The WFD has recognized this need with regard to international sign and has recently founded the IS Interpreting Working Group in order to develop regulation and assessment for IS interpretation at international events (Turner & Napier, 2014).

Not surprisingly, Whynot's (2015) thesis confirms that audience members' previous experience with IS has a significant effect on comprehension. Apart from instituting training of IS interpreters, providing some type of training for potential audience members at international events is another possibility. Apart from periodic workshops and preparatory seminars ahead of large international events, resources for autodidactic training are scarce. For the lexical level, the official DVD of IS signs frequently used in WFD contexts (WFD, 2008) and an online dictionary of IS signs (DeafPlus, 2012, in Whynot, 2015, p. 121) exist but do not seem to reach the (potential) audience successfully, according to Whynot's (2015) lexical frequency study. A positive exception is the Signs2Cross project (see http://signs2cross.signwiki.org/index.php/Main_Page), which aims to provide access to IS via videos of a wide variety of signers.

Considering the high context dependency of the form of IS presenters or interpreters use (McKee & Napier, 2002; Rosenstock, 2004; Whynot, 2015; inter alia), any research conducted outside of the immediate setting will lose reliability. Methodologically, Zeshan's (2015) study on meaning making in cross-signing can also inform comprehension testing of IS, as it documents the process of meaning making. Both investigations of IS comprehension to date have attempted to quantify comprehension post hoc, that is removed from the actual context of production. Whynot (2015, p. 202) notes: "At times, some nuances about the make-up of the audience and degree of formality of the presentation were missed, because study participants were not actually at the conference and were merely observing a video recording of the conference context." While certainly challenging, an in situ investigation of ongoing co-construction of meaning by presenter/interpreter and audience would recognize both context dependency of IS features as well as the online comprehension by audience members. Winston and Roy (2015, p. 98) describe this for lectures in general and point out that "while we are in the middle of discourse, we have only part of the text, and we build our interpretation of it based only on what we have, not the text as a whole." Napier's (2007) study of cooperation in interpreted discourse between a Deaf presenter and a hearing interpreting team suggests capturing this process via a multiple method approach might be possible.

CONCLUSION

Ladd (2008, p. 51) considers international events where people interact through IS a "site in which we can locate some of the deepest manifestations" of deaf collectivity. Zeshan's (2015) recent paper describes some concrete mechanisms by which this collectivity can be created through joint meaning making through cross-signing. The review of literature in this essay attempts to give an overview and make explicit some of the mechanisms at work when attempting to comprehend IS. Many past papers have focused on either the linguistic status or specific features of IS. Detailing the two attempts to date to systematically identify and correlate different factors influencing comprehension (Rosenstock, 2004; Whynot, 2015) provides a starting point for training, interpreter certification, and potentially a shift in our perception of IS.

In 1990, Ansgar Bergmann poignantly stated:

> WFD provides international interpreters for those countries that cannot afford their own interpreters. Provision is not perfect, but it is important to emphasize that it is an emergency solution, which does not give satisfactory benefit. If deaf people get 50% benefit from lectures, it is better than no access to information. (Bergmann, 1990, p. 3)

The widespread and increasing usage of IS today suggests that it is no longer an emergency solution. Nevertheless, results in Rosenstock (2004) and Whynot (2015) show that overall comprehension is far less than lecture comprehension in NSLs (as reported by Marschark et al., 2005), albeit higher than Bergmann's estimate.

As a trainer of IS, Oyserman (this volume) suggests several strategies for novice interpreters of IS, namely visual thinking, use of space, and employing English mouthings where the audience requires. Whynot (2015) and Rosenstock (2004) identify linguistic as well as sociodemographic factors positively influencing comprehension of IS (see above). Certainly, this knowledge should be communicated to IS (interpreter) trainers and be part of a possible certification process for IS interpreters. However, comprehension of IS seems to be more than just the decoding of a code: "Participants observing IS presentations seem to integrate the forms differently from how they process discourse in their NSL, mainly from the contextual knowledge that they are attending to a mixed language system. Additional research on processing differences between NSL reception and IS or other contact language reception is needed to verify this intuition" (Whynot, 2015, p. 218). Methodologically, creative ways of testing comprehension in situ, at the event and during IS usage might provide a window into the more global processes involved.

Finally, (non)comprehension has a cultural and political implication. This is referenced by Baumann and Murray (2009, p. 6): "Because of their constant interaction with others, Deaf people can become a model of a cosmopolitan community. Through the use of gesture and international sign language and through their empathetic bond that is a product of the shared Deaf experience, Deaf people are models of human interaction in a globalized world." Green (2014, p. 461) is more cautious and points out the moral resposibility that comes with using IS: "Communication in IS is neither effortless nor pre-given; signers must engage in linguistic but also, and more fundamentally, moral labor, predicated on and productive of expected and valued forms of relationality. It is this value that motivates and gives meaning to deaf people's commitment to and, even in dissent, use of IS" (p. 461).

REFERENCES

Adam, R. (2012). Language contact and borrowing. In R. Pfau, M. Steinbach, & B. Woll (Eds.), *Sign language: An international handbook* (pp. 841–861). Berlin, Germany: De Gruyter Mouton.

Bauman, H.-D., & Murray, J. (2009). Reframing: From hearing loss to deaf gain. *Deaf Studies Digital Journal, 1*, 1–10.

Bergmann, A. (1990). Extra rational responses: International sign – language? *SignPost*, 4(3), 2–3.

Coppock, P. (1990a). Internationalsignlanguageagain. *SignPost, 3*(1), 14–15.

Coppock, P. (1990b). ISL, Insign'n'Interps. *SignPost, 3*(4), 12–13.

Frishberg, N. (1986). *Interpreting: An introduction.* Silver Spring, MD: RID Publications.

Fusillier-Souza, I. (2006). Emergence and development of signed languages: From a semiogenetic point of view. *Sign Languages Studies, 7*(1), 30–56.

Green, E. M. (2014). Building the tower of Babel: International Sign, linguistic commensuration, and moral orientation. *Language in Society*, 43(4), 445–465.

Hiddinga, A., & Crasborn, O. (2011). Sign languages and globalization. *Language in Society*, 40(4), 483–505.

Ladd, P. (2008). Colonialism and resistance: A brief history of Deafhood. In H.-D. Bauman (Ed.), *Open your eyes: Deaf studies talking* (pp. 42–59). Minneapolis. MN: University of Minnesota Press.

Marschark, M., Sapere, P., Convertino, C., & Seewagen, R. (2005). Access to postsecondary education through sign language interpreting. *Journal of Deaf Studies and Deaf Education, 10*(1), 38–50.

Marschark, M., Sapere, P., Convertino, C., Seewagen, R., & Maltzen, H. (2004). Comprehension of sign language interpreting: Deciphering a complex task situation. *Sign Language Studies*, 4(4), 345–368.

McKee, R., & Napier, J. (2002). Interpreting into international sign pidgin: An analysis. *Journal of Sign language and Linguistics, 5*(1), 27–54.

Mesch, J. (2010). *Perspectives on the concept and definition of International Sign* (Unpublished report). World Federation of the Deaf. Retrieved from http://www.wfdeaf.org/wp-content/uploads/2012/03/Perspectives-on-the-Concept-and-Definition-of-IS_Mesch-FINAL.pdf

Moody, W. (2002). International Sign: A practitioner's perspective. *Journal of Interpretation*, 1–47.

Napier, J. (2002). *Sign language interpreting: Linguistic coping strategies.* Coleford, UK: Douglas McLean.

Napier, J. (2006). A time to reflect: An overview of signed language interpreting. In R. Locker McKee (Ed.), *Interpreter education and interpreting research: Diversity and community in the worldwide sign language interpreting profession* (pp. 12–24). Gloucestershire, UK: Douglas McLean.

Napier, J. (2007). Cooperation in interpreter-mediated monologic talk. *Discourse & Communication, 1*(4), 407–432.

Pizzuto, E., & Volterra, V. (2000). Iconicity and transparency in sign languages: A cross-linguistic cross-cultural view. In K. Emmorey & H. Lane (Eds.), *The signs of language revisited: An anthology in honor of Ursula Bellugi and Edward Klima* (pp. 261–286). Hillsdale, NJ: Lawrence Erlbaum.

Rodriguez Ortiz, I. R. (2007). Sign language comprehension: The case of Spanish Sign Language. *Journal of Deaf Studies and Deaf Education, 13*(3), 378–390.

Rodrıguez Ortiz, I. R., & Mora Roche, J. (2008). The efficiency of information transmission for sign and spoken language. *American Annals of the Deaf, 152*(5), 480–494.

Rosenstock, R. (2004). *An investigation of international sign: Analyzing structure and comprehension* (Unpublished doctoral dissertation). Gallaudet University, Washington, DC.

Rosenstock, R. (2008). The role of iconicity in international sign. *Sign Language Studies, 8*(2), 131–159.

Roy, C. 1989. *A sociolinguistic analysis of the interpreter's role in the turn taking exchanges of an interpreted event* (Unpublished doctoral dissertation). Washington, DC: Georgetown University.

Scholl, S. (2008). A twisted brain: Interpreting between sign language and a third language. In C. Kellett Bidoli & E. Ochse (Eds.), *English in International Deaf Communication* (pp. 331–342). Bern, Switzerland: Peter Lang.

Scott Gibson, L., & Ojala, R. (1994, August). *"International Sign" interpreting.* Paper presented at the Fourth East and South African Sign Language Seminar, Uganda.

Stone, C. (2012). Interpreting. In R. Pfau, M. Steinbach, & B. Woll (Eds.), *Sign language: An international handbook* (pp. 980–998). Berlin, Germany: De Gruyter Mouton.

Supalla, T., & Webb, R. (1995). The grammar of International Sign: A new look at pidgin languages. In K. Emmorey & J. Reilly (Eds.), *Language, gesture, and space* (pp. 333–352). Hillsdale, NJ: Lawrence Erlbaum.

Turner, G. H., & Napier, J. (2014). On the importance of professional sign language interpreting to political participation. In A. Pabsch (Ed.), *UNCRPD implementation in Europe—a deaf perspective: Article 29: Participation in political and public life* (pp. 54–71). Brussels, Belgium: EUD.

Whynot, L. A. (2015). *Assessing comprehension of International Sign lectures: Linguistic and sociolinguistic factors* (Unpublished doctoral dissertation). Macquarie University, Sydney, Australia.

Winston, E., & Roy, C. (2015). Discourse analysis and sign languages. In A. Schembri & C. Lucas (Eds.), *Sociolinguistics and deaf communities* (pp. 95–120). Cambridge, UK: Cambridge University Press.

Wit, M. de. (2010). Sign language interpreting in multilingual international settings. In R. Locker McKee & J. Davis (Eds.), *Interpreting in multilingual, multicultural contexts* (pp. 226–246). Washington, DC: Gallaudet University Press.

Woll, B. (1990). International perspectives on sign language communication. *International Journal of Sign Linguistics, 1*(2), 107–120.

Woll, B., Sutton-Spence, R., & Elton, F. (2001). Multilingualism: The global approach to sign languages. In C. Lucas (Ed.), *The sociolinguistics of sign languages* (pp. 8–32). Cambridge, UK: Cambridge University Press.

World Federation of the Deaf (WFD). (2008). *Suggested International Signs for use at the World Federation of the Deaf (WFD) General Assembly* (DVD). Helsinki, Finland: World Federation of the Deaf, Norwegian Association of the Deaf and Ål Experiential College and Conference Center for Deaf People, and Døves Media.

Zeshan, U. (2015). "Making meaning": Communication between sign language users without a shared language. *Cognitive Linguistics, 26*(2), 211–260.

Zeshan, U., Keiko, S., & Bradford, A. (2013, July). *Multilingual and multimodal aspects of "cross-signing"—A study of emerging communication in the domain of numerals.* Poster session presented at TISLR 11, London, UK. Retrieved from http://www.ucl.ac.uk/dcal/tislr/tislr-programme

Zimmer, J. (1989). Toward a description of register variation in American Sign Language. In C. Lucas (Ed.), *The sociolinguistics of the deaf community* (pp. 253–272). San Diego, CA: Academic Press.

Part III **Usage**

International Sign: An Exploration Into Interpreter Preparation

Maya de Wit and Irma Sluis

The number of sign language interpreters varies per European country, depending on the available educational programs for interpreters and existing accessibility legislation. National deaf[1] associations, as well as national sign language interpreter associations, still report a lack of qualified sign language interpreters to meet the demand, especially interpreters with special skills such as in health-care interpreting (de Wit et al., 2012).

Not only national sign language interpreters are needed; there is also a demand for international sign interpreters within Europe.[2] Because of the increased involvement of the European Union of the Deaf (EUD) and stakeholders at the European level, the request for international sign interpreters has increased within EU institutions and in the political arenas in Brussels, Strasbourg, and Geneva (Turner & Napier, 2014).

In this essay, we take a closer look at international sign interpreters working at EU institutions and European level organizations. First, we provide an overview of the current status of international sign interpreters at the European level, the need for international sign interpreters, and the hiring and recruitment process. The overview is based on a literature review, analyses of public and organizational information, and a questionnaire on the background profiles of international sign interpreters. Second, we take a closer look at the preparation for an assignment by international sign interpreters. In particular, we consider the questions if preparation is needed and, if so, which preparation techniques are needed for an international sign assignment in comparison to an assignment in

1. In this article we use lowercase *deaf* to refer to any deaf person regardless of community or cultural affinity.

2. There are different ways to define *Europe*. It can be defined by geographical location, by the members of the European Union (http://europa.eu/about-eu/countries/index_en.htm), or by the states of the Council of Europe. (http://www.coe.int/en/web/portal/country-profiles). In this article, *Europe* is defined by its geography, unless stated otherwise.

a national sign language. The data on preparation techniques were collected through personal diaries of international sign interpreters. Finally, we describe our research findings and make recommendations on the various aspects of interpreter preparation.

INTERNATIONAL SIGN INTERPRETERS IN THE EUROPEAN CONTEXT

Development of the Profession

Sign language interpreting is still a relatively young profession. Traditionally, sign language interpreters are educated to interpret between their national spoken and signed languages (Calle, 2012; Napier, 2006). Training of national sign language interpreters usually does not include international sign interpreting. To understand the need for and the development of international sign interpreters in Europe, first we take a closer look at the historical development of the sign language interpreter profession in Europe.

From a global perspective, sign language interpreting became a profession in the 1960s in the United States, followed by Sweden. Sweden was the first European country to establish a national association of sign language interpreters in 1969. Prior to these developments, deaf people relied on family members or neighbors to assist them in communication with those who did not know sign language (Cokely, 2005). The first sign language interpreters provided their services on a voluntary basis. The deaf community (i.e., deaf people who share a sign language and deaf culture) started to select those whom they thought to be trustworthy and skilled. The growth and development of the profession in the United States had an impact on the profession across the globe (Napier, 2006). Other countries emulated the developments in the United States by establishing and lobbying for professional sign language interpreting education and services in their country.

In this essay, we look particularly at the development of the profession in Europe, while at the same time acknowledging the American counterpart. Development of the sign language interpreting profession as a whole took place in European countries in various stages. The Scandinavian countries, the United Kingdom, and France were the first countries to develop sign language interpreter training programs and interpreting services. Formal training of sign language interpreters started to appear first with weekend courses and over time expanded to the current full-time, three- to four-year educational programs (de Wit, 2012).

The EUD, as well as national associations of deaf persons, lobbied for the legal, sociological, and cultural recognition of their national sign languages (Timmermans, 2005), encouraged by the resolutions of the European parliament in 1988 and 1998 and the 2003 recommendation[3] of the Council of Europe. The right to sign language as a human right was reiterated by the EUD in the Brussels Declaration,[4] a nonlegislative document adopted in November 2010 at the European Parliament, in the presence of Adam Kosa, deaf member of the European Parliament, and representatives from all national deaf associations across Europe (Wheatley & de Wit, 2014).

In summary, the developmental stages of the sign language interpreter profession in European countries can be generally described as follows: first steps were taken to secure (partial) funding for the sign language interpreting services, simultaneously defining the entitlement to these services by national law or provisions. Second, educational programs were established, followed by lobbying for the recognition of the national sign language. The third and current developmental stage is the establishment of a national registry, often an independent agency responsible for ensuring the quality and maintaining the national registration of all sign language interpreters in the country (de Wit, 2012).

The profession of sign language interpreters has no official status in Europe (de Wit, 2012). Any person who claims to be an interpreter can carry out interpreting services. There is no quality control on interpretation services through European legislation. If there is quality control, then this is carried out at the national level. The one European directive in relation to interpreting services is the 2010 European Directive on the right to interpretation and translation in criminal proceedings (2010/64/EU[5]). According to this directive, the member states of the European Union are bound to safeguard quality control for all spoken and signed language interpreters in criminal proceedings. Article 5 of the directive states that quality control should be carried out through the establishment of a national register of interpreters, but no definitions or guidance are provided on how this should be conducted.

3. http://assembly.coe.int/documents/adoptedtext/ta03/erec1598.htm.

4. http://www.eud.eu/Brussels_Declaration-i-305.html.

5. http://ec.europa.eu/justice/criminal/criminal-rights/right-translation/index_en.htm.

Currently there are approximately 7500 sign language interpreters in nearly 40 European countries (de Wit, 2012). According to EUD and the European Forum of Sign Language Interpreters (efsli), the number and quality of national sign language interpreters needs to be increased (Wheatley & de Wit, 2014). Moreover, there is a great need for interpreters with additional skills, such as an additional spoken or signed language.

International Sign Interpreters

Next to the need for national sign language interpreters, there is also a demand for international sign interpreters within Europe (EUD, 2013). The request for international sign interpreters within EU institutions and the political arena in Brussels and Strasbourg has increased because of the intensified involvement and participation of the EUD and other stakeholders at the European level (Turner & Napier, 2014).

The linguistic status of international sign is vigorously debated. International sign is not an official language but is widely used at international meetings where participants do not share one common sign language (EUD, 2012). The first international communication arose in the beginning of the 19th century at deaf sport events. In the late 1950s, during the World Federation of the Deaf (WFD) Congress, the participants expressed the need for a more standardized language. As a result, the WFD set up a commission to collect the international signs used during the past 50 years, which resulted in the publication of Gestuno, a photographic lexicon (Moody, 2002).

At the WFD Congress in 1977, interpreting in Gestuno was offered for the first time. Two years later, a group of primarily teachers of the deaf attended a preconference training in Gestuno signs in order to interpret at the WFD Congress in 1979 in Bulgaria. Their interpretation was not considered successful by the participants because they used the Gestuno lexicon in spoken Bulgarian word order (Moody, 2002). After discussing the use of Gestuno versus national sign languages at the WFD Congress, both were offered at following Congresses. By 1991, the term *Gestuno* was dropped and the term *international sign* became more commonly used. For an in-depth description of the change from Gestuno to international sign, please see Moody's discussion (Moody, 2002).

International sign has been described and discussed in various studies. The most frequently asked question is if international sign is a language. According to Moody (1994), international sign is a contact language and is not conventionalized; nevertheless, researchers found that utterances in international sign are complex (Allsop, Woll, & Brauti, 1994; Bergmann, 1990; McKee & Napier, 2002; Moody, 2002; Supalla & Webb, 1995; Webb & Supalla, 1994; Woll, 1990).

In 1991, at the World Congress in Tokyo, Fischer and Supalla presented on the topic of international sign and stated that international sign has a rich and complex grammar. Supalla called it a pidgin language that is, however, more complex than its spoken language counterparts. A few years later, Supalla and Webb (1995) called international sign a *koine*, because it is used as a contact language, made between closely related languages that have a shared grammar.

Moody (2002, p. 37) states: "International sign is not a language. It has no stable community of users who depend on it for daily communication. It is a pidgin, although research has shown that the grammatical structures are much more complex than the typical spoken language pidgin." Rosenstock (2004) found that international sign has a strong component of role playing and limited lexicon, and that the users tend to use the iconic signs from their own national sign language.

In the context of this chapter, the linguistic status of international sign is not foregrounded. Rather, the practical application and usage in the context of European institutions and European level organizations by interpreters of international sign is described. We follow the EUD, which refers to international sign as an auxiliary language and has published a disclaimer on their website (EUD, 2012), which affirms the importance of national sign languages: "International sign is—albeit not being the perfect solution—a good option when working with a diverse audience."

The EUD uses international sign at their annual general meeting and their conferences as one of the main forms of communication in order to meet the needs of participants from various countries typically present in the audience.

There is no formal educational program to learn international sign or international sign interpreting. To become an international sign interpreter, the interpreter ideally needs to be fluent in more than one sign language (Moody, 2008). Knowing more than one sign language creates language flexibility and allows the interpreter to quickly adapt to the language needs of the users. McKee and Napier (2002) acknowledge this, furthermore stating that international sign interpreters are to be more than conduits. The conduit model arose when interpreting in sign language became more professional. A shift occurred from a model in which the interpreter acted as a helper into a model in which the interpreter was neutral, objective, and acted as a relay between the source and target language: "The sign language interpreter acts as a communication link between people, serving only in that capacity" (Solow, 1981, p. ix).

Interpreting into international sign demands a greater use of background knowledge and consideration of relevancy and efficiency in the interpreting process, and therefore international sign interpreters are more than conduits (McKee & Napier, 2002). International sign interpreters tend to convey a message for a mixed audience. To be comprehensible for a mixed audience, the interpreters need to understand the background and culture of the audience: "Effective IS interpreters appear to demonstrate an awareness of the communicative demands this places on an audience, and make adaptations in their output according[ly]" (McKee & Napier, 2002, p. 31).

Because of the lack of formal education, international sign interpreters are not officially registered and do not have official professional recognition. The EUD recognizes that there is no standard for international sign interpreters, and also understands that an international sign interpreter is not always able to interpret in each situation for every international sign interpreter user (EUD, 2012). Associations of deaf people and interpreters worldwide (efsli, EUD, World Association of Sign Language Interpreters [WASLI], and WFD) would therefore like to instigate this formal recognition by setting up a register for international sign interpreters.[6] This would create a standard and engender quality control (Nardi, 2008). To determine qualifications for such a register, WASLI and WFD set up a taskforce to develop an accreditation system for international sign interpreters.[7]

International Sign Interpreter Work Settings

International sign interpreters work in a variety of settings. This article focuses on EU institutions, the United Nations (UN) in Geneva, the Council of Europe, and other European-level organizations. The three main institutions within the European Union that sign language interpreters work

6. WFD and WASLI Term of Reference, Task Group on International Sign, process for hiring, March 15, 2013.

7. http://wasli.org/wp-content/uploads/2013/09/WFD-WASLI-IS-Interpreter-Statement.pdf.

for are the European Parliament, the European Commission, and the Court of Justice (at an informal meeting of the EU institutions and AIIC-EU-ND committee on November 13, 2013). Sign language interpreters are not employed by the institutions but work on a freelance basis. The three institutions list a total of 3200 freelance interpreters, of which approximately 900 are active, including sign language interpreters. The European Parliament, as one of the European institutions, recognizes only the 23 spoken languages in the European Union as official working languages within the parliament, and none of the European sign languages.[8] The sign language interpreters working at the parliament initially struggled to be recognized (Wheatley & de Wit, 2014).

The Directorate General for Interpretation of the European Commission, also known as SCIC (Service Commun Interprétation-Conférences), is responsible for organizing interpreting services for the European Commission. Spoken language interpreters can work as a staff interpreter or on a freelance basis for the European institutions. To work as a freelance interpreter, the interpreter must pass an interinstitutional accreditation test,[9] after which his or her name is added to the list of accredited freelance interpreters. In contrast, sign language interpreters are not on staff and do not take the accreditation test. In 2013, SCIC contracted a total of approximately 60,000 days of freelance interpreting work for all interpreters.

Until 2012, SCIC took care of all the requests for sign language interpreters within the three institutions. This was due to the small number of requests for sign language interpreters and the experience SCIC had gained. To fulfill the requests, SCIC uses a provisional ad hoc list, a so-called common list of freelance interpreters, which in February 2014 had approximately 41 sign language interpreters. This list, which has no formal status, was created throughout the years, based on ad hoc requests. To be on the common list, the interpreter must have a university degree, have completed interpreting studies, and have provided an overview of worked hours as an interpreter. SCIC states that they do not know if all of these 41 interpreters are still active and if their language combinations are still up to date (Donald Tait, head of ACI recruitment at the European Commission, personal communication, October 23, 2013). Of the 41 interpreters, 13 are listed as interpreting from and to different national

8. http://europarlamentti.info/en/European-parliament/working-languages/.

9. http://europa.eu/interpretation/accreditation_en.htm.

sign languages and a total of 10 interpreters are also listed as international sign interpreters.

The interpreting requests SCIC receives mostly concern international sign, not national signed languages, and are almost always fulfilled. On average, sign language interpreters are booked 20 to 30 days a year by the EU institutions. This only shows the number of times the bookings go through SCIC, but it does not reflect the actual frequency that sign language interpreters work within EU institutions. More often, international sign interpreters are not booked through SCIC but by other European organizations hosting an event at the EU institutions with participants who are deaf sign language users.

When a sign language interpreter is requested, SCIC sends out an email to the sign language interpreters on the aforementioned common list, on the basis of the language combinations requested and the interpreters' domiciles. When selecting the interpreter for the assignment, SCIC does not look at the number of worked hours or the completed education of the interpreter, although it does check to see that the interpreter does not have any negative reports in their SCIC file.

Another major European-based institution working regularly with international sign interpreters is the United Nations (UN) in Geneva. The UN Convention on the Rights of Persons With Disabilities (UNCRPD), which was ratified by the UN in 2007, is being reviewed through hearings in Geneva. At these hearings, the UN agency in Geneva provides sign language interpreters in those signed languages that are "derived" from the official UN languages. So, for example, they provide national sign language interpretation for Wallonian Sign Language (LSFB) because French is an official language, but not for Flemish Sign Language (VGT), because Dutch is not. All public UNCRPD committee sessions are interpreted into international sign nonetheless (also certain Human Rights Council sessions and other human rights instruments). This does not include private meetings, break times, or other nonpublic events (Annika Pabsch, EUD policy officer, personal communication, 2014). The UN agency in Geneva currently has no set selection procedure for international sign interpreters.

Many of the spoken language interpreters working at EU institutions and the UN are members of the International Association of Conference Interpreters (AIIC), which negotiates the working conditions[10] and fees of freelance interpreters working for these groups. Within AIIC, a work-

10. http://europa.eu/interpretation/doc/conv_en_2008.pdf.

ing group called the Sign Language Network (SLN) was established in 2009 to work toward accepting sign language interpreters as AIIC members. The European Forum of Sign Language Interpreters (efsli) worked closely together with the AIIC SLN to prepare documentation for the AIIC membership (Monfort & de Wit, 2012). In January 2012, the AIIC members agreed at their general meeting to allow sign language interpreters to become members of AIIC. The acceptance of these interpreters to AIIC has been an important step in the international recognition and status of sign language interpreters. As of May 2015, two sign language interpreters are members of AIIC. To deliver quality interpreting services within the EU institutions and the UN, one of the requirements is that interpreters prepare for their assignments.[11]

Interpreter Preparation

Interpreting is a process consisting of different components. One of these components is preassignment preparation (Napier, 2002). The interpreter needs to prepare him- or herself in order to deliver a quality interpretation. In this essay we take a closer look at preparation of the international sign interpreter, how this is conducted, and if the preparation techniques and methods are different than from preparing for an assignment in a national sign language. Preparation by the interpreter provides a higher quality of performance (Campbell, Rohan, & Woodcock, 2008; Dean & Pollard, 2001; Diriker, 2011; Frishberg, 1990; Humphrey & Alcorn, 1996; Janzen & Korpiniski, 2005; Kauling, 2012; Napier, 2002; Neumann Solow, 2000; Nolan, 2005; Pollard & Dean, 2008; Seleskovitch, 1978; Stewart, Schein, & Cartwright, 1998; Stone, 2007; de Wit, 2010b).

Kauling (2012) explored how sign language interpreters prepare for their assignments in regard to the preparation material that they receive. According to Kauling (2012), interpreters could have two different methods of preparing for an assignment:

1. To focus on the understanding of the source text, and
2. To strive to enlarge extralinguistic knowledge.

To understand the source text the interpreter will study the terminology prior to the assignment. A further understanding of the text can also be

11. http://aiic.net/page/628/practical-guide-for-professional-conference-interpreters/lang/1#21,article2.

developed during the interpreting process. It is important that interpreters learn about the topic and jargon used in a specific setting (Nolan, 2005). The interpreter can do this by requesting and studying the materials available, for example, the program, background documents, and speeches. Comprehending the terminology results in understanding the relationships between terms. As a result, the interpreter has a better understanding of how the knowledge in a text is organized (Cabré, 2010). Furthermore, Nolan (2005) states that it is advisable to attend interpreter meetings at the event in which the interpreter has the opportunity to ask for clarifications and address any concerns with colleagues.

The second strategy, according to Kauling, is used mainly during the assignment, where the interpreter must gain a full understanding of the concept in order to interpret accurately. Extralinguistic knowledge is related to the situation, speakers, audience, power relations, etc. An interpreter may have thought this over before the assignment, but the interpreter will enlarge his or her knowledge during the assignment.

The preparation for an assignment concerns the gathering of extralinguistic knowledge (Gile, 1995). This is the knowledge specific to the interpreted setting, which will assist the interpreter in a better understanding of the discourse. This knowledge is, for example, information on the goals and intentions of the speaker, which will result in a more accurate interpretation. If possible, an interpreter could attend a workshop or lecture of the speaker in order to observe the speaker (Nolan, 2005). The interpreter can then learn about how the speaker uses specific terms, how he or she moves, and what kind of speech-supported gestures are made. Knowing if the speaker is a native speaker of the language in which he or she is presenting is also of importance (Gile, 1995), because the native language could interfere with the language spoken.

Dean and Pollard (2013) suggest a wider preparation approach by focusing on using available controls in the setting. To master the situation, an interpreter could gain knowledge of the setting by using the demand-control schema. Dean and Pollard found that during an interpreting assignment an interpreter is confronted with demands, which can be divided into four domains: environmental, paralinguistic, interpersonal, and intrapersonal demands. To control these demands, an interpreter should prepare herself in each domain. For environmental demands, the interpreter could prepare herself on, for example, the goal of the environment and the physical surroundings. For interpersonal demands, the interpreter explores the communication goals and the cultural dynamics. To prepare for the paralinguistic demands, the interpreter could consider the volume, pace, accents, etc. The fourth demand category is intrapersonal. To prepare for that demand, the interpreter could reflect on her feelings, thoughts, and possible psychological responses.

Preparation of the interpreting setting, specifically information about the environment and other extralinguistic factors, is also mentioned by McKee & Napier (2002) in relation to international sign interpreters: "International interpreters are shown to be more than conduits, as their interpreting decisions indicate extensive use of contextual knowledge, inferencing, audience awareness, and considerations of relevance and efficiency in the process of interpretation" (p. 1).

Moody (2002) states that in conjunction with, and as a result of, the limited lexicon of international sign, the interpreter needs to "act out" the speeches. This indicates the need for the international sign interpreter to prepare before the assignment and to obtain the aforementioned extralinguistic knowledge.

Working at the European level, interpreters need not only to prepare the content of the speech, background of the speakers, and extralinguistic knowledge but also to gain knowledge about how these institutions function and what the current related issues are. They need to take notice of the different bodies such as the European Commission, the Council of Europe, the European Parliament, and the Court of Justice. In addition, interpreters have to learn about the decision-making process and the special terms used in this environment. In the case of international sign interpreting, comprehension of the processes and system is important, because interpreting in international sign is considered "free interpreting" (McKee & Napier, 2002, p. 31). As is mentioned with free translation, this is considered a translation in which as few or as many words are used in an accessible register in the target language in order to convey the same notion as the source language (Kauling, 2012). McKee and Napier state in regard to international sign and free interpreting: "In the case of IS interpreting, the main aim is to re-create an approximation of the essential message in a hybrid language, which may, at times, necessitate some reduction of content" (McKee & Napier, 2002, p. 31).

When an event is planned, the EU institutions follow their established recruitment process for international sign interpreters, as mentioned earlier. These institutions have little knowledge of working with sign language interpreters, and as a consequence, the interpreter needs to clarify the role of the sign language interpreter, as well as explain and assist in arranging practical conditions on site. To guide the institutions, representatives of the AIIC Sign Language Network and the AIIC Negotiating Delegation to the EU created, in early 2014, two new guidelines. These guidelines provide detailed information for sound engineers[12] and spoken language interpreters[13] when working with sign language interpreters. The aim of the guidelines is to provide concise information on how sign language interpreters work and how they are used within EU institutions when sign language interpreters are booked for specific events.

METHODOLOGY

To collect data for this article, a less traditional approach was adopted. Generally researchers do not participate in their own research; data are gathered and analyzed by an independent third party. However, considering the small number of international sign interpreters working at the European level and at the EU institutions, the researchers deemed it necessary to participate in order not to influence the outcome of the research. Our nonparticipation might have had a visible effect (Hale & Napier, 2013). In addition, considering that if validity of qualitative inquiry is interpretation and understanding of the social world, there is no need for the researcher to neutralize herself or suppress her knowledge and experience (Fendt & Sachs, 2008).

This research is a first exploration of international sign interpreting and preparation. To discover patterns of meaning in the collected data set, the unstructured data drew on the principles of content analysis (Joffe, 2012). This method was especially useful to obtain information from responses to the "unstructured" or "open-ended" questions (Smith, 2000, p. 314).

Especially within the field of social sciences, a researcher has to take into account in what context a respondent has stated something. This in contrast with a field where a researcher is able to measure something, or more traditional methods in which first a theoretical framework is chosen (Joffe & Yardley, 2004).

Within this method, the first step was to collect the data. The data were collected and coded, themes were sought, and categories were made. After

12. http://aiic.net/page/6700/guidelines-for-sound-engineers/lang/1

13. http://aiic.net/page/6701/guidelines-for-spoken-language-interpreters-working-in-mixed-teams/lang/1

establishing the categories, the researchers counted how many times key themes were mentioned.

Participants and Process

Using network and snowball sampling, a total of 32 interpreters were directly contacted to participate in the research. The contacted interpreters were all international sign interpreters on an informal list of the WFD and EUD, as well as international sign interpreters known to work at the European level. All interpreters were contacted individually with a request to participate in the research during a three-month period. The interpreters were also asked if they knew other international sign interpreters who matched the profile.

From the 32 interpreters contacted, 16 interpreters filled out their background profile as international sign interpreters and 5 interpreters completed the diary. Out of the 16 interpreters, 11 hearing and 5 deaf interpreters participated. There were 8 male and 8 female international sign interpreters who filled out the background profile. The respondents were from the Netherlands, the United Kingdom, Germany, Belgium, France, Denmark, Finland, and the USA. The years that the interpreters had been working as a national sign language interpreter varied from 0 (deaf interpreter) to 33 years. Twelve interpreters had worked less than 15 years and 4 for more than 15 years. Their experience in international sign interpreting ranged from 1 to 25 years. Twelve international sign interpreters had less than 10 years of experience working as international sign interpreters; the other 4 had more than 11 years. Figure 1 provides an overview of the native languages of the interpreters.

The Data

The research consisted of two data sets collected through a questionnaire (Appendix 1) and a diary study (Appendix 2). The questionnaire was designed to acquire information on the profile of international sign interpreters. The respondents were asked to fill out a questionnaire on their general background profile. The questions included whether participants were male/female, deaf/hearing, in which country they lived, how many years of experience as a sign language interpreter they had, and how many years they worked as an international sign interpreter. In addition, questions on their language skills were posed: their native language, which languages they know, and into and from which languages they interpret.

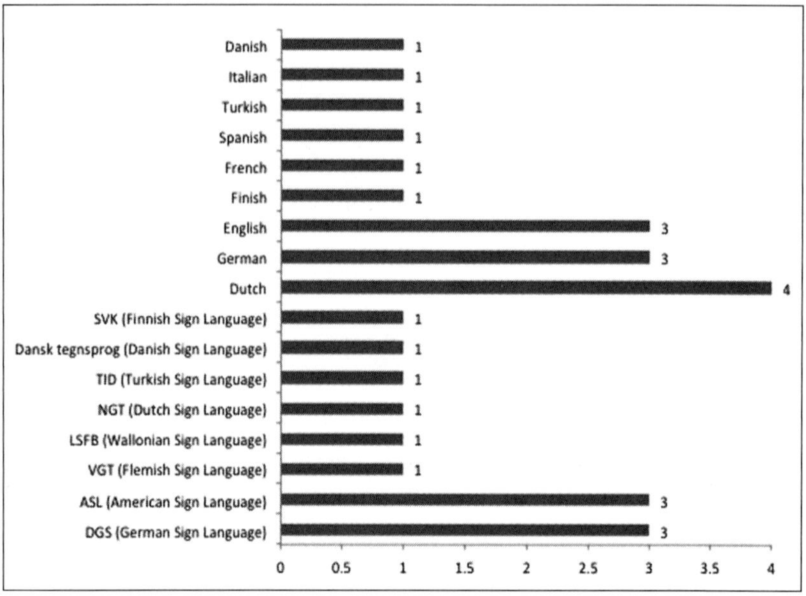

FIGURE 1. *Native languages of international sign interpreters.*

Furthermore, a question on which institutions and organizations they have worked for in Europe was included.

The second data set consisted of diary entries. The researchers collected data by providing access to an online diary to each of the interpreters. With the use of diaries the perspectives of the respondents were collected, which are more difficult to obtain by interviews or observations. Nunan (1997, cited in Horvath, 2005, p. 115), states that diaries give the opportunity to the researcher to concentrate "more on the cognitive processes underlying human performance and ability" and the "mental processes underlying observable behavior." The international sign interpreters kept semistructured diaries during three months of their international sign assignments at the European level and collected their experiences within these assignments regarding the setup of the assignment and their preparation.

The diary (Figure 2) was introduced with guidelines on how to use it and contained questions to lead the respondent as well as to seek for more structured data. The first part of the diary was comprised of structured questions that looked more closely at the event languages and logistics (how were you contacted, what were the duration and the setup), and interpreter-related questions: In which languages was interpretation

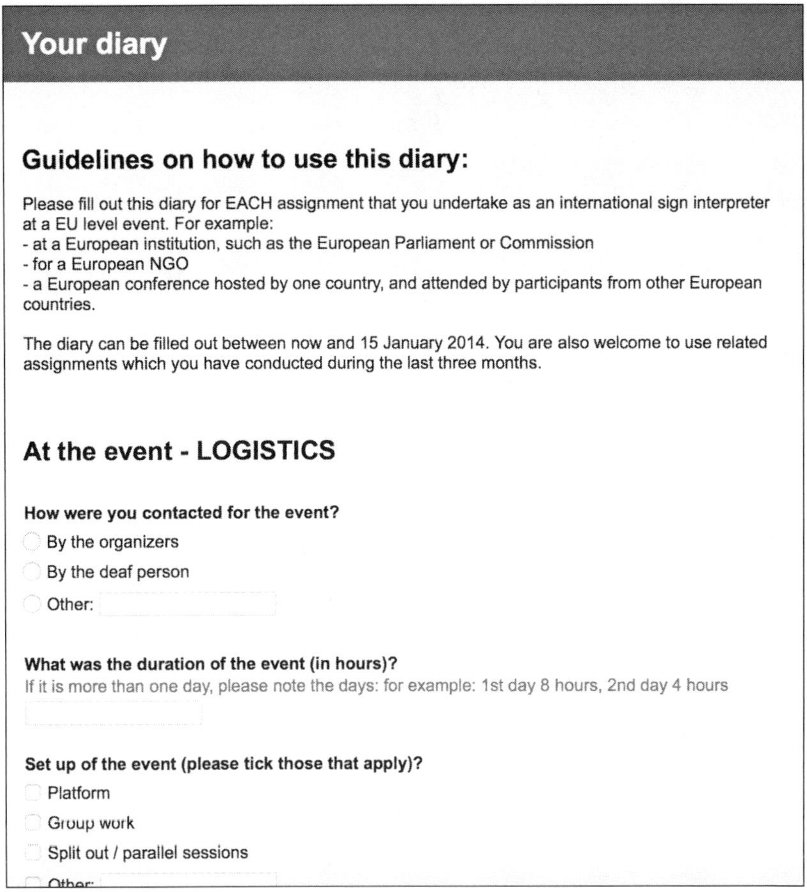
Your diary

Guidelines on how to use this diary:

Please fill out this diary for EACH assignment that you undertake as an international sign interpreter at a EU level event. For example:
- at a European institution, such as the European Parliament or Commission
- for a European NGO
- a European conference hosted by one country, and attended by participants from other European countries.

The diary can be filled out between now and 15 January 2014. You are also welcome to use related assignments which you have conducted during the last three months.

At the event - LOGISTICS

How were you contacted for the event?

- By the organizers
- By the deaf person
- Other:

What was the duration of the event (in hours)?
If it is more than one day, please note the days: for example: 1st day 8 hours, 2nd day 4 hours

Set up of the event (please tick those that apply)?

- Platform
- Group work
- Split out / parallel sessions
- Other:

FIGURE 2. *Diary study.*

offered? How many interpreters were working in a team (spoken and signed)? Was there an interpreter coordinator? In addition, a question on the topic of the event was included to see if the interpreter was familiar with the topic and how this had an effect on the possible preparation.

The second part of the diary contained open questions concerning whether the respondents had prepared for the assignment and the steps they undertook. If they had prepared, they were asked about the preparation materials and how easily these were made available. In addition, they were asked whether they would have prepared differently had the assignment been in their native national sign language. Lastly, the interpreters were asked if they would do something differently next time. Before completing the diary, the respondents had the opportunity to note any additional comments.

RESULTS

The highest educational degrees of the 16 interpreters were as follows: 8 of the interpreters had a vocational or associate degree, 3 had a bachelor's degree, 3 had a master's degree, 1 was currently attending a master program, and 1 had completed a training conducted by a governmental agency. Figure 3 gives an overview of the European level institutions and organizations the international sign interpreters have worked for.

A total of 13 diary entries by 5 interpreters were made, an average of 2.7 per interpreter. For these 13 events, the interpreters were contacted for their services directly by the organizers of the event more than half of the time (Figure 4). The duration of the events varied from less than 4 hours to a 9-day event. During the events, the interpreters primarily needed to perform platform work, but also in combination with interpreting during breakout sessions and networking moments (Figure 5). The most used languages at the 13 events were English and international sign, followed by French, Spanish, and German (Figure 6). At the events, the international sign interpreters worked in teams of two to six interpreters. For 10 of the events, there was a team of two interpreters, 2 events had three interpreters, and 1 event had six interpreters. All of the interpreters working in teams had worked with each other before.

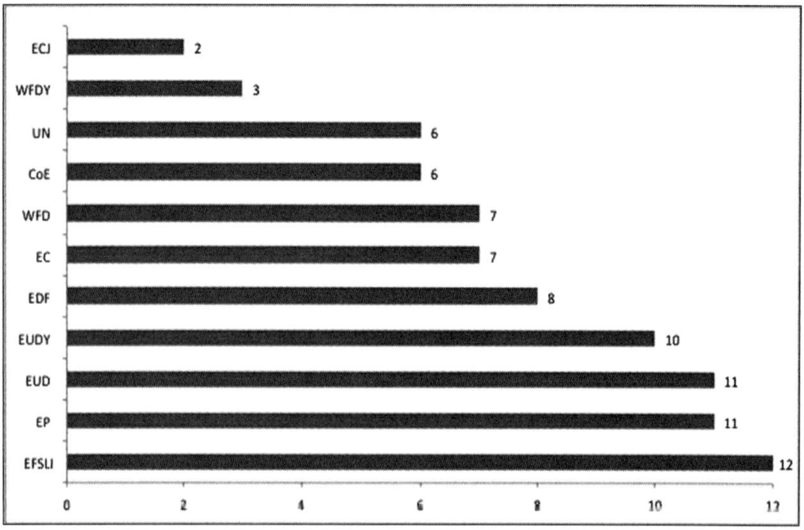

FIGURE 3. *Organizations for which international sign interpreters work.*

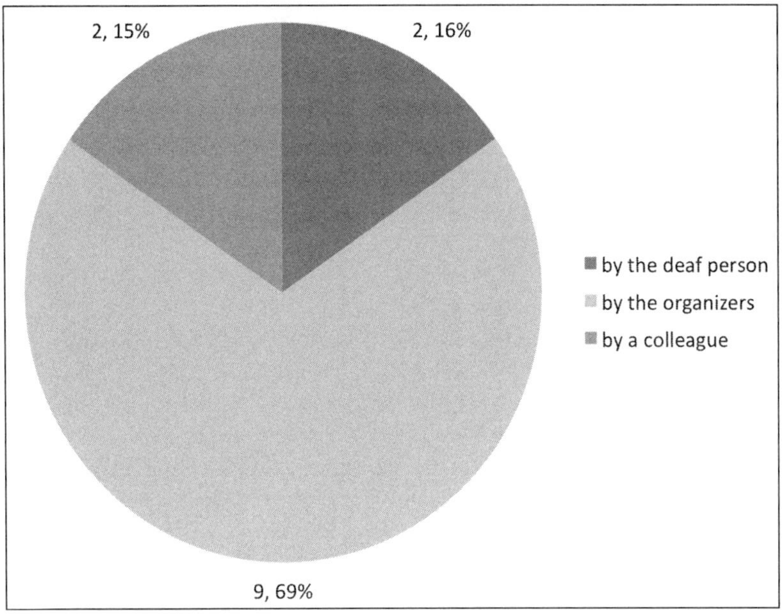

FIGURE 4. *"How were you contacted for the event?"*

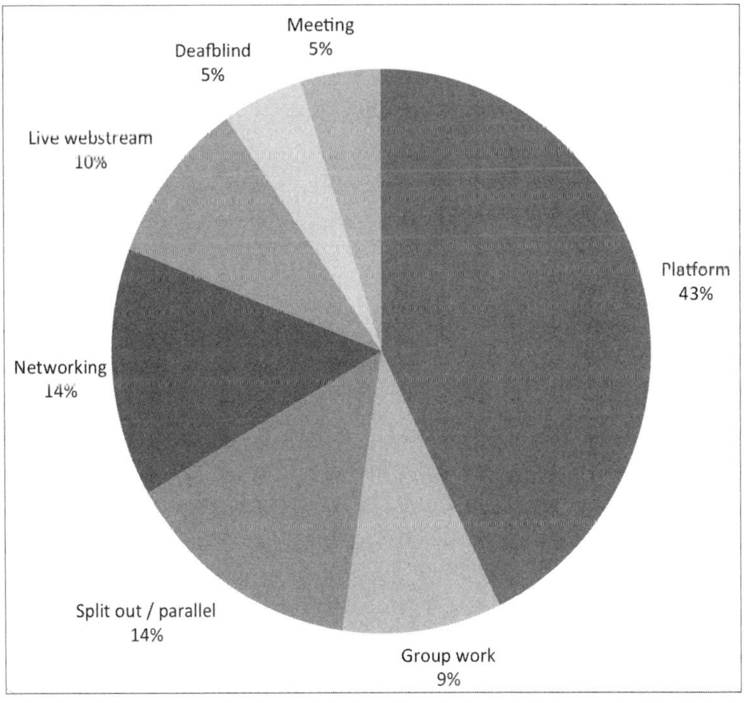

FIGURE 5. *Set up of the events.*

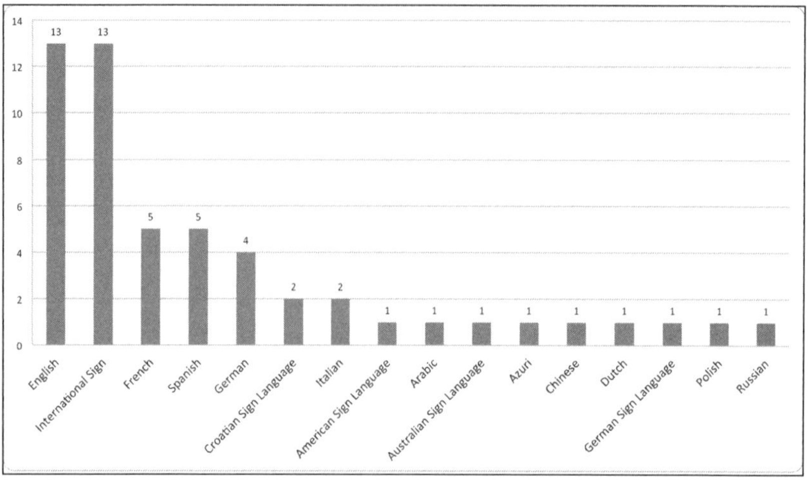

FIGURE 6. *Languages used at events.*

When looking more closely at the content and the logistics of the events, the respondents reported that of all the events, seven had a formal announcement about the presence of international sign interpreters.

Following the content analysis approach for the analysis of the unstructured data collected from the respondents in regard to the topic of preparation, several key issues were identified: (a) great variety in preparation techniques, (b) difficulty in obtaining preparation materials, (c) different views on adequate preparation, (d) increased stress level and complexity, and (e) lack of awareness among conference organizers.

Great Variety in Preparation Techniques

In nearly half of the events, the interpreters were very familiar with the content of the event, and only in one case not familiar at all. The interpreters mentioned that they had prepared themselves for all of the events; however, the way they prepared differed. One respondent mentioned: "The only thing I prepared was research on the signs that are used for different countries and this was for Mandela's commemoration, so I researched the accepted sign name for him and events surrounding his life."

The most frequently mentioned preparation method was the reading of the program or agenda, background information, and available presentations and abstracts. Second, the interpreters prepared with their colleagues the international signs to use for specific event related terminology. Other preparation strategies mentioned were online searches on the topic, background information on the hosting organization, requesting preparation materials, and preparation with deaf clients on signs and terminology. Other strategies included early arrival at the event to ensure the necessary technical and logistical arrangements, agreement with a colleague on teamwork, communication and clarifications with clients, and further information on the program and side events.

Difficulty in Obtaining Preparation Materials

As mentioned previously, reviewing materials such as presentations and background information was considered the most important preparation technique. The interpreters indicated that those materials were not easy to come by. At half of the events, they had to ask the organizers repeatedly or search for the information themselves. As one of the respondents stated: "There was none, only the agenda. I had to explain and ask repeatedly. I took this on me, since the first interpreter had not asked (I had come in late to the assignment). After explaining and also sending the EUD guidelines, most of the presentations were sent."

Different Views on Adequate Preparation

Looking back after the interpreted event, the interpreters noted that at nine of the events they had prepared adequately. At one event this was not the case and at another event it was considered acceptable but could have been better, and at two of the events the interpreters mentioned that it could have been different. The reasons named were as follows: (1) Changing of the interpreter's role with different expectations from the client. (2) The interpreter was not fully briefed that interpreting was not needed at the event, just for networking during breaks. (3) Preparation by different members of the team differed. It appeared that not all interpreters shared the same view on how much or what kind of preparation was needed. One interpreter confirmed she felt pressure and would try to avoid this next time: "Be tougher on getting breaks, because at times, I had to work longer than I normally would in normal circumstances, but I felt under pressure to keep interpreting because the meeting was so important (and I had no co-worker)."

Increased Stress Level and Complexity

Had an event been in their national sign language, interpreters would have prepared differently in 6 out of the 13 events. The reason given by the respondents for this is that for the international sign interpreting, they needed more time to prepare and agree on the terminology and the determination of the related international signs. The international sign events were also perceived as more stressful due to their high level status and the linguistic and cultural complexity, including the variety of languages and cultures. One respondent stated: "Yes, in that sense that the concepts in IS had to be discussed and agreed on prior to interpreting. In my national sign language there is not such a need for that, unless they are unusual concepts."

Lack of Awareness Among Event Organizers

In the diary, respondents could indicate if they were contacted by the event organizers or by the deaf participant, or give a different answer. There was no given answer provided to indicate if the event was organized by a deaf-led organization. The respondents made several suggestions on how to handle certain aspects differently at a future assignment. Most of the suggestions involved informing the organizers what the interpreters need in order to conduct their work, such as adequate break times, the importance of good sound, proper seating, and technical requirements when working with camera positions. Because of the lack of this information, the conditions under which the interpreters needed to work were more difficult, as stated in one example: "We need to inform the technicians even better of what is needed in the room to make it run smoothly. Now there was a deaf panel member and deaf audience members and that did not work well with the camera, there was a delay, which meant needing to concentrate even further on what was happening. And we lost concentration on switching positions every time because of the angle of the camera."

DISCUSSION AND CONCLUSIONS

To enhance the quality of the interpretation, interpreters need to prepare for their assignment. The participating international sign interpreters in this study all confirmed they had prepared for the assignment in various ways. Their most frequently mentioned method of preparation was studying of informational materials, such as the program and presentations. As McKee and Napier (2002, p. 31) mentioned, international sign interpreters need to have a broader understanding of the context, the relevance thereof, and the awareness of the audience members in order to produce an interpretation. Their interpretation is more often an acting out, and making conscious choices of reduction of content to produce an interpretation that is understandable to a wider audience (Moody, 2002). This relates to the second most often mentioned preparation technique, namely the determination and selection of international signs to be used for the specific terminology and jargon related to the setting. Prior to the event, the interpreters within their team, and at times with the deaf clients, discussed the choice of international signs for the specific concepts. Another recommended strategy was a preparatory meeting with the speakers and presenters at the event (Nolan, 2005). During this meeting, the interpreters are able to hear in more detail the goals and intentions of the speakers, learn about their background, and familiarize themselves with their speaking style. This preparation method was not often mentioned by the respondents. One interpreter did mention briefing with the deaf presenter and informing all the presenters of the role of the interpreter.

For half of the events, the international sign interpreters stated that if this had been an assignment in their national sign language, they would have prepared differently. They would have experienced it as less stressful and less time would have been invested in terminology and corresponding international signs. Overall, the interpreters working as international sign interpreters at the European level experience a high stress level due to the status of the event, the large diversity of international sign users, and the inexperience of the event organizers. The latter is reflected in the suggestions of the interpreters for improvement following the event. The suggested changes mainly concern logistics and professional factors, such as proper seating arrangements and headsets, but also appropriate break times and more information for the organizers on what the interpreters need to perform their tasks.

RECOMMENDATIONS

This study is a first exploration into the preparation interpreters undertake when working as international sign interpreters. The results give insights into what kind of preparation techniques interpreters use. The results of this study demonstrate the various ways international sign interpreters prepare for an assignment, including different strategies in comparison to an assignment carried out in their national sign language. The international sign interpreters report that they invest substantially more time preparing for international sign events by studying the preparation materials and selecting international signs.

Next to the preparation techniques mentioned by the interpreters, thorough preparation appears also to be needed in order to lower the intensity and interpreter's stress level during assignments. The participants report that their heightened stress level is created by, among other things, the complex event logistics in combination with the lack of knowledge of the event organizers as to the interpreter's professional requirements. This inexperience of the organizers is currently addressed primarily by the interpreter who guides the organizers through the process, which is an additional responsibility for the interpreter. To reduce the interpreter's stress level and additional responsibility, education of the event organizers needs to be addressed. The 2014 AIIC guidelines for technicians and spoken language interpreters within the EU institutions are a first step, but attention needs to be given to a wide implementation and use of these guidelines.

To change the interpreter's challenging working conditions, some of the respondents suggested that the event organizers and the EU institutions be made aware of the specific needs of interpreters by creating an additional document explaining the need for adequate break times, the importance of good sound, proper seating, and technical requirements when working with a camera and live web streaming. Another essential requirement for the interpreter is extensive preparation materials. This detailed information is needed in order for the interpreter to thoroughly understand the topic and the jargon and consequently determine the appropriate international signs. These materials should be provided as a matter of course by the event organizers, rather than the interpreters having to ask for it repeatedly, as indicated by the respondents.

In addition to an improvement in the logistics, the international sign interpreters should try to arrange a meeting with the speakers prior to the event. The respondents hardly mentioned this possibility, but according to Nolan (2005), this will create an opportunity for the interpreter to become used to the voice and speaking style of the presenter. The interpreters did indicate that they at times consult both deaf presenters for clarification and process agreement and also deaf participants to agree on the international signs in the context.

As only five of the contacted international sign interpreters filled out the questionnaire, there is an opportunity to learn more through a follow-up study. This subsequent study could include as many respondents as possible by conducting individual interviews in addition to the online diary. Further research on the possible effects of the various preparation methods for an international sign assignment could be useful. For example, it would be helpful to discover whether preparation of the extralinguistic knowledge results in quality improvement or an increase in the comprehension of the interpretation.

Being an international sign interpreter is a demanding occupation that requires additional skills, other than working in national contexts, to deal with the complexity at hand. Considering the increasing demand for international sign interpreters within Europe, further recognition and acceptance at the European level is needed, as well as ensuring equal working conditions to spoken language interpreters. Additional awareness raising and dissemination of expertise is required among the EU institutions. The increased knowledge at the European level should result in less additional responsibilities and tasks which are now carried out by the international sign interpreter, as a consequence shifting the focus of the interpreter to the quality of the interpretation instead of the complexity of the logistics.

REFERENCES

Allsop, L., Woll, B., and Brauti, J. M. (1994). International sign: The creation of an international deaf community and sign language. In H. Bos & T. Schermer (Eds.), *Sign language research 1994: Proceedings of the European Congress on Sign Language Research* (pp. 171–188). Hamburg, Germany: Signum Press.

Bergmann, A. (1990). Extra rational responses: International sign language? *Signpost, 3*(3), 2–3.

Cabré, M. (2010). Terminology and translation. In Y. Gambier & L. van Doorslaer (Eds.), *Handbook of Translation Studies* (Vol. 1, pp. 356–365). Amsterdam, the Netherlands: John Benjamins.

Calle, L. (2012). *Sign language interpreter training programmes* (efsli report 2011, updated 2012). Retrieved from http://efsli.org/efsliblu/wp-content/uploads/2012/09/R1101-The-right-to-sign-language-interpreting-services-when-working-or-studying-abroad.pdf

Campbell, L., Rohan, M., & Woodcock, K. (2008). Academic and educational interpreting from the other side of the classroom: Working with Deaf academics. In P. Hauser, K. Finch, & A. Hauser (Eds.), *Deaf Professionals and Designated Interpreters* (pp. 81–105). Washington, DC: Gallaudet University Press.

Cokely, D. (2005). Shifting positionality: A critical examination of the turning point in the relationship of interpreters and the deaf community. In M. Marschark, R. Peterson, E. A. Winston, P. Sapere, C. M. Convertino, C. R. Seewagen, & C. Monikowski (Eds.), *Sign language interpreting and interpreter education: Directions for research and practice* (pp. 3–28). Oxford, UK: Oxford University Press.

Dean, R., & Pollard, R. (2001). Application of demand-control theory to sign language interpreting: Implications for stress and interpreter training. *Journal of Deaf Studies and Deaf Education, 6*(1), 1–14.

Dean, R., & Pollard, R. (2013). *The demand control schema: Interpreting as a practice profession*. North Charleston, SC: CreateSpace.

Diriker, E. (2011). User expectation surveys: Questioning findings and drawing lessons for interpreter training. İstanbul Üniversitesi Çeviribilim Dergisi 3. Retrieved from http://www.journals.istanbul.edu.tr/iuceviri/article/view/1023011090/1023010348

Eisenhardt, K. (1989). Building theory from case study research. In *Academy of Management Review, 14*(4), 532–550.

EUD. (2012). *International sign guidelines*. Retrieved from http://www.eud.eu/International_Sign_Disclaimer-i-206.html

EUD. (2013). *UNCRPD report* Retrieved from http://www.eud.eu/uploads/EUDUNCRPDWWW_1.pdf

Fendt, J., & Sachs, W. (2008). Grounded theory method in management research users' perspectives. *Organizational Research Methods, 11*(3), 430–455.

Frishberg, N. (1990). *Interpreting: An introduction*. Silver Spring, MD: RID.

Gile, D. (1995). *Basic concepts and models for interpreter and translator training*. Amsterdam, the Netherlands: John Benjamins.

Glaser, B., & Strauss, A. (1967). *The discovery of grounded theory: Strategies for qualitative research*. New York, NY: De Gruyter.

Hale, S., & Napier, J. (2013). *Research methods in interpreting: A practical resource*. London, UK: Bloomsbury.

Horvath, I. (2005). *The cognitive components of autonomous learning in post-graduate interpreter training*. Retrieved from http://www.independentlearning.org/uploads/100836/HOR05034.pdf

Humphrey, B., & Alcorn, J. (1996). *So you want to be an interpreter: An introduction to sign language interpreting*. Amarillo, TX: H & H Publishing.

Janzen, T., & Korpiniski, D. (2005). Ethics and professionalism in interpreting. In T. Janzen (Ed.), *Topics in signed language interpreting* (pp. 165–199). Amsterdam, the Netherlands: John Benjamins.

Joffe, H. (2012). Thematic analysis. In D. Harper & A. R. Thompson (Eds.), *Qualitative research methods in mental health and psychotherapy: A guide for students and practitioners* (pp. 209–223). Chichester, UK: Wiley.

Joffe, H., & Yardley, L. (2004). Content and thematic analysis. In D. Marks & L. Yardley (Eds.), *Research methods for clinical and health psychology* (pp. 56–68). London, UK: Sage.

Kauling, E. (2012). *Keeping the surprises to a minimum* (Unpublished MA thesis). Utrecht University of Applied Sciences, Utrecht, the Netherlands.

McKee, R., & Napier, J. (2002). Interpreting in international sign pidgin. *Sign language and Linguistics, 5*(1), 27–54.

Monfort, A.-V., & de Wit, M. (2012, March). The International Association of Conference Interpreters (AIIC) opens its doors to sign languages. *efsli Newsletter,* 14.

Moody, B. (1994, April). International sign: Language, pidgin, or charades? Paper presented at the Issue in Interpreting 1 Conference, University of Durham, Durham, UK.

Moody, B. (2002). International Sign: A practitioner's perspective. *Journal of Interpretation,* 1–47.

Moody, B. (2008). The role of international sign interpreting in today's world. In C. Roy (Ed.), *Diversity and community in the worldwide sign language interpreting profession* (pp. 19–32). Gloucestershire, UK: Douglas McLean.

Napier, J. (2002). *Sign language interpreting: Linguistic coping strategies.* Coleford, UK: Douglas McLean.

Napier, J. (2006). A time to reflect: An overview of signed language interpreting. In R. Locker McKee (Ed.), *Proceedings of the Inaugural Conference of the World Association of Sign Language Interpreters* (pp. 12–24). Coleford, UK: Douglas McLean.

Nardi, M. (2008). To boldly go . . . abroad!? In C. J. Kellett Bidoli & E. Ochse (Eds.), *English in international deaf communication* (pp. 279–305). Bern, Switzerland: Peter Lang.

Neumann Solow, S. (2000). *Sign language interpreting: A basic resource book.* Burtonsville, MD: Linstok Press.

Nolan, J. (2005). *Interpretation, techniques, and exercises.* Bristol, UK: Multilingual Matters.

Pollard, R., & Dean, R. (2008). (Eds.) Applications of demand control schema in interpreter education. In *Proceedings of the pre-conference meeting at the national convention of the Registry of Interpreters for the Deaf, August 3, 2007.* Rochester, NY: University of Rochester.

Rosenstock, R. (2004). *An investigation of international sign: Analyzing structure and comprehension* (Unpublished doctoral dissertation). Gallaudet University, Washington, DC.

Scott Gibson, L., & Ojala, R. (1994, August). International sign interpreting. Paper presented at the Fourth East and South African Sign Language Seminar, Kampala, Uganda.

Seleskovitch, D. (1978). *Interpreting for international conferences*. Washington, DC: Pen and Booth.

Smith, C. P. (2000). Content analysis and narrative analysis. In H. T. Reis & C. M. Judd (Eds.), *Handbook of research methods in social and personality psychology* (pp. 313–335). Cambridge, UK: Cambridge University Press.

Solow, S. N. (1981). *Sign language interpreting: A basic resource book*. Silver Spring, MD: National Association of the Deaf.

Stewart, D., Schein, J., & Cartwright, B. (1998). *Sign language interpreting: Exploring its art and science*. Boston. MA: Allyn and Bacon.

Stone, C. (2007). Deaf translators/interpreters rendering processes: The translation of oral languages. *Sign Language Translator and Interpreter, 1*(1), 53–72.

Supalla, T., & Webb, R. (1995). The grammar of international sign: A new look at pidgin languages. In K. Emmorey & J. Reilly (Eds.), *Language, gesture, and space* (pp. 333–354). Mahwah, NJ: Lawrence Erlbaum.

Timmermans, N. (2005). *The status of sign languages in Europe*. Strasbourg, France: Council of Europe.

Turner, G. H., & Napier, J. (2014). *UNCRPD implementation in Europe: A deaf perspective—Article 29: Participation in political and public life*. Brussels, Belgium: European Union of the Deaf.

Webb, R., & Supalla, T. (1994). Negation in international sign. In I. Ahlgren, B. Bergmann, & M. Brennan (Eds.), *Perspectives on sign language structure: Papers from the Fifth International Symposium on Sign Language Research 1* (pp. 173–185). Durham, UK: ISLA.

Wheatley, M., & de Wit, M. (2014). Joint co-operation: The only way forward. In B. Costello, M. Thumann, & R. Shaw (Eds.), *WASLI 2011 Conference Proceedings* (pp. 119–128).

Wheatley, M., & Pabsch, A. (2012). *Sign language legislation in the European Union*. Brussels, Belgium: Churchill's.

Wit, M. de. (2010a). *Linguistic coping strategies from international sign to English* (Unpublished MSc research report, EUMASLI). Heriot-Watt University, Edinburgh, UK.

Wit, M. de. (2010b). Sign language interpreting in multilingual international settings. In R. Locker McKee and J. Davis (Eds.), *Interpreting in multilingual, multicultural contexts* (pp. 226–242). Washington, DC: Gallaudet University Press.

Wit, M. de. (2012). *Sign language interpreting in Europe* (Self-published report).

Wit, M. de, Salami, M., & Hema, Z. (2012). Educating sign language interpreters in healthcare settings: A European perspective. In L. Swabey & K. Malcolm (Eds.), *In our hands: Educating health care interpreters* (pp. 229–259). Washington, DC: Gallaudet University Press.

Woll, B. (1990). International perspectives on sign language communication. In *International Journal of Sign Linguistics, 1*(2), 107–120.

Appendix 1:

Survey—Your Background as an International Sign Interpreter

In support for the research "International Sign: An Exploration into Interpreter Preparation"

You are:

- ☐ Man
- ☐ Woman

You are:

- ☐ Deaf
- ☐ Hearing
- ☐ Hard of hearing

Which country do you live?

How many years have you been working as a sign language interpreter in your national sign and spoken language?

How many years have you been working as an international sign interpreter (approx.)?

What is your native language(s)?

Which languages (spoken and signed) do you know and at which level?

Please use: http://europass.cedefop.europa.eu/en/resources/european-language-levels-cefr

Which spoken and sign languages do you interpret from and into?

Do you have a degree or diploma in sign language interpreting?
Check all that apply

- ☐ No
- ☐ Vocational / Associate degree
- ☐ BA
- ☐ MA
- ☐ Other:

With which of the following institutions and organisations have you worked in Europe?
Check all that apply

- ☐ European Union of the Deaf (EUD)
- ☐ European Union of the Deaf Youth (EUDY)
- ☐ World Federation of the Deaf (WFD)
- ☐ World Federation of the Deaf Youth (WFDY)
- ☐ European Forum of Sign Language Interpreters (efsli)
- ☐ European Disability Forum (EDF)
- ☐ European Parliament (EP)
- ☐ European Commission (EC)
- ☐ European Court of Justice (ECJ)
- ☐ Council of Europe (CoE)
- ☐ United Nations (UN) in Geneva

Appendix 2:

Individual Diary—International Sign Interpreter

Guidelines on how to use this diary:

Please fill out this diary for EACH assignment that you undertake as an international sign interpreter at an EU level event. For example:

- at a European institution, such as the European Parliament or Commission
- for a European NGO
- a European conference hosted by one country, and attended by participants from other European countries.

The diary can be filled out between now and 15 January 2014. You are also welcome to use related assignments which you have conducted during the last three months.

AT THE EVENT—LOGISTICS

☐ How were you contacted for the event?

☐ By the organizers

☐ By the deaf person

☐ Other:

What was the duration of the event (in hours)?

If it is more than one day, please note the days: for example: 1st day 8 hours, 2nd day 4 hours

Set up of the event? (please tick those that apply)

☐ Platform

☐ Group work

☐ Split out / parallel sessions

☐ Other:

AT THE EVENT—LANGUAGES

Which language(s) were used at the event?

AT THE EVENT—INTERPRETERS

In which languages (spoken & signed) was interpretation offered?

How many spoken language interpreters per spoken language were working at the event?

How many national sign language interpreters per national sign language were working at the event?

How many international sign interpreters were working at the event?

Was there an interpreter coordinator (or head of team) present for all interpreters?

Did the event announcement state the provision of international sign interpreters?

Did you work with your team interpreter before?

AT THE EVENT—TOPIC

How familiar were you with the topic of the event?

- ☐ Not familiar
- ☐ Somewhat familiar
- ☐ Very familiar

DIARY

Below are questions that we kindly ask you to use to fill out your diary.

Did you prepare for this assignment?

What did you do to prepare for this assignment? Describe the steps.

Preparation materials: Were these easily available or did you have to ask for them (repeatedly)?

Looking back at the assignment: Was the preparation adequate for the assignment?

If this assignment was in your national sign language would you have prepared differently?

Would you do something different next time?

COMMENTS

If you have any other comments, please note them here.

From a Koine to Gestalt: Critical Points and Interpreter Strategies in Interpretation From International Sign Into Spoken English

Brett Best, Jemina Napier, Andy Carmichael, and Oliver Pouliot

National Deaf communities around the world, and particularly in Europe, are now enjoying an increase in international exchange (de Wit, 2010a). This is in part due to the higher levels of education that Deaf people have achieved in recent decades, enabled by interpretation and other support services (Lang, 2002), increased recognition of signed languages, and advancing technology (de Wit, 2010a). This type of international exchange among Deaf people has impacted the types of assignments that sign language interpreters are hired to undertake (de Wit, 2010a), for example, to enable political participation at a European level (Turner & Napier, 2014). Such assignments may require interpreters to have additional linguistic skills and cultural knowledge (de Wit, 2010a) and convey the core of a message to a mixed audience who have different national signed languages (Moody, 2002), a situation that may require the use of International Sign (IS).

The status of IS as a language is hotly debated in literature (see Rosenstock & Napier, Hansen, this volume). Regardless of the linguistic status of IS, it is often used at international conferences and academic gatherings (Hiddinga & Crasborn, 2011; Supalla et al., 2010) and international meetings (Turner & Napier, 2014). Hiddinga and Crasborn (2011) state that IS is unlikely to ever be standardized because the form of IS varies depending on the addressees and their language backgrounds. While the form of IS may never be delineated by conventionalized standards, the World Federation of the Deaf (WFD) and the World Association of Sign

Language Interpreters (WASLI) have recently formed the IS Interpreting Task Group in an effort to regulate and monitor the standards of IS interpreting in international contexts (Turner & Napier, 2014). Such an endeavor shows that there is a demand for IS and a need to ensure professional interpretation services between IS and English. Though questions have been raised about the overall average comprehension level of International Sign (Whynot, 2015) and particularly in regard to interpreted IS (Rosenstock, 2004), Turner and Napier (2014) state that it is possible that "the resources required for sufficient interpreter-mediation [*sic*] across the European public sphere will primarily be delivered in the shape of high-quality IS interpreting provision" (p. 64). With the growing demand for IS interpreting, more research needs to be done into best practices on this form of interpreter-mediated communication.

To date, comparatively little linguistic research has been conducted on IS interpreting, and the research that has been carried out has predominantly focused on interpreting from spoken English into IS (McKee & Napier, 2002; Rosenstock, 2004, 2008) or on the linguistic strategies used by a deaf-hearing interpreting team when working at an international conference in IS (Stone & Russell, 2014). Therefore, the case study discussed in this chapter will contribute to understanding the processes involved in IS interpreting by focusing on the linguistic strategies employed by two professional IS interpreters when working from IS into spoken English.

LITERATURE REVIEW

Here we provide an overview of the relevant literature to frame our case study, and we focus on investigations into the definition and nature of IS, interpreting from spoken English into IS, and interpreting from a national signed language into a spoken language.

International Sign

Although sign languages are different in every country, deaf people can "communicate across mutually unintelligible language boundaries" (Supalla & Webb, 1995, p. 334) using "cross-national signed communication" (Adam, 2012, p. 852), known as International Sign (IS). Essentially, IS is a form of "foreigner talk" (Quinto-Pozos, 2007), where different sign languages come into contact and signers exploit their awareness of gesture, iconicity, and visual-spatial expression. Although IS displays many linguistic features similar to other established sign languages (such as grammatical features), it does not have a consistent, established vocabulary. It lacks transmission from one generation to the next and has an unstable community of users, which are two very important factors in considering the linguistic status of IS (Suppalla & Webb, 1995; Rosenstock, 2004). Thus, "use of the term International Sign, rather than International Sign Language, emphasizes that IS is not recognised as having full linguistic status" (Adam, 2012, p. 853).

IS has been described as a pidgin by some researchers (Moody, 2002; McKee & Napier, 2002) and as a koine by others (Supalla & Webb, 1995). There is a general consensus that IS lacks an established lexicon and is flexible (Allsop, Woll, & Brauti, 1995; Moody, 2002). Furthermore, the lexicon that is used may be dependent on the specific interlocutors as a form of language contact (Adam, 2012): IS relies heavily on borrowing lexical items from various sign languages, which is influenced by the nationality of the signer and also the context where the signer is using IS (Whynot, 2015). IS often necessitates the conveyance of broader generalities in lieu of specifics (Allsop, Woll, & Brauti, 1995), and given the lack of established lexicon, complex meanings are not easily conveyed (Adam, 2012). For these reasons, Mesch (2010) reports that it is "easier to process information received in a national sign language than in IS" (p. 8).

There are conventions, however, in using IS that do appear to have some level of standardization: aspects of the grammatical structure and key established signs (such as WORK, IMPORTANT, DEAF, HEARING, and INTERPRETER). Thus describing it as a koine—a new, mixed language variety that has arisen as a result of contact between two or more mutually intelligible varieties (Kerswill & Williams, 2000)—may possibly be appropriate. Hansen discusses which labels to use when discussing IS in her chapter in this volume.

As a koine, IS is increasingly used as the lingua franca at international meeting places, including academic and political conferences, seminars, and meetings (de Wit, 2010a; Supalla et al., 2010; Turner & Napier, 2014). One such meeting place is a postgraduate program delivered jointly by Heriot-Watt University (UK), the University of Applied Sciences Magdeburg-Stendal (Germany), and Humak University of Applied Sciences (Finland): the European Masters of Sign Language Interpreting (EUMASLI), which was an ideal site to collect data for this case study.

As mentioned earlier, there are very few empirical studies of IS, and even fewer on IS interpreting. Existing studies of IS interpreting have concentrated on interpreting from English into IS, apart from one unpublished research paper (de Wit, 2010b). There is a wide range of literature in spoken and signed language interpreting research that recognizes that interpreters produce reduced or expanded renditions (e.g., Major & Napier, 2012; Wadensjö, 1998) as a linguistic coping strategy (Napier, 2002). Thus we take that as a given strategy in IS interpreting. However, we are interested in the specific strategies used by IS interpreters, given that IS is not an established language, such as strategies to account for a lack of direct equivalences or lack of a "database" of established lexicon from which to draw.

Interpreting from English into IS

According to Scott Gibson and Ojala (1994), to competently interpret into IS, an interpreter must possess knowledge of the universal linguistic structures of sign language, such as "localization, verb modification, question forms, facial expression, negation, borrowed signs and pantomime" (cited in McKee & Napier, 2002, p. 31). Until the publication of this volume, there were only two studies that had examined the linguistic features of IS used by interpreters: McKee and Napier (2002) and Rosenstock (2008). The contribution of Stone and Russell (this volume) in their comparative analysis of the use of depicting verbs by IS interpreters is a third.

McKee and Napier (2002) analyzed six interpreted passages from three sources: authentic footage from the World Games for the Deaf (now known as the Deaflympics) held in Denmark, the Congress of the International Federation of Deaf Sports (CISS) held in Finland, and the official video of the 1995 Congress of the World Federation of the Deaf. The data totaled 14 minutes and featured four hearing interpreters—two from English-speaking countries and two from other European countries. Rosenstock (2008) analyzed a total of 10 minutes of data from two different presentations at the Deaf Way II conference held in July 2002, in Washington, DC. These presentations were given in American Sign Language (ASL), interpreted into spoken English, and two hearing interpreters worked from the spoken English interpretation to produce the message in IS.

McKee and Napier (2002) and Rosenstock (2008) found many of the same characteristic forms in the IS interpreted output in their respective studies. Production features observed included a slower rate of articulation, an increased signing size and space, and lip patterns accompanying nouns, proper nouns, and some words in the English source message to disambiguate meaning (McKee & Napier, 2002). Grammatical features such as locating referents in space (McKee & Napier, 2002), using surrogate space and token space (Rosenstock, 2008), adverbial inflection (McKee & Napier, 2002), nonmanual grammatical markers (McKee & Napier, 2002; Rosenstock, 2008), referential (role) shifting, and providing context through actions were also noted in the interpreters' IS output (McKee & Napier, 2002). According to Napier and McKee (2002), these linguistic structures serve to make the interpretation succinct and somewhat predictable in form, which facilitates the audience's ability to decode the message; this is necessary because audience members will not be native users of the target output and ordinary strategies of comprehension (such as making closure on meaning through prediction of language forms and collocation) are not as readily available.

The IS interpreters in both studies used depicting signs (classifiers), which were used in place of fixed vocabulary for nouns (McKee & Napier, 2002) or to replace prepositional phrases in English (Rosenstock, 2008). Rhetorical questions were also used either as a linking device (McKee & Napier, 2002) or in lieu of relative clauses or declaratives (Rosenstock, 2008). One strategy observed was that IS interpreters appeared to delete information that they inferred to be redundant (McKee & Napier, 2002) or not crucial to the understanding of the content (Rosenstock, 2008). Other types of reductions also occurred: "Several longer phrases in the English text are reduced to shorter constructions in the IS translation" (Rosenstock, 2008, p. 4). McKee and Napier (2002) report examples of certain information, such as numbers and names of unfamiliar people and places, that were omitted if they were inessential to the message, not able to be easily transmitted, or could not be retained during processing time.

Conversely, strategies of expansion were also observed. Rosenstock (2008) reported that many English lexical items were expanded into phrases in IS, as the interpreter judged it beneficial to expand or paraphrase English words, so that the audience had a better understanding of the concept in the corresponding context. Different types of repetitions were also noted by Rosenstock (2008). One type was the production of more than one form of a sign for the same concept, perhaps to reach as wide an audience as possible. Another type of repetition was the reiteration of the topic of a paragraph. As Rosenstock (2008) explains,

"By introducing the concept, expanding on it, and then repeating it, the interpreter ensures that the audience understands that the expansion still belongs to one topic" (p. 7).

Other strategies that the interpreters in the studies used to enhance understanding of the target output and manage information flow included having an extended lag time for more effective message analysis, highlighting salient information, making relationships between elements more graphic by anchoring the topic on the nondominant hand, highlighting parts of the message by extending the final hold on signs that show important information, making the abstract more concrete, making explicit what is implicit, and choosing generic signs more likely to be understood such as signs that are iconic, have a simple form, or show a basic concept (McKee & Napier, 2002). Signs using metaphorical constructions such as metonymy were used to depict abstract concepts, for example, BAG-OF-MONEY as a substitute for funding (McKee & Napier, 2002; Rosenstock, 2008); and instead of using a lexical item, IS interpreters used constructed action and dialogue, depicting signs, an example, or paraphrase (McKee & Napier, 2002). Interpreters also used their knowledge of contextual and local information, such as the physical appearance of important people and places and previous related events, to depict information visually in their interpretation (McKee & Napier, 2002).

Interestingly, Rosenstock (2004) reports that how interpreters and presenters use IS seems to differ, which is confirmed by Whynot (2015). Given Mesch's (2010) statement that IS is more difficult to receive than a national sign language, it is particularly interesting to delve into the strategies employed by professional interpreters when making lexical choices for such visually rich, situation-specific, communicative renditions.

Interpreting from IS into English

To our knowledge, there is only one pre-existing study of IS to English interpreting, which is an unpublished research report (de Wit, 2010b). In her study, de Wit analyzed a spoken English interpretation of almost 6 minutes of video taken from an authentic 20-minute presentation given in IS by a deaf man to a mixed European audience. The interpreter was an experienced IS interpreter, who was familiar with the content of the presentation. The analysis of the interpretation was focused on examining a range of strategies used by the interpreter at the sentence level, which de Wit drew from existing literature, including omissions, additions, reformulations, summaries, use of fillers, paraphrases, reverse paraphrases [what Wadensjö (1998) would refer to as reduced renditions], alterations of lag time, and repairs. She noted that omissions tended to occur when reformulations were made, and, when additions were made to provide clarifying information, this sometimes created the omission of other information. She also found some occurrences of summarizing, paraphrasing, and reverse paraphrasing and one incident of repairing.

One of the key strategies that de Wit (2010b) noted was the interpreter's use of time lag, which was averaged at 5 seconds, so she concluded that

> a long lag time is a starting point for the International Sign interpreter to produce the best interpretation possible. Because International Sign is not conventionalized, there will be signs or expressions that are uncommon to the interpreter, for which the interpreter needs more source message information in order to interpret it into an equivalent target message. (p. 16)

De Wit noted that because she was not able to interview the interpreter-participant, she could not interrogate her classifications of the strategies used. Thus one of her recommendations was that any future research should incorporate a follow-up interview with interpreters in order to get insight into their interpreting decisions.

Interpreting From a Signed Into a Spoken Language

Because there is only one other small study on interpreting from IS into English, it is helpful to consider work that has been carried out on the analysis of interpretation from a national signed language into a spoken language. One such study involved the analysis of compression strategies used by ASL/English interpreters (Finton & Smith, 2004; Finton, 2005). The authors maintain that certain information conveyed in ASL is inherently expanded visually and therefore must be reduced to adhere to linguistic appropriateness in spoken English and create meaning, and therefore interpreters use compression strategies (Finton & Smith, 2004; Finton, 2005). Through the use of compression strategies while interpreting ASL to English, the authors state that the following types of common errors may be reduced: Intrusion of source language features, wordiness, redundancies, register mismatch, inappropriate use of first person dialogue, and loss of speaker style. Finton and Smith mention different types of expansion in ASL and the corresponding compression strategy employed by interpreters when working from ASL into English. These strategies include recognizing the function of expansions in ASL, such as contrasting information to emphasize an opposing idea and realizing that the contrast need not be interpreted literally into English. Other areas of expansion seen in ASL are techniques such as faceting, which function to narrow a concept to a particular image—something that can be done adequately by adverbs, qualifiers, and vocal intonation in spoken English—and the fact that reiteration in ASL may simply serve as a form of emphasis, which can be done by other means in spoken English. Finton and Smith also mention the utilization of three-dimensional space and note that "the amount of detail in a message, the use of referential space, and the figure-ground relationships provide particular challenges when interpreting between ASL and English" (p. 131). The amount of detail considered linguistically appropriate in ASL may differ from considerations of appropriateness in English. They assert that interpreters must take into account the function of the message and demonstrate willingness to change the structure of the message in such instances. Finton and Smith also explain that although English may have a specific lexical item to describe a concept, ASL may lack one such lexical item and instead list various examples: explaining by example or "couching." Lastly, they state that ASL exhibits a type of expansion that can be referred to as "describe, then do" (p. 135), wherein a short description of something is followed by an enactment either through reported dialogue or a "verb sandwich," when a verb in a sentence occurs twice. They suggest that the corresponding compression strategy when interpreting these ASL expansions into English would be, in the former circumstance, to let go of the need to report the entire interaction in detail and instead report the gist of the story; and in the latter, to recognize that the reappearance of the verb adds more information about how the action is being performed.

While compression strategies may be necessary when providing a spoken interpretation of a national signed language, expansion strategies may also be required. Hema (2002) analyzed the decisions behind his lexical choices when interpreting from a presentation from British Sign Language (BSL) into English and focused his analysis on the first few introductory utterances of the signed presentation and his corresponding interpretation. Hema justified the expansion strategies in English interpretation as necessary to match the register and the linguistic and cultural norms of the hearing audience. Drawing on Wadensjö's (1998) work, Hema explains that it is important for interpreters to adopt an approach centered not just on message transfer, but on performing various communicative activities (such as expansion) to facilitate the intended message impact.

One of the first studies of interpretation from a signed into a spoken language was conducted by Roy (1987), who analyzed the discourse style and paralinguistic features of an interpretation of a lecture delivered in ASL into English. She also played the recording of the English interpretation to a group of hearing nonsigners and asked them to comment on what they heard. Her analysis found that, although the interpreter had provided an accurate interpretation in terms of matching the propositional content, she had neither adequately represented the register nor matched the affect of the sign language lecture and this was as a result of inappropriate use of intonation, rhythm, stress marking, and pitch. In sum, the hearing listeners noted that (based on listening only to the English text) they perceived the presenter as talking to children, rather than giving an academic lecture.

More recently, Fitzmaurice and Purdy (2015) found that disfluent pausing (i.e., pausing in the wrong places or for too long when speaking in English) also has a negative effect on listener judgements of ASL-to-English interpretations. Fitzmaurice and Purdy explain that one might expect more pauses in a spoken interpreted message because the cognitive load of interpreting may necessitate some time to formulate the next articulation, so they were interested in how pauses are perceived by listeners. An ASL monologue on the cardiovascular system was interpreted by a nationally certified interpreter, with more than 20 years of professional interpreting experience. The recording was then edited to eliminate or reduce any atypical pauses. Participants were randomly assigned to listen to the audio either with or without the pauses. Baseline data was collected by asking Deaf participants to watch the source text in ASL and judge the speaker on certain qualities. Listeners of the audio versions were asked their thoughts on the speaker, their manner of speaking, and general impressions of the speaker. Fitzmaurice and Purdy found that the atypical pauses negatively impacted listener judgments of the speaker and that those who directly watched the presenter had more positive judgments. Interestingly, however, those listening to the original audio with atypical pauses were not told that they were listening to an interpretation, so Fitzmaurice and Purdy state that further research is needed to explore whether participants are able to distinguish between the qualities of the speaker and the interpreter when they are aware that what they are hearing is not the product of a single person.

This study is interesting and applicable to this case study of an interpretation of IS into English because it highlights that such atypical, disfluent pauses do happen when working from a signed to a spoken language, even when the interpreter is qualified and experienced.

Macías (2006), in the analysis of spoken language simultaneous interpretation, has suggested that disfluent pauses may be an indication of a problem with the interpreter's fluency. Napier (2007) and Napier, Carmichael, and Wiltshire (2008), however, analyzed how pauses can be used strategically to enhance an interpretation. In a case study of the cooperative strategies between a Deaf presenter and the interpreters providing a spoken English interpretation of his monologue from Auslan (Australian Sign Language) into English, Napier (2007) found that cooperation occurs through strategic use of eye gaze, pausing, and nodding as "paralinguistic cues to co-construct meaning and negotiate smooth delivery of talk" (p. 427). Participants used such cues with intentionality to convey comprehension, mark episodes, clarify content, control the pace of the presentation, or establish the footing of the presenter. Cooperative principles based on Gricean maxims of cooperation in spoken conversation (Grice, 1975) were suggested for interpreter-mediated monologic talk. Napier, Carmichael, and Wiltshire (2008), in a discussion of the same case study with a focus on the prepresentation briefing and postmeeting debriefing, suggest that the level of preparation between the presenter and interpreters enabled the enhanced cooperation during the delivery of the spoken English interpretation to meet the intent of the presenter, and the expectations of the audience. In his case study, Hema (2002) also reported on the importance of being able to prepare with his Deaf client beforehand and mentioned the use of cues, such as eye contact with panelists, which informed his interpretation. This research on preparation with presenters when working from a signed to a spoken language is particularly relevant to our exploration of working from IS to English, because, as de Wit (2010a, p. 241) states, "a successful interpretation in the multilingual international setting also depends on a good cooperation between the interpreter and the client."

Moody (2002) explains that all signed languages use referential, topographical, and structural space and that these elements, in conjunction with others such as facial expressions, present three-dimensional, "simultaneous bundles of information" (p. 31). While Moody concedes that all languages have examples of simultaneous information, he argues that signed languages are able to incorporate a great deal of simultaneous information that must be presented differently in a linear, sequential spoken language. While Moody explains that bundled simultaneous information is common to all signed languages, because IS is typified by an impoverished lexicon (Allsop, Woll, & Brauti, 1995), more iconicity and gesture (Moody, 2002), and possible dependence on a cultural framework (McKee & Napier, 2002), a communicative utterance in IS may more frequently exhibit compact bundles of simultaneous information, requiring additional cognitive processing to untangle the bundled information and express it in a linear language.

Moody (2002) identifies use of three-dimensional space as a significant component of these "simultaneous bundles of information" (p. 31) in national signed languages, and Finton and Smith (2004, p. 131) state that "because the use of space is such a significant component of ASL, it can present some unique challenges for . . . interpreting into English." Therefore, the strategies an IS interpreter utilizes when handling a significant portion of bundled simultaneous information in a visual-gestural communicative utterance may be borne from strategies acquired from interpreting from a national signed language into a spoken language.

Considering these strategies that are used when interpreting from a signed into a spoken language, this case study will make a contribution toward understanding the strategies involved when interpreting IS into spoken English, and the additional challenges that may be present when interpreters are working from a koine into an established language.

METHOD

Modeling our study on that used by Napier (2007) and Napier, Carmichael, and Wiltshire (2008) in their linguistic case study of a signed to spoken English interpretation, we used a descriptive linguistic case study approach (Hale & Napier, 2013) to analyze authentic qualitative data and draw on interpreter reflections of their decision making, in order to provide a "thick description" (Geertz, 1973) of strategies utilized by two professional sign language interpreters working simultaneously in an interpreter-mediated classroom environment.

Data Collection Site

The official language of instruction of the EUMASLI program is English. During the 2.5-year program, which is targeted at experienced interpreters of national sign languages, students are taught British Sign Language (BSL), Finnish Sign Language, German Sign Language, and IS;

develop skills in translating and interpreting between English and IS; and learn research skills (Hessmann et al., 2011). The teaching team is made up of Deaf and hearing lecturers from the three partner universities.

The second cohort of the program, who were enrolled between 2013 and 2015, included both Deaf and hearing students; therefore not only did students learn, communicate in, translate, and interpret IS, but there were two languages of instruction: IS and English. Thus two IS-English interpreters were present to interpret at every module, and the interpreting direction would depend on the language used by the teacher. The interpreting services were provided through the same agency, so there was a level of consistency in provision across the modules (i.e., at least one of the interpreters had worked in previous modules).

The fact that IS was being used and interpreted regularly in this context made an EUMASLI classroom a prime site for collecting authentic IS interpreted data. Given the lack of previous research examining linguistic strategies for interpreting from IS into English, we decided to focus this case study on the analysis of an excerpt of interpretation in that direction. The four coauthors of this chapter were all involved in the EUMASLI program: as a teacher (Jemina), a student (Brett), and two of the regular interpreters (Andy and Oliver).

The Data

The data was comprised of a video recording of a lecture given in IS to a mixed international group of hearing and Deaf postgraduate students at Heriot-Watt University, Edinburgh, Scotland, in September 2014, and which was simultaneously interpreted into spoken English. The clip used for analysis is an excerpt chosen from a video that is approximately 67 minutes long. The excerpt is approximately 11 minutes long and was chosen because it is comprised mostly of monologic segments.

Participants and Context

The presenter using IS (Jemina) is a hearing, fluent signer and a native user of BSL who is also fluent in Auslan, proficient in American Sign Language (ASL), and works as an interpreter between English and BSL, Auslan, or IS. Both interpreters are also native signers. One interpreter (Andy) is a native signer of BSL, is also fluent in Auslan, and works between English and BSL, Auslan, or IS; the other interpreter (Oliver) is a native signer of ASL, is also conversant in BSL, and works as an interpreter between English and ASL or IS. Moody (2002) cites the importance of knowing more than one signed language when working with IS in an international environment so that an interpreter has the mental flexibility to adapt to new and different vocabulary. Both interpreters are also native English users and experienced working professionally with IS. The interpreters and presenter had worked together many times previous to the context of this study and were familiar with one another's signing styles and personalities.

While IS does not have an established lexicon (Allsop, Woll, & Brauti, 1995; Moody, 2002), Adam (2012) explains that the lexicon used in IS may be dependent on the interlocutors involved. In this case, the participants in this program had previously established a great deal of their own lexicon, which was used in classroom lectures, discussions, and informal interaction. McKee and Napier (2002) cite Moody (1994) when they state that "an important requirement for IS interpreting is close knowledge of the context in which one is working" (p. 49). The interpreters had regularly interpreted for this course, so they were familiar with the specific lexicon often used in this context. Thus all the coauthors are familiar with the lexicon used by this group, which was essential to allow a thorough analysis of the data.

Process

The video clip was imported into ELAN, a computer program that allows the precise alignment of transcription with video data (Wittenburg et al., 2006) and is widely used by sign linguists (Johnston & Crasborn, 2006; Perniss, 2015). First, on one tier, an English gloss was recorded for each individual sign produced in IS. This was done before listening to the spoken English interpretation in order not to bias the transcription. Next, a verbatim transcript of the interpreters' spoken English was produced in a Microsoft Word document, and the transcribed spoken sentences were then entered into ELAN on a separate tier to correspond with the units of IS glosses. An additional tier was also added to enable comments on observations of the interpretation choices or any other interesting aspects of the data. The document transcript of the English interpretation was also used to identify potentially interesting areas (see the Analysis section) for deeper examination by highlighting segments with noticeable pauses in bold font. Pauses were manually annotated in the ELAN software.

Professional interpreters generally have a high level of metalinguistic awareness, that is, the ability to focus attention on language use and reflect upon its nature, structure, and functions "because they must constantly analyze the linguistic structure of the source language, the semantic message presented within that linguistic structure, the message's potential impact, and the equivalents in an alternative linguistic structure that will provide the same message impact to users of the target language" (Napier & Barker, 2004, p. 372). Thus, an important part of the process was for the analysis to be considered by the interpreters, in order to provide an additional layer of metalinguistic commentary on the data.

Analysis

Munday (2012) refers to "critical points" in a translation as "points in a text which require interpretation and in some cases substantive intervention by the translator" (p. 2), and such points may be identified by a hesitation or disfluency as the interpreter decides how to proceed. Angelone (2010) refers to such critical points as a "problem nexus" (p. 18). It could be argued that IS—which is not a language and lacks an established lexicon—may present interpreters with the need to perform "substantive intervention" (Munday, 2012, p. 2) in order to reformulate a message produced in a highly visual, spatial koine with limited lexicon into a linear, spoken language with an extensive established vocabulary.

Two approaches were used to analyze the data. The first approach focused on the identification of disfluent pauses (Fitzmaurice & Purdy, 2015) in the spoken English interpretation. Fitzmaurice and Purdy (2015) explain that while some pauses have purposes and functions in speech, speakers will sometimes pause when they are experiencing difficulty with devising or articulating their utterance. Fitzmaurice and Purdy explain that such hesitations may occur at an unnatural time in an utterance or have a longer duration than normal, and they cite Bortfeld, Leon, Bloom, Schober, and Brennan (2001) when they state that "pausing disfluencies are more common with increased cognitive load" (quoted in Fitzmaurice & Purdy, 2015, p. 2). These statements are in regard to noninterpreted, conversational situations. However, Angelone (2010) applies pauses to interpretation and heightened cognitive load and specifically identifies "pauses in target text generation" (Angelone, 2010, p. 18) as a criterion for identifying the occurrence of problem nexuses in the source text. He explains that these pauses, caused by encountering a problem nexus, indicate a heightened cognitive load for the interpreter. Jefferson (1989) found that native speakers of English tend to accept up to 1.0 seconds of silent pause in conversation, and Fitzmaurice and Purdy (2015) cite Trudgill (2000) when they state that pauses of 4 seconds may cause embarrassment in American communicative exchanges. The maximum standard that native speakers of English are willing to accept, without discomfort for a message that they know is being interpreted, has not been explored, so for the purposes of this study, anything exceeding Jefferson's (1989) maximum standard of 1.0 seconds was considered a disfluent pause. Filled pauses (Lallgee & Cook, 1969) such as "uh" or "ah" were not considered as pauses in this data. Periods of silence lasting more than 1.0 seconds in the target text were noted, and the corresponding segment of the source text was then analyzed in the hope that identifying such instances in the target text would reveal areas where interpreters may have experienced a heightened cognitive load (perhaps due to trying to decipher ambiguity in the koine) and hence employed particular linguistic strategies. The source text transcription was then compared to the target text transcription in ELAN and evaluated.

RESULTS AND DISCUSSION

In this case study, we have found instances of the working interpreter using strategies mentioned by Finton and Smith (2004) in their study of interpretation from ASL into English. We have also identified examples where the interpreter utilized some of the same strategies, when working from IS into spoken English, that McKee and Napier (2002) and Rosenstock (2008) identified interpreters using, when working from English into IS. The examples here are not inclusive of every occurrence of a certain observed phenomenon but rather simply serve to illustrate our findings.

Pausing

Fitzmaurice and Purdy (2015) explain that with the cognitive load of interpreting, one might expect more pauses when interpreting a message from a signed into a spoken language, because it may necessitate some time to formulate the next articulation. Finton and Smith (2004) state that when the number of signed lexical items varies significantly from the number of lexical items in a spoken interpretation, "there is always potential for awkward and unnatural periods of silence" (p. 137). De Wit (2010a) reports that working in international, multilingual settings increases the demands on an interpreter's cognitive processing capacity. Thus, one might expect to hear even more atypical pausing when an interpreter is working from IS into English.

Angelone (2010) identifies a pause as a verbal indicator of uncertainty on the part of an interpreter when he or she is faced with a problem nexus, which Munday (2012, p. 2) refers to as a "critical point." Because different interpreters may individually experience different problem nexuses or critical points in a source text, the aim of the research was not to identify potential problem nexuses in IS but rather to analyze the strategies that these professional interpreters utilized to produce a coherent spoken English interpretation of IS. Identifying disfluent pauses in the target text drew our attention to instances where processing strategies may have been utilized.

While pauses were effectively used as a means for identifying moments of interpreter strategizing, we realized that pauses in the target text may actually originate from pauses in the source text, or it may also be the case that some pauses are actually an intentional tactic utilized by an interpreter when waiting for enough information to coherently produce an English sentence. It also seemed that other strategies for extending processing time were utilized instead of outright pauses. There were instances of the interpreter slowing the rate of speech production at certain points or drawing out certain words. When asked to reflect on this strategy, the interpreters commented as follows:

> I've heard [Oliver] use it as a regular strategy. . . . I do it too, as do many other interpreters I suspect. (Andy)
>
> Perhaps a slowing down of speech indicates the opposite of a problem nexus: a smooth sailing point? It could also be closer to what we are perceiving to be an easier rate to receive by those who are listening. When we have a heavier processing load, it often feels like we are "chasing" the source language with our "hearing" tongues, sometimes blindly trusting that what is coming out of our mouths is making any sense. I would not rule out that it can be used to lessen the silence between points—it would be interesting to see if this slowing down typically happens at the beginning or end of interpreted utterances. (Oliver)

Thus there is a potential drawback in this case study when attempting to apply Angelone's (2010) theory of pauses as signifying a problem nexus and therefore heightened cognitive load on the part of the interpreter in order to identify areas of possible strategizing. To numerically quantify a pause as something more concrete than a subjective, innate linguistic sense, the criterion used in this case study for identifying a disfluent pause is based on what is typically tolerated for native speakers of English during a conversation. This situation, however, was an interpreted, expository lecture with a target audience that had a mix of native and nonnative English speakers. More research needs to be done to determine the maximum, standard pause comfortably accepted by individuals who realize that they are listening to an interpreted message, as the tolerated baseline may be different for simultaneous interpretations, particularly because these specific audience members were almost all interpreters themselves.

Moreover, Fitzmaurice and Purdy (2015) cite Shigemitsu (2005) when they state that perception of pause length may be dependent on culture and language, so even if a baseline for tolerated pause duration in simultaneous interpretations can be established in future research, its relevance may be compromised in an international context. Nonetheless, in this study, identifying disfluent pauses by the criterion set did reveal interesting areas of interpreter strategy utilization. Here we provide examples from the data using principles from the horizontal transcription method as suggested by Gallez (2010) and Metzger and Roy (2011). Rather than use the horizontal method to depict the interpreter mediated turns in a dialogue, we illustrate the lengths of pauses when interpreting from a monologic IS text into English.

Illustrative Examples of Findings

IS often necessitates the conveyance of broader generalities in lieu of specifics (Allsop, Woll, & Brauti, 1995; Whynot, 2015). In order to create meaning and be linguistically appropriate, such general utterances may need to be expanded when working into spoken English. An example of one such utterance can be seen in Table 1.

In Table 1, the interpreter chooses lexicon that offers more specificity than the IS source text, such as *checklist* for the sign glossed as LIST and *taxonomy* for the long list of evaluative criteria, glossed as MANY CRITERIA-LIST. It is particularly interesting in both of these words that in the audio of the target text, the supporting interpreter can be heard offering these specific lexical suggestions to the working interpreter. Also interesting is that the cointerpreter can be detected offering the lexical suggestion of "taxonomy" during the 1.7-second pause before the working interpreter articulated "taxonomy," which arguably gives some credence to Angelone's (2010) criterion of pausing for detecting points in a translation that requires a heightened cognitive load and the need for an interpreter to make a decision in a problem nexus.

TABLE 1. *Expansion for Specificity and Making the Implicit Explicit.*

Participant	Time					
			4-s pause		1.7-s pause	2-s pause	
Lecturer*	ONE EXAMPLE LIST CLEAR QUOTE EASY TICK POINT-POINT-POINT GUIDELINES OTHER MANY CRITERIA-LIST					
Interpreter-English		So, one example would be	a kind of easy but more straightforward checklist of what should be included, and another way to do it is to have a much more in depth look at	the taxonomy of		what a translation involves

*Back translation: One example is a list that is clear and "easy" with a few specifics. The other is a long list of criteria.

In this situation, we can see that perhaps both interpreters were cognizant of a need to assign specifically differing descriptive lexicon to the contrastive types of lists mentioned in the source text. This is indicated both by the more specific English lexicon selected to differentiate the two lists and by the pause as the working interpreter bore the cognitive load of processing the source message while searching for linguistically appropriate, expansive vocabulary in the target language.

McKee and Napier (2002) state that when working from English to IS, interpreters may also make explicit what is implicit. This is another way to add specificity and may be observed in this example. Because the second list of criteria mentioned is visually depicted as being a much longer list than the first, it follows that using such a list would provide one with a "much more in-depth look" at what a translation involves, which is what the interpreter said in his interpretation (see Table 1). Hence this inference was made explicit in the English interpretation. In Table 2, the interpreter also expands on the source text to make it more specific to the academic situation.

In Table 2, the interpreter expands on what is offered in IS with lexical choices that add more specificity to the academic context such as *hybrid* and *gestalt*. In addition to the interpreter expanding on what was offered in IS, we also see instances of pausing as he cognitively processes the receiving of the source text, fleshes it out, and produces it in spoken English. Interestingly, the instances of the longest lag times happened during the times when expansion was being employed.

The signed portion of this utterance begins at 4:28.8 and continues until 5:01.8. The interpretation for this segment begins at approximately 4:46.6, around 18 seconds into the utterance. Prior to beginning the interpretation for this segment, the interpreter was still interpreting a previous segment into English. Cokely (1992) found that average lag time is 2.8 seconds with an upper limit of 6–8 seconds for sign language interpreters. McKee and Napier (2002) found that IS interpreters "routinely stretch the outer limits of processing and memory capacity for simultaneous interpreting in order to maximize effective message analysis and reconstruction of a conceptually equivalent TL message," often working with a lag time of 10–16 seconds and sometimes more (p. 42 ff.). When working from IS to spoken English, we see that this may also be the case, as in the example in Table 2.

This is an interesting example because, while expanding on the source text by offering more specific lexicon in English, we also see some

TABLE 2. *Expansion for Specificity and Couching Compression Strategy.*

Participant	Time			
	4:28.8	4:46.6	1.7-s pause	
Lecturer*	CAN GROUP GROUP GROUP DISCUSS READ THINK PT+rt WANT SAME ENVISION WHAT MANY-CRITERIA-LIST+rt CRITERIA LIST–lf CAN PICK+ PICK+lf PICK+rt PICK+lf PUT-TOGETHER PRO-1 FEEDBACK-TO-ME FROM ALL WE PUT-DOWN PUT-DOWN PUT-DOWN AIM ALL-AGREE POINT POINT POINT GUIDELINES rt			
Interpreter-English		I think what we can do is pick from both lists and come up with a kind of hybrid, um, detailed and more gestalt type of, um,		evaluation

*Back translation: In small groups, you can discuss this, read about it, think about it, and then when we have the same understanding, we can look at both lists, pick things from each, you can give me your feedback, and once we've done that, I will write it down and it will become our guidelines for evaluation.

compression strategies as explained by Finton and Smith (2004). These authors describe *couching* in ASL (Finton & Smith, 2004, p. 134) as happening when a signer would like to convey a concept for which a single ASL lexical item does not exist, so the concept is conveyed by grouping several signs together. Perhaps similarly, Adam (2012) states that in IS, several gestures and signs may be combined to indicate a single referent. The compression strategy for interpreting couching in ASL would be to identify the appropriate, equivalent, lexical item or concept in English rather than produce a spoken word for each individual sign produced: "An awkward and stilted interpretation could result if the ASL-to-English interpretation included the ASL description" (Finton & Smith, 2004, p. 135). In Table 2, the lecturer gives many examples of working together: DISCUSS READ THINK . . . WANT SAME ENVISION. This could be an example of couching because a general concept of working together is being formed. The compression strategy identified by Finton and Smith (2004) is to identify the appropriate English concept, which this interpreter does. Instead of providing an English lexical item for each example signed, the interpreter conveys the overall concept of collaboration and mutual agreement by stating "we" will pick from both lists to "come up with" the evaluative criteria, thereby effectively utilizing one of Finton and Smith's (2004) strategies for compression.

While this may be an example of couching and the corresponding compression strategy, given the lag time, it may also be indicative of cognitive processing strategies. When asked to reflect on this example, the interpreters noted that

> [This is] a great example of why longer decalage [time lag] is needed in IS work. By staying back, Oliver was able to compress with economy, allowing him time to devote to other parts of his process and to taking feeds from me. (Andy)
>
> Thinking back, this is a rather predictable moment. Jemina would have told us that she would have them working in groups, as she often does. So, as I was finishing what I most likely sensed was the end of the monologic portion of her intervention, the transition to the comparatively more direct instruction came with less pressure. Another consideration is the fact that all of the individuals in the room were signers. There is a contextual element at work as well I think. You notice that I did not say, "Can you now get into groups"—and perhaps I thought this was implicit in the message but perhaps I saw her sign-

TABLE 3. *Reductions.*

Participant	Time	
Lecturer*	EVERYTHING ME-GIVE-YOU-ALL DROP-IN DROP-IN DROP-IN DROP-IN DROP-IN DROP^BOX FINISH FINISH DROP-IN DROP-IN	
Interpreter-English		Okay, so everything I'm giving you is in the Dropbox as well.

*Back translation: Everything I've given to you all has been put in, put in, put in, put in the Dropbox. It has already been put in there.

ing and [decided] not to worry about GROUP GROUP GROUP because everyone in the room knows what that means. (Oliver)

While expansion may be one technique that interpreters working from IS to spoken English may need to utilize, reduction is a technique that may be applied as well. IS shares many elements of "foreigner talk" such as repetition and summaries of previous utterances (Adam, 2012; Quinto-Pozos, 2007). Rosenstock (2008) found that interpreters working from spoken English use repetition in their interpretations into IS to clarify certain concepts. Given the possibility of repetition in IS, reduction may be necessary in some instances when producing an interpretation of these types of repetitions to maintain linguistic appropriateness in spoken English. An example of repetition is noted in Table 3.

While the literature states that repetition does occur in IS, what is happening in this particular example may be more akin to a phenomenon observed in national signed languages. Finton and Smith (2004) state that in ASL certain signs may be repeated in a text, typically as a way to mark emphasis. In this example, the lecturer seems to be emphasizing the fact that the materials in reference have also been made available through the application called Dropbox. The corresponding compression strategy for dealing with such reiterations is to use other means to accomplish the emphasis in spoken English instead of a literal interpretation of the repetition as it was signed (Finton & Smith, 2004, p. 130). This is the compression strategy utilized by this interpreter as he conveys the reiterated information into a sentence in spoken English without providing an exact interpretation of the actual repetition that occurred in the source text. As commented on by Oliver:

TABLE 4. *Strategic Omissions.*

Participant	Time	
	7:17.9	7.20.3
Lecturer*	YOU-ALL EXPERIENCE POSS-2 THINK IMPORTANT WE EVALUATE PUT-DOWN PUT-DOWN PUT-DOWN WE THINK CONNECT THEORY FIRST listing #S-T+lf #T-T+rt EQUAL SECOND listing PT+rt IMPACT MATCH AUDIENCE PT+rt INFORM ALL FINISH TEXT #W-F-D WANT WHAT CRITERIA-LIST	
Interpreter-English		In your experience—from your experience, I would like to hear your opinions about how you think about whether or not this kind of criteria matches the theory we've been looking at in terms of ST to TT and so on and so forth.

*Back translation: From your experience, I want to know what you think is important to put on our evaluative list. We need to consider the application of theory, source text and target text equivalence, if the impact on the audience matches, and criteria for the translation such as in the WFD example.

> Prosody plays a big role here. The combination of repetition for emphasis as well as nonmanual markers for further clarity in the source text will lend itself to a very specific, prosodic interpretation in English.
>
> Andy states:
>
> This is not only a common strategy, but a necessary one as the repetition rendered into English would be incongruent to target text norms.

McKee and Napier (2002) and Rosenstock (2008) found that interpreters working from English to IS may delete information deemed unessential or redundant or information that cannot be retained during processing time. Table 4 shows how the interpreter omitted some information presented in IS, namely matching audience impact and a reference to a hypothetical World Federation of the Deaf (WFD) commission for a translation that had been explained earlier and then referenced several times previously in class.

In this instance, this particular utterance began at 7:17.9, and the interpretation of this segment began at approximately 7.20.3. This is within the average 2.8 seconds of lag time for simultaneous interpretation as reported by Cokely (1992), so it does not seem that this omission was due to pressures of lag time. Perhaps, it was what Napier (2002) would term as a *conscious, strategic omission.*

The presenter in this case could be said to be employing what Finton and Smith (2004, p. 133) might refer to as a compression strategy for "explaining by example," an occurrence in which a concept is expressed through signing several different examples. One could argue that the interpreter utilized the compression strategy for explaining by example by opting not to mention each example signed but instead refer to "what we've been looking at" because these specifics had already been previously mentioned in class and also served to form the general concept of appropriateness of selected criteria for the assignment.

> This may be an unconscious omission in terms of Oliver grasping the "impact on the audience matches" bit, then gets presented with the repetition of the WFD information, so he elects to go generic with his "and so on and so forth"? (Andy)
>
> This segment could also be labeled as direct instruction to the class, similar to the "get into groups and discuss" example of Table 2. Should we as interpreters be aware of these changes in discourse narrative? [So it may be] not so much conscious strategic omission as much as it is cognitive overload. Sometimes you should hang back but you don't due to processing "momentum." (Oliver)

When explaining how International Sign works and offering recommendations for using it, Moody (2002) states, "Use common experiences" (p. 36). He encourages interpreters to know their audience and to take advantage of what may be commonly known. Likewise, McKee and Napier (2002) report that when working from English to IS, interpreters use their knowledge of relevant people, contextual information, and local places—knowledge which they also know to be shared by the target audience—to make their interpretations more clear. In Table 5, we see evidence of the interpreter using his knowledge of the building to make the interpretation more specific.

The IS source text first spatially refers to an area nearby, then mentions a room indicated as being further away, and lastly specifically names the lounge and places it as even further away. The interpreter uses his

TABLE 5. *Application of Personal Knowledge for Clarification.*

Participant	Time	
Lecturer*	FIRST THINK MAYBE 3 4 3 4 GROUP GROUP CL: bent V SIT-IN-CIRCLE CAN PT+lf HAVE PT+lf ROOM PT+lf OR PT+lf far LOUNGE EAT CAKE CAN CL: legs walking WALK-THERE SPACE HERE HOT HAVE CAKE PT+lf	
Interpreter-English		And I'd like you to get into groups of 3 or 4 and you're okay to leave the, um, room to go into the lounge room or go to the other computer room or to the student common room because it's, uh, a little uncomfortable, and there is still cake in there, I guess.

*Back translation: First, I think that you should get into groups of 3 or 4 people. You can go out there. We have a room, or go to the lounge and eat cake. You can walk there. There is space there. It is hot here. There is cake there.

knowledge of the facility to assign specific names to these areas—"the other computer room" and "the student common room"—in the English interpretation to make it more clear in the interpretation which areas are being referenced, but this is not necessarily a strategy that is used only when interpreting from IS into English.

As noted earlier, preparation between a presenter and interpreters is paramount to ensure that a spoken interpretation faithfully represents the message and intent of the signing presenter and also meets the norms of the situation and expectations of a hearing audience. The importance of IS/English interpreter preparation is discussed by de Wit and Sluis in this volume. In the context of our study, the interpreters were provided with copies of any PowerPoint slides for lectures prior to the teaching block. However, in the excerpt featured in this chapter for analysis, the lecturer was not using any PowerPoint and in fact was prompting discussion from students. Thus the interpreter preparation was minimal for this particular segment. Although the interpreters had the advantage of working regularly in that context with the lecturer and students, they note that preparation influences their interpretation choices in the following ways:

> If the presenter has a working knowledge of written English and can provide either background papers, PowerPoints or any other prepara-

tory materials, then it allows us to use the vocabulary that they themselves have chosen to express their concepts when producing a spoken interpretation. It's interesting to note that this specific vocabulary often comes up in the feeds given by the team interpreter, who can sometimes be looking at the screen whilst the working interpreter is looking at the IS source. Not only does preparation allow us to reflect our clients' linguistic choices better, but we also have a greater appreciation of the overall view and of the goals of their communication. (Andy)

> There is also the factor of knowing that the person that you are interpreting for can hear. I don't think this changed our interpretation, but we also have the advantage of listening to her speak, perhaps even give the same lecture in English, perhaps preparing us beforehand in English. This is atypical, yes, but nonetheless may have an influence on preparation. An important part of preparation is knowing the language of the institution, of the department, and of that specific cohort. (Oliver)

The level of preparation and the familiarity of the interpreters with each other and the context have impacts on the teamworking strategies between the interpreters and how they feed information to each other when interpreting into English, as commented on by Andy:

> Oliver and I actively overfeed each other (if possible) as we've both discovered that we're neither of us put off by our respective feeds and will disregard as often as accept them based on a variety of factors such as (i) time constraints, i.e., that was too long ago now for me to crowbar it back in somehow; (ii) memory constraints, e.g., after those three dates, four names, and a list of countries a page long, I've no space for THAT!; (iii) for classroom dynamic changes, e.g., they've already got[ten] up and started leaving by the time you get to that point; (iv) we simply didn't hear the feed amongst the classroom noise; or (v) we disagree with the feed. But . . . most of the time it's welcome, precise, and appreciated.

CONCLUSION

IS may present complex challenges for interpreters when simultaneously interpreting into a spoken language. IS signers frequently produce bundles of simultaneous information for which clear and quick interpretation may prove difficult. The professional interpreters in this case study utilized various strategies to produce an interpretation including preparation, teamwork, pausing to buy time to receive or process adequate information to produce a coherent English sentence, expansion, reduction, strategic omission, application of personal knowledge, and compression strategies corresponding to reiteration, couching, and explaining by example, all of which are strategies that have been identified in working with national signed languages.

Many of these strategies are the same types of strategies utilized by interpreters working from spoken English to IS or from a national signed language into a spoken language, though greater lag time and an enhanced knowledge of the context, information, speaker, and linguistic skills may be necessary when working in contexts where IS is being used. Given that an interpreter may develop such strategies when working from a national signed language into a spoken language, perhaps it is not surprising to see the same strategies utilized when working with IS.

This linguistic case study is limited by the fact that it is a single, brief excerpt of interpreters working in one situation. Furthermore, the duration of the clip features the work of primarily one interpreter, though with support from a co-interpreter. These interpreters work together often and are very familiar with the presenter, audience, physical location, and content of the lecture. Different strategies may be necessary and observed in IS interpreters working in environments with which they are less familiar or working with individuals with whom the interpreters have less familiarity. There was no media used by this presenter, such as a PowerPoint, so strategies that interpreters may utilize when media is present and accessible also could not be considered. Another issue to consider is whether the fact that both interpreters and the presenter are native bimodal-bilinguals with a shared spoken language was an important factor in this interpretation.

Also, while Napier (2007) explores cooperation strategies in interpreter-mediated monologic talk, it was not possible to visually observe the interpreters in this data as the camera was focused only on the presenter, so it is not entirely clear what visual cooperation strategies they may have utilized when working with this presenter (e.g., use of eye gaze).

We suggest that future research could focus on how the setting and audience might affect an interpreter's pausing and overall performance. How much does the interpreter care about how the audience judges the intricacies of his or her interpretation? How much difference is there between interpreters working from a national sign language into English as compared to IS into English?

Though there are limitations to the study, it does serve as an introductory exploration into an area that has hitherto remained uninvestigated. If strategies for interpreting from IS do indeed stem from those that are utilized when interpreting national signed languages, this has implications for training IS interpreters. As the use of IS continues to broaden and the need for IS interpreting grows, an awareness of the strategies utilized in interpreting IS into spoken English will begin to pave the way for the high-quality IS interpretation services that Turner and Napier (2014) predict will become increasingly necessary in the future.

REFERENCES

Adam, R. (2012). Language contact and borrowing. In R. Pfau, M. Steinbach, & B. Woll (Eds.), *Sign language: An international handbook* (pp. 841–861). Berlin, Germany: De Gruyter Mouton.

Allsop, L., Woll, B., & Brauti, J. M. (1995, July). *International sign: The creation of an international deaf community and sign language.* Paper presented at the Sign Language Research 1994 Fourth European Congress on Sign Language Research, Hamburg, Germany.

Angelone, E. (2010). Uncertainty, uncertainty management, and metacognitive problem solving in the translation task. In G. Shreve & E. Angelone (Eds.), *Translation and cognition* (pp. 17–40). Amsterdam, the Netherlands: John Benjamins.

Cokely, D. (1992). *Interpretation: A sociolinguistic model.* Burtonsville, MD: Linstock Press.

Finton, L. (2005). Compression strategies: ASL to English interpreting. *Journal of Interpretation*, 49–64.

Finton, L., & Smith, R. (2004). The natives are restless: Using compression strategies to deliver linguistically appropriate ASL to English interpretation. In E. Maroney (Ed.), *Proceedings of the 15th National Convention Conference of Interpreter Trainers* (pp. 125–143). Fremont, CA: CIT.

Fitzmaurice, S., & Purdy, K. A. (2015). Disfluent pausing effects on listener judgment of an ASL-English interpretation. *Journal of Interpretation*, 24(1). Retrieved from http://digitalcommons.unf.edu/joi/vol24/iss1/3

Gallez, E. (2010, July). *Advantages of a horizontal transcription format for interpreter-mediated exchanges.* Paper presented at the Critical Link Interpreting in the Community Conference, Birmingham, UK.

Geertz, C. (1973). *The interpretation of cultures.* New York, NY: Basic Books.

Grice, H. P. (1975). Logic and conversation. In P. Cole & J. L. Morgan (Eds.), *Speech acts* (pp. 41–58). New York, NY: Academic Press.

Hale, S., & Napier, J. (2013). *Research methods in interpreting: A practical resource*. London, UK: Bloomsbury.

Hema, Z. (2002). Dialogism. *Deaf Worlds, 18*, 62–65.

Hessmann, J., Salmi, E., Turner, G. H., & Wurm, S. (2011). Developing and transmitting a shared interpreting research ethos: EUMASLI—A case study. In B. Nicodemus & L. Swabey (Eds.), *Advances in interpreting research: Inquiry in action* (pp. 177–198). Amsterdam, the Netherlands: John Benjamins.

Hiddinga, A., & Crasborn, O. (2011). Sign languages and globalization. *Language in Society*, 40(4), 483–505.

Jefferson, G. (1989). Preliminary notes on a possible metric which provides for a "standard maximum" silence of approximately one second in conversation. In Bull, P. (Ed.), *Conversation: An interdisciplinary perspective* (pp. 166–196). Clevedon, UK: Multilingual Matters.

Johnston, T., & Crasborn, O. (2006). The use of ELAN annotation software in the creation of signed language corpora. In *Proceedings of the EMELD'06 Workshop on Digital Language Documentation: Tools and standards: The state of the art*. Lansing, MI: EMELD. Retrieved from http://emeld.org/workshop/2006/papers/johnston-crasborn.pdf

Kerswill, P., & Williams, A. (2000). Creating a new town koine: Children and language in Milton Keynes. *Language in Society, 29*(1), 65–115.

Lallgee, M. G., & Cook, M. (1969). An experimental investigation of the function of filled pauses in speech. *Language and Speech*, 12(1), 24–28.

Lang, H. G. (2002). Higher education for deaf students: Research priorities in the new millennium. *Journal of Deaf Studies and Deaf Education, 7*(4), 267–280.

Macías, M. (2006). Probing quality criteria in simultaneous interpreting: The role of silent pauses in fluency. *Interpreting*, 8, 25–43.

Major, G., & Napier, J. (2012). Interpreting and knowledge mediation in the healthcare setting: What do we really mean by "accuracy"? In V. Montalt & M. Shuttleworth (Eds.), *Linguistica antiverpiesa: Translation and knowledge mediation in medical and health settings* (pp. 207–226). Antwerp, Belgium: Artesius University College.

McKee, R., & Napier, J. (2002). Interpreting into international sign pidgin: An analysis. *Journal of Sign Language and Linguistics, 5*(1), 27–54.

Mesch, J. (2010). *Perspectives on the concept and definition of International Sign* (Unpublished report). World Federation of the Deaf. Retrieved from http://www.wfdeaf.org/wp-content/uploads/2012/03/Perspectives-on-the-Concept-and-Definition-of-IS_Mesch-FINAL.pdf

Metzger, M., & Roy, C. (2011). The first three years of a three-year grant: When a research plan doesn't go as planned. In B. Nicodemus & L. Swabey

(Eds.), *Advances in interpreting research: Inquiry in action* (pp. 59–84). Amsterdam, the Netherlands: John Benjamins.

Moody, W. (2002). International sign: A practitioner's perspective. *Journal of Interpretation*, 1–47.

Munday, J. (2012). *Evaluation in translation: Critical points of translator decision making*. London, UK: Routledge.

Napier, J. (2002). *Sign language interpreting: Linguistic coping strategies*. Coleford, UK: Douglas McLean.

Napier, J. (2007). Cooperation in interpreter-mediated monologic talk. *Discourse and Communication*, *1*(4), 407–432.

Napier, J., & Barker, R. (2004). Sign language interpreting: The relationship between metalinguistic awareness and the production of interpreting omissions. *Sign Language Studies, 4*(4), 369–393.

Napier, J., Carmichael, A., & Wiltshire, A. (2008). Look-pause-nod: A linguistic case study of a Deaf professional and interpreters working together. In P. C. Hauser, K. L. Finch, & A. B. Hauser (Eds.), *Deaf professionals and designated interpreters: A new paradigm* (pp. 22–42). Washington, DC: Gallaudet University Press.

Perniss, P. (2015). Collecting and analysing sign language data: Video requirements and use of annotation software. In E. Orfanidou, B. Woll, & G. Morgan (Eds.), *Research methods in sign language studies: A practical guide* (pp. 55–73). London, UK: Wiley Blackwell.

Quinto-Pozos, D. (2007). Outlining considerations for the study of signed language contact. In D. Quinto-Pozos (Ed.), *Sign languages in contact* (pp. 1–30). Washington, DC: Gallaudet University Press.

Rosenstock, R. (2004). *An investigation of international sign: Analyzing structure and comprehension* (Unpublished doctoral dissertation). Washington, DC: Gallaudet University.

Rosenstock, R. (2008). The role of iconicity in international sign. *Sign Language Studies, 8*(2), 131–159.

Roy, C. (1987). Evaluating performance: An interpreted lecture. In M. McIntire (Ed.), *New dimensions in interpreter education: Curriculum and instruction: Proceedings of the Sixth National Convention of the Conference of Interpreter Trainers* (pp. 139–147). Silver Spring, MD: RID.

Stone, C., & Russell, D. (2014). Conference interpreting and interpreting teams. In R. Adam, C. Stone, S. D. Collins, & M. Metzger (Eds.), *Deaf interpreters at work: International insights* (pp. 140–156). Washington, DC: Gallaudet University Press.

Supalla, S., Clark, P., Neumann Solow, S., & Muller de Quadros, R. (2010). Developing protocols for interpreting in multilingual international conferences. In R. L. McKee & J. Davis (Eds.), *Interpreting in multilingual, multicultural contexts*. Washington, DC: Gallaudet University Press.

Suppalla, T., & Webb, R. (1995). The grammar of international sign: A new look at pidgin languages. In K. Emmorey & J. S. Reilly (Eds.), *Language, gesture, and space: International conference on theoretical issues in sign language research* (pp. 333–352). Hillsdale, NJ: Erlbaum.

Turner, G. H., & Napier, J. (2014). On the importance of professional sign language interpreting to political participation. In A. Pabsch (Ed.), *UNCRPD implementation in Europe: A deaf perspective—Article 29: Participation in political and public life* (pp. 54–71). Brussels, Belgium: EUD.

Wadensjö, C. (1998). *Interpreting as interaction.* London, UK: Routledge.

Whynot, L. A. (2015). *Assessing comprehension of international sign lectures: Linguistic and sociolinguistic factors* (Unpublished doctoral dissertation). Macquarie University, Sydney, Australia.

Wit, M. de. (2010a). Sign language interpreting in multilingual international settings. In R. Locker McKee & J. Davis (Eds.), *Interpreting in multilingual, multicultural contexts* (pp. 226–246). Washington, DC: Gallaudet University Press.

Wit, M. de. (2010b). *Linguistic coping strategies from International Sign to English* (Unpublished MSc research report, EUMASLI). Heriot-Watt University, Edinburgh, UK.

Wittenburg, P., Brugman, H., Russel, A., Klassmann, A., & Sloetjes, H. (2006). *ELAN: A professional framework for multimodality research.* Retrieved from http://www.lat-mpi.eu/papers/papers-2006/elan-paper-final.pdf

The Complexities of Interpreting International Conferences: A Case Study

Naomi Sheneman and Pamela F. Collins

The goal of this case study, conducted by a Deaf and a hearing research team, was to investigate preparation and communication strategies that interpreters use to deal with the unique dynamics of working at an international conference. Additionally, this study looked at the logistics of working at a conference and in teams of hearing and Deaf interpreters. This case study specifically analyzes translation and simultaneous interpretation products and interview data that give insight into the processes and experiences of interpreters working at a specific international conference with several sign languages and mixtures.

The data reported here are the result of a research internship project in which Pamela, a hearing interpreter researcher, was asked to create transcriptions from recorded relayed simultaneous interpretations of spoken English based on lectures and a panel discussion given in sign by three African Deaf presenters in the United States at a transnational conference in spring 2012. Naomi, a Deaf interpreter researcher, was asked to create transcriptions translating the source text (signed) to written English. Conference attendees were primarily Americans who wanted to learn how Deaf communities within African nations fight for language recognition and removal of barriers. The presenters used a mixture of their own country's sign language and American Sign Language (ASL). One of the presenters mentioned that he was presenting in a mixture of South African Sign Language (SASL), ASL, and International Sign (IS). The presenter did not explain his understanding of IS in detail. However, from our observations of all three presenters and two of five panelists, they used a mixture of their own sign language and ASL to varying degrees, along with borrowed words from other sign languages. In our view, this mixture of various sign languages in itself constitutes IS. Thus, the presenter was using IS composed of elements from SASL and ASL, not a third language, IS, as he implied. The three Deaf presenters had varying fluency in ASL. We observed mixing between ASL and their own native sign language along with use of specific lexical items from other sign languages such as British Sign Language (BSL). Deaf presenters at this conference had one very specific aim: to communicate information and their own experience using available resources. There were no sign language interpreters fluent in the presenters' native sign languages on site. Thus, the use of IS, considered as a mixture of their own native sign language and the hosting country's sign language, along with loan signs from other sign languages, was the most ideal way to communicate. Given the circumstances, they adjusted IS usage in a way that was best tailored to the conference attendees. As we discuss in the literature review, IS is a system agreed upon by people who meet in a particular context. Our case study confirms this and demonstrates that the use of IS is a continual, dynamic process of finding the best way to effectively relay information; therefore, the interpreters constantly struggle to find a working synergy.

The simultaneous interpretation transcription and the translation products were compared in spring 2013. Through the comparison of products, we discovered a difference of register as well as losses of important content in the simultaneous translation products. Through interviews, we investigated if the team interactions differed for each of the three presentations and the panel discussion or if a standard setup was established prior to the event. Deaf interpreters were part of the interpreting process. For the Deaf presenters who used more ASL, Deaf interpreters were utilized to offer support off the platform to the hearing interpreters interpreting into spoken English. For one Deaf presenter who used more Ugandan Sign Language (USL) and BSL than ASL, more interpreters were needed: a Deaf interpreter translated the presenter's presentation into ASL, another Deaf interpreter standing on the platform mirrored the interpretation for the audience, and hearing interpreters interpreted into spoken English.

The deconstruction of simultaneous interpretation and translation products led to questions about the process. The ontological stance associated with this interpretative approach, according to Glesne (1999), "portrays a world in which reality is socially constructed, complex, and ever changing" (p. 5) and it is important to understand how people perceive the meaning of a particular situation. Semistructured interviews were conducted with the coordinator, a hearing interpreter, and a Deaf interpreter who worked the conference to learn about their experience of working in a conference setting that included a mixture of ASL, different African sign languages, and contacts with other sign languages to spoken English. A summary of interviews conducted with the interpreters who worked at this conference includes their reflections on the whole process. Specifically, we focus on detailing their preparation experiences and interpreting strategies as well as the teaming dynamics of hearing and Deaf interpreters.

We believe that insights gained from analyzing the placement process at this particular event can be applied to experiences of similar groups in other contexts. By learning more about the experiences of these interpreters, we might better tailor interpreter training opportunities to address unknown issues and preparation needs for the interpreters to ensure effective simultaneous interpretation at international conferences and thereby minimize obstacles that may impede team performance. Specific training is needed to best prepare interpreters for this type of simultaneous interpretation setting, which involves demanding cognitive performance (Christoffels & De Groot, 2005; Gile, 1997). For research and attention given to team interpreting (Forestal et al., 2012; Hoza, 2010), a holistic concept of Deaf-hearing teaming is not well understood. Ressler (in Forestal et al., 2012) states that research has just begun on how Deaf and hearing teams prepare together. This study was designed to explore the implications for interpreting at international events. Interpreters have the responsibility of facilitating communication between individuals who do not speak the same language or share the same culture at the moment they are face to face (Pöchhaker, 2004). In recent years, there has been an increase of information exchange opportunities between different nations that use different sign languages (Hiddinga & Crasborn, 2011). The traditional training model of sign language interpreters cannot be clearly applied to interpreting international conferences largely due to additional complexities and demands (de Wit, 2010). It is crucial to promote awareness of unique dynamics of multilingual conferences that exist outside of traditional conference interpreting. By learning more about the experiences of these interpreters, we might better prepare interpreters to address issues and preparation needs and ensure effective simultaneous interpretation at international conferences, thereby minimizing obstacles that impede team performance.

REVIEW OF THE LITERATURE

To date, there has been little attention paid to the implications for interpreting at international events dealing with a mixture of sign languages, International Sign, and cultures (but see de Wit, 2010). An additional layer of complication is working with Deaf interpreters in this type of setting (Stone & Russell, 2013). Deaf interpreting is an emerging profession with limited literature on how Deaf interpreters' involvement may influence the interpreting process.

Competency of Sign Language Interpreters in Multicultural and Multilingual Settings

Traditionally, interpreters are trained in their native spoken and the national sign language (de Wit, 2010). Interpreters rely on their own knowledge of the language and culture in the communities that they work with (Reagan, 2010). That is based on the premise that they are to work between two languages and cultures. Additional skills are needed for the interpreter to be able to work in multicultural and multilingual settings such as the ability to "switch smoothly between more than two languages, without interlanguage interference" (de Wit, 2010, p. 231). The interpreters in these settings deal with two challenges: the different types of audiences and the cognitive demands of managing more than two languages at the same time (Christoffels & De Groot, 2005; Gile, 1997).

The traditional training methodology does not sufficiently prepare interpreters to work in multilingual settings. There are training programs available in Austria and Spain that train interpreters in multilingual interpreting (de Wit, 2010). It is believed that the interpreter's language agility would improve if the interpreter acquires fluency in more than two spoken languages (Seleskovitch, 1978), which was supported by de Wit (2010): "The more languages and cultures the interpreter is familiar with, the more flexibility the interpreter has, and the easier it will be for the interpreter to function" (p. 231). De Wit (2010) observes that native speakers of English struggle to understand nonnative English speakers. She theorizes that nonnative English listeners have the ability to decipher nonnative English speech, especially if the speaker comes from the same language family. Furthermore, having knowledge and capacity in additional languages gives them the skill to decipher what is being uttered (de Wit, 2010). By knowing more than one sign language, an interpreter can expand his or her understanding of a variety of signs used in different situations (de Wit, 2010; Moody, 2008). It is not realistic to expect interpreters to know every language, but it is beneficial to recognize other languages and be comfortable with presenters who are not presenting in the two languages that the interpreter is accustomed to working with (Seleskovitch, 1978). Grammatical features common to most sign languages are part of a contact sign system referred to as International Sign (IS; Moody, 2008); hence it might be beneficial for interpreters to be familiar with more than one sign language. Moody (2008) claims that interpreters who want to be fluent in IS should be fluent in at least two sign languages.

Other than needing knowledge of additional languages and cultures, the interpreter needs to have a variety of flexible interpreting strategies to respond to the unique demands in a multilingual and multicultural setting. Some such strategies are to take a more active role in facilitating the turn-taking process (de Wit, 2010) or to communicate their own needs in order to provide effective interpretations. Reagan (2010) argues that consumers depend on the interpreters' sensitivity and judgement to effectively mediate the interpreting process. De Wit (2010) describes sensitivity as the interpreter's awareness of the consumers' linguistic and cultural needs without receiving direct signals from them while accurately rendering the information. Furthermore, this sensitivity is based on the ability to know whether to follow or avoid traditional interpreting practices in a multilingual interpreting setting (de Wit, 2010).

ASL has been described as a lingua franca (Stone & Russell, 2013). Although ASL has gained dominance in international conferences, "it does not occupy a central position, as it does not serve to connect whole language communities" (Hiddinga & Crasborn, 2011, p. 497). It remains an open question whether the dominance of ASL could affect the interpreter's sensitivity and judgment, identified as a necessary component by Reagan (2010) in the interpreting process, if the conference was held in United States.

With our increasing mobility and mixture of languages, it becomes more likely that speakers' intended messages may be lost in the layers of political, social, and cultural dynamics (Edwards, 2010). Cross-cultural competency is an essential skill for an interpreter who works in a multilingual and multicultural setting (de Wit, 2010). Edwards (2010) claims that bilingualism is not a linguistic identity but a social and psychological one that could influence the interpreting process. The interpreter's cultural identity has influence on the interpretation when the interpreter feels compelled to negotiate the process rather than facilitate the language-based meaning in the communication process (Kent, 2004). A cross-cultural mediation strategy that interpreters in such settings incorporate is to find message equivalence by being aware of what connotations exist for a specific word in different cultures (de Wit, 2010). If interpreters are not aware and sensitive to the fact that the addition of interpreters can potentially create cultural struggles for all parties involved, Kent (2004) cautions that the audience may experience feelings of inequality as a result.

De Wit (2010) identifies three reasons why interpreting in multilingual international settings is even more challenging. First, as mentioned before, interpreters are usually trained in two languages and cultures. Working in international settings exposes interpreters to different levels of fluency in the various languages used at the event, which can range from near native to none in the additional languages. Next, additional complexities impact the interpreter's cognitive processing capacity as more effort is required. Third, the interpreter is tasked with working with nonnative users of both languages that she is trained in.

The role of an interpreter is fluid and determined by the goal of the interpreted event (Pöchhaker, 2004). This causes the interpreter to change his or her set of strategies. However, some of the strategies are due to cultural differences and could be perceived as oppressive (Kent, 2004). Kent (2004) reports interpreters can be criticized for managing cross-cultural differences in their work. Mindess (1999) reports differently. Kent (2004) further suggests that when addressing cultural conflicts that emerge, the interpreters' decisions should be guided by strategies on how to mediate the relationships in an interpreted event. Maintaining a positive open rapport with the consumers can make a multilingual interpreting event a positive one (de Wit, 2010).

Besides having the linguistic and cross-cultural competency, interpreters assigned to work at international events should also possess a considerable amount of professional interpreting experience and knowledge of the subject matter. They need to be prepared for the presentation topic including terminology (Seleskovitch, 1978) and obtain materials from the presenters (de Wit, 2010). If they do not have access to formal training, they should be encouraged to attend international conferences as participants to achieve greater understanding of this type of work environment. Interpreters are advised to slowly work their way into this type of assignment by starting with observations (de Wit, 2010). This recommendation is supported by Aquiline (2006), who states that interpreters need to have sufficient experience interacting with Deaf people at international events before being able to interpret at similar events. Thus interpreters should be encouraged "to attend international conferences and Deaf events" (Aquiline, 2006, p. 146).

Sign Language Interpreting at International Conferences

IS is described as "another linguistic form that is commonly used at international Deaf conferences" (Supalla et al., 2010, p. 212). Provision of IS is not ideal; rather it is a solution because participants are unable to bring interpreters from their own countries (Moody, 2008). Moody (2008) emphasizes that the use of IS does not ensure full access to the information that is being provided. Interpreters working in IS appear to render their interpretations a bit more slowly than those working in a national sign language (McKee & Napier, 2002). Interpreters cannot simply learn a list of IS vocabulary to provide effective communication access (Moody, 2008, p. 27): "Becoming fluent in the IS used in such conferences requires several years of on-going exposure to these gatherings, especially because the signs are always evolving." In addition, in order to achieve fluency, IS interpreters need to be willing and capable of creatively expressing concepts and continue learning during the process (Moody, 2008).

In recent years, there has been a rise in international meetings between Deaf communities that intrigues sign language interpreters and might attract them to accept assignments there even if they are not ready (de Wit, 2010). Quite commonly, sign language interpreters claim that they can interpret in IS although they cannot (Aquiline, 2006). Thus, Aquiline suggests that the World Association of Sign Language Interpreters (WASLI) and the World Federation of the Deaf (WFD) collaboratively create a training curriculum for interpreters, conduct assessment and accreditation of IS-qualified interpreters, create standards of practice for IS interpreters, and maintain a registry of accredited IS interpreters for international conference planners. A task force was created in 2014 by WASLI and WFD to address just these issues (Turner & Napier, 2014). This would certainly be a positive step because, according to Moody (2008), "skilled and experienced IS interpreters can capture up to 90% of the information if they are well prepared" (p. 25). The sole aim of IS interpreters is to provide equivalence through free interpretation. Free interpretation is a process in which the interpreter creates inferences based on what he or she understands from the source language to determine the meaning and make predictions of what the information means to the target audience (McKee & Napier, 2002).

Just recently, attention has been given to successful protocols needed to ensure quality sign language interpreting at conferences (Supalla et al., 2010). International events bring a new layer of challenges to the profession of sign language interpreting (de Wit, 2010). The challenge also lies with the coordination and collaboration of all the interpreters at the events (Supalla et al., 2010). To date, only very few empirical studies have investigated the IS interpretation process and outcome, with the work by McKee and Napier (2002) and Rosenstock (2004, 2008) being the exceptions.

A model protocol for interpreting at an international conference was recommended by a group of United States researchers, Deaf and hearing, and sign language interpreters to ensure success at the 2006 Theoretical Issues in Sign Language Research conference (TISLR9). This document follows the International Association of Conference Interpreters (AIIC) guidelines for consultant interpreters and conference planners (Supalla et al., 2010). Rather than publishing an open call for interpreters, it was recommended that an advisory committee be established to identify and appoint qualified interpreters. This protocol also formulated guidelines to be shared with all presenters on how to work with interpreters as well as plan for preparation meetings. Moody (2008) highly recommends preparing before interpreting to ensure familiarity with the presenters and presentations. Scheduling practices were also included in the protocol. The protocol suggested that interpreters are scheduled efficiently to allow them to have breaks. This recognizes that interpreting dense material at an international conference without proper break times can affect interpreting performance. Coordination suggestions regarding logistics and troubleshooting were included as well (Supalla et al., 2010). Deaf interpreters who are well versed in interpreting in IS should be placed to accommodate those who do not have access to their native sign language (Supalla et al., 2010).

Hearing and Deaf Interpreting Teams

Deaf interpreters have worked within the Deaf community for many years but have only gained official recognition recently (Collins & Walker, 2006). Teamwork between Deaf and hearing interpreters was established via trial-and-error processes as they learned to create an effective system (Forestal et al., 2012). This continues to be a topic of inquiry as evidenced by various studies in the recent years (Bentley-Sassaman, 2010; Nicodemus & Taylor, 2014; Sheneman, 2015; Stone & Russell, 2013, 2014). There were initial questions about whether Deaf interpreters are expressing the same thing as hearing interpreters. The misunderstanding lies with whether hearing interpreters are supposed to produce interpretations for the Deaf interpreters or give feeds to the Deaf interpreters. Both are different functions, and training is required for both (Ressler, 1999). Forestal et al. (2012) claim that Deaf and hearing interpreters have different foci in the interpreting process; hearing interpreters focus on making sure the hearing consumers are following the process whereas Deaf interpreters focus on the Deaf consumers. Ressler's (1999) study found differences in the interpretation products of Deaf and hearing interpreters in pausing, eye gaze, head nods, number of signs per minute, use of fingerspelling, and clarifications. She concludes that Deaf-hearing teams require training to facilitate collaboration (Ressler, 1999).

Exploration of how Deaf-hearing interpreter teams work in multicultural and multilingual settings began only recently. Interpreters must collaboratively work with other interpreters that are responsible for relaying the information because the first interpretation influences what is rendered in the one following it (de Wit, 2010). De Wit (2010) argues that the first interpretation must be grammatically and semantically clear. Deaf interpreters have to deal with high expectations because they are perceived as experts on sign language (Collins & Walker, 2006). However, interpreting between two sign languages requires specialized skills, according to Collins & Walker (2006), that are not available in training opportunities for Deaf interpreters. This is also true for hearing sign language interpreters. There is no formal academic instruction program in IS interpreting (Moody, 2008). In addition, Deaf-hearing teams need training in how to prepare together and how to develop communication strategies for supporting each other during the interpreting process (Stone & Russell, 2013).

In recent years, there has been an increase of Deaf-hearing interpreting teams working at conferences, including the type that occurred at this conference, in which the Deaf interpreter watching the Deaf presenter feeds to the hearing interpreter to interpret in spoken English (Stone & Russell, 2014). Previous studies focused on the ASL or IS products produced by Deaf-hearing interpreter teams (Ressler, 1999; Stone & Russell,

2014). There have been no studies analyzing the spoken (or written) outcome of conference interpretation by Deaf-hearing teams to date.

To ensure effective interpretation in a multilingual setting with a Deaf-hearing team, it is important that both interpreters in the team are fluent in the same sign language, have previously worked with each other in regular interpreting tasks, and are comfortable with processing interpretations via feeds (Stone & Russell, 2013). Trust is instrumental in effective Deaf-hearing teams (Forestal et al., 2012; Stone & Russell, 2013). Furthermore, the teams interviewed in Stone and Russell's 2014 study emphasized the importance of ongoing collaboration between team members. Deaf-hearing interpreter teams are found to incorporate strategies for chunking, accommodations, and affirmations in their interpreting work that involves use of IS (Stone & Russell, 2014). A team in Stone and Russell's 2013 study reported that they had developed an idiosyncratic system of signals to communicate with each other. Therefore, Stone and Russell (2013) recommend that Deaf and hearing interpreters meet beforehand to communicate how to feed to each other and how to work through the interpretations with each other's support. They also recommend that the teams meet the audience members to determine how to best present interpretations.

METHODOLOGY

This case study uses textual analysis and semistructured interviews to address the following research questions:

1. What differences between simultaneous interpretation and translation products of discourse in a multilingual setting can be observed?
2. What issues emerge during interpreting at multilingual international events?
3. What issues emerge while working in Deaf-hearing interpreting teams at multilingual international events?

Data Collection

Three monologic source texts by three Deaf African presenters were recorded. The dialogic source text was a discussion between two of five panelists (both Deaf African females) with two audience members (one white American female and one black male who immigrated to the United States from Africa). Both researchers were given permission to use the simultaneous interpretation and translation products from their research internship for this case study. The first text was a monologic text 19 minutes long, which was a mixture of SASL, ASL, and IS, although SASL seemed to be the dominant language. The hearing interpreter doing simultaneous interpretation utilized the presenter and feeds from the Deaf interpreter and the hearing interpreter next to her for support as needed.

The second text was a monologic text 11 minutes and 50 seconds in length, which appeared to be a mixture of SASL and ASL, with more ASL usage, possibly to best accommodate the American audience. The hearing interpreter was watching the Deaf presenter with the support of a hearing interpreter and a Deaf interpreter. Also, in contrast to the other two lecture situations, the hearing interpreter had a chance to prepare with the Deaf presenter.

The third lecture, 10 minutes and 55 seconds long, was monologic with the Deaf presenter using a mixture of USL, SASL, and ASL, although ASL usage was minimal. The interpretation process had several steps: a Deaf interpreter seated in the front row, supported by another Deaf interpreter seated next to him, translated the presentation into ASL for another Deaf interpreter standing on the platform. The Deaf interpreter on the platform, who was next to the Deaf presenter, was mirroring the final product given to her by the two Deaf seated interpreters. The hearing interpreters were watching the Deaf interpreter on the platform to render interpretation into spoken English although the Deaf interpreter respondent in this study reported that at times hearing interpreters were looking at the Deaf interpreters seated next to them in the front row.

The last text analyzed (8 minutes and 28 seconds) was dialogic, involving six different signers: four females and two males. This text had a mixture of sign languages: SASL, USL, one unidentifiable African nation sign language, and ASL. It appears that ASL was used most in this situation. The hearing interpreters were watching the speakers, with Deaf interpreters offering support as needed. However, the Deaf interpreters were placed too far from hearing interpreters in this room. While the audience members were signing, there was a hearing interpreter who was mirroring in the front. There were numerous interruptions from audience members wanting to say something. Much of the distraction was due to the audio picking up laughter and visual sight lines were not always clear.

Text Comparison

Based on the four source texts, both translations and recorded simultaneous interpretations were produced and, in the case of simultaneous interpretations, transcribed. These two written versions were then compared for textual and stylistic differences in a side-by-side comparison. Three themes emerged: dysfluencies (pauses, truncations, false starts); changes in register; and additions/omissions. Details and examples are given.

Interview Participants and Procedure

Four hearing and four Deaf interpreters worked at the conference in spring 2012. All eight were invited to participate in the interview via e-mail. However, due to scheduling constraints and other hesitations, only three agreed to participate in the study. Each of the three individuals focused on their own work at this specific conference. This case study gathered data from the interpreter coordinator for the conference, one hearing interpreter, and one Deaf interpreter. Upon completion of the informed and video consent paperwork, each interview lasted approximately half an hour and was videotaped. The video data was later transcribed and analyzed for common themes.

Consistent with traditional methods of qualitative inquiry, the primary mode of data collection used interviews to address the second and third research questions (Creswell, 2007). Each interview was semistructured in nature, yet detailed enough to provide exhaustive data about the scheduling of interpreters and the interpreting process. A basic interview protocol was developed, but other questions arose from the participants' responses. The interviews allowed for elaboration and clarification of the questions.

Interviews produced a significant amount of data and were analyzed using a coding process. Creswell (2007) explains that "qualitative researchers often 'learn by doing'" (p. 150). As a frame of reference, Maxwell (2005) offers two primary steps for data analysis. The first step is to code data into organizational categories and subsequently organize them into substantive categories. Once these substantive or organizational categories have been defined, Yin (2003) encourages analysis for themes common to all. In other words, a within-case analysis is completed followed by a cross-case analysis (Creswell, 2007).

Through analysis of interpreter data from semistructured interviews, two emergent themes appear in and across the data: coordination and training. A discussion of each theme follows, accompanied by examples found in the data and discussion of the data found across the data of the study.

RESULTS

Textual Analysis

The simultaneous interpretation transcripts included *false starts* such as "so" and "and" or starting a sentence with a verb, "was," which are unusual features for public-speaking situations. There was evidence of awkward *pauses* in between concepts as the interpreter attempted anticipating the next section of the source text. *Fillers* such as "ummm," "ahh," and "soooo" were used. *Repetitions* occurred such as "within those countries . . . within those provinces" (text 2), indicating the working interpreter or a combination of the team was anticipating a different concept. "These elec . . . to these elected" (text 1) and "training . . . um . . . training of" (text 2) demonstrate the interpreter's online processing. The use of run-on sentences in the text was another issue that emerged when two or more complete sentences were used without clear sentence boundaries (see Tables 1–4).

Pauses and *intrasentential dysfluencies* were the most common such as "described . . . arti . . . that is descry . . . these are four articles" (text 1) and "adap . . . adaptations" (text 2).There were also some instances of the interpreter articulating an utterance and at some point becoming inaudible. This seemed to be caused by exceeding processing capacity.During the third monologic text, the interpreter was struggling with pronouncing African country names. This was a good example of successful teamwork, as the interpreter's teammate took over voicing. In the dialogic text, there were numerous instances of the interpreter pausing, seemingly trying to grasp what was being said.

TABLE 1. *False Start.*

	Simultaneous interpretation product	Translation product
Monologic text 1 (16:46)	Mi casa is an or . . . that actually make sure that the SAPC is following through on providing access to deaf persons.	The ICASA is in charge of making sure that the SABC's television license is in good standing.

TABLE 2. *Intrasentential Dysfluencies.*

Monologic text 2 (1:06)	**Simultaneous interpretation product** We had another person who was partially blind, and then we had someone who was completely blind who was a man, and then we had someone who was . . . was actually in a handicap.	**Translation product** The five prospects included a woman and a man with low vision, a man with legal blindness, a man in a wheelchair.

TABLE 3. *Dropping Formal Register.*

Monologic text 1 (9:36)	**Simultaneous interpretation product** So we can go to government and say, well, you guys are not knowledgeable about these articles?	**Translation product** We requested a meeting with the Department of Social Development. They said they knew nothing.

TABLE 4. *Substitutions and Omissions.*

Monologic text 1 (8:49)	**Simultaneous interpretation product** So here with the CRPD regarding the Congressional Rights of People with Disabilities. These are 4, ah, points that are described . . . arti . . . that is descri . . . these are 4 articles from the CRPD which we go and present about so we actually have to educate Parliament and Congress because they are not aware of the UN articles that have already been ratified.	**Translation product** The United Nations Convention on the Rights of Persons with Disabilities (CRPD) proposes framework that focuses on different areas for individuals with disabilities: accessibility, freedom of expression and opinion, and access to information, education, participation in cultural life, recreation, leisure, and sport
Monologic text 3 (5:25)	**Simultaneous interpretation product** When we look at education once we have sign language in the schools we can spread that as the medium of instruction in schools that are all over the country.	**Translation product** They currently offer sign language classes in college so there is an increased recognition of sign language. This has a positive effect on Deaf education in recognizing that sign language can be the medium of instruction.

There were several occurrences of the interpreter dropping the formal register, possibly due to processing overload.

There were some substitutions and omissions to the target texts that were not present in the source texts, most likely because the interpreters were struggling to understand the information being delivered in a mixture of sign languages. Specific details from the source text were reproduced in the target text with a temporal delay when the interpreter realized that the previous utterance did not include all the points, so a new utterance was created to include the remaining points. There were no aligning translation products for those. Another type of addition was when information was not comprehended so new information was added (possibly a closure strategy). In the context of this essay, the term *deletion* is used to include any information significant enough to change the message that was either substituted or completely omitted.

Interview Results

As mentioned previously, two themes emerged from the analysis of the interview data: coordination and training. Interpreters are expected to work together by interacting with one another to achieve a common goal: communication access.

COORDINATION

Supalla et al. (2010) identify tasks of coordination to include recruitment and scheduling of qualified interpreters as well as communicating interpreting protocols with all parties (p. 202). Coordination of interpreting services at this particular conference includes individual parts that work together as an inseparable whole: preparation, logistics, collaboration, and rapport.

Preparation

The coordinator reported that the Deaf presenters were helpful in getting all the presentations to her, which she passed on to the interpreting team. She also interpreted one presentation and she felt well prepared because she reviewed the PowerPoint and met with the Deaf presenter for more than an hour to discuss the presentation. She also had the advantage of having interpreted for the same presenter before.

The hearing interpreter reported that she walked into the job without any helpful information other than it was an international conference and that the African Deaf experience would be discussed. She was able to meet with one of the presenters for preparation, but only for 10 to 15 minutes. This interpreter did utilize other resources to prepare (i.e., Internet and informal exchanges with other African Deaf people).

The Deaf interpreter expressed that the request for interpreters came on very short notice and consequently preparation materials arrived late. She was able to refer to the PowerPoint presentation slides and notes on her iPad. However, there was not much time to prepare. She wished she had had a chance to meet with the presenters. She believes that meeting with presenters for any conference is the biggest challenge. She felt that she was not allowed to interact with the presenters; she believes it was because the Deaf presenters were interacting with the hearing interpreters and were unaware that Deaf interpreters were also involved in the task.

Logistics

The coordinator expressed that everything was done in a very narrow time frame and there were impromptu actions. Logistics were discussed within the same week of the conference. Budget constraints prevented her from doing more to prepare. Some interpreters from a different agency were doing this job on a pro bono basis and other interpreters were dispatched from her own agency. She deferred to the Deaf interpreters to decide how they were going to be incorporated.

The hearing interpreter felt the interpreting team did not discuss logistics thoroughly as a team to gain clear understanding of what the setup was going to be. This conference was atypical of her previous interpreting experiences. She wished there had been an opportunity to do a planning meeting before the conference.

The Deaf interpreter recalled that the conference was operating on a small budget. The coordination team had to organize interpreters for the event in a very short time span. Thus, the team was formed based on availability of interpreters.

Collaboration

The coordinator felt she was in charge of trying to communicate everything to the team. There were a number of aspects to consider such as positions of the interpreters, identification of active and supporting interpreters, teaming, interpreting process, and break times. In addition, several of the hearing interpreters had a preferred Deaf interpreter as a teammate, which complicated the efforts to collaborate.

The hearing interpreter expressed her disappointment that the preconference did not take place formally. She was surprised that it happened spontaneously in this particular setting. She also wished she had had more support from her team in ensuring appropriate word choice, accuracy of information, and filling in gaps in her interpretation.

The Deaf interpreter stated that ASL was announced as the official language of the conference. The realization that presenters from several different countries and language backgrounds would participate necessitated a coordinator, so someone was assigned. The Deaf interpreter also articulated disappointment that a certain Deaf interpreter who has experience with interpreting international conferences was not included.

Rapport

The coordinator was impressed with the selection of Deaf interpreters and believed that they were more experienced in interpreting international conferences than the hearing interpreters: "I mean, we could not have done it without the Deaf interpreters." The hearing interpreter appreciated working with the assigned coordinator, as she was a respected colleague. The coordinator was the reason why she took the job. She felt that things worked out as well as they did because of the coordinator.

The Deaf interpreter thought the team worked together nicely. Everyone was focused on ensuring sufficient interpreting coverage. She expressed frustration that because IS is not an official sign language, her task was to find a happy medium between the Deaf presenter and the capabilities of the interpreters.

TRAINING

Training on how to deal with multilingual/multicultural settings with IS is needed. The interpreters interviewed for this study expressed the need for additional training on working in Deaf-hearing teams. As indicated by Forestal et al. (2012), there is a difference between working in a hearing-hearing team, being able to switch roles of active and support interpreter, and working with a team involving feeding. The hearing interpreter commented that it would have been instrumental to be trained on how to work in Deaf-hearing teams:

> It seems that there are some people who just do it and it just happens and it seems that it works well for them. The times that I have done

> it, it has worked well for the most part . . . but there's been no formal training. It's kind of like, oh, yeah, this seems right. Let's do this. This seems right. Let's do that. And as far as I know, I don't know of any interpreter training programs, any formalized training in working with Deaf interpreters.

In conclusion, the respondents were asked to share the lessons they learned from this particular experience. The hearing interpreter expressed:

> It was fabulous and fantastic. And it was great to see what our Deaf interpreters do. You know, see their work. Working from an international sign, South African Sign Language and ASL. And the kind of processing that it takes. It was amazing. It was an amazing experience. . . . We wouldn't have been able to do it without the Deaf interpreters, professionalism, the skill—it was amazing. An amazing experience that bonded myself with a particular colleague, you know, that we enjoy working together now on a professional basis. We really do. And I would really love to have more experiences like that.

The Deaf interpreter stated:

> I think it was a wonderful experience. I think it was a breakthrough topic. I think we recognized a lot of our weaknesses. I think we wish there were a lot of things we knew before. I wish that we could have come together as a team to discuss some of our weaknesses. That would have made us stronger. I wish we would have had preparation. You know, and now the fact that it's over, you can't practice that again. . . . That is disappointing. I wish that we could take advantage of the good and bad experiences for the future. And I look forward to continued work in this area.

DISCUSSION

The results of the text comparison show clearly the textual and stylistic differences between a translation and an interpreted product. Translation work offers the luxury of time to interact with the source text before finalizing the target text (Pöchhaker, 2004), whereas simultaneous interpretation requires online processing and carries a heavy cognitive load (Christoffels & De Groot, 2005). Our deconstruction of simultaneous interpretation and translation products offered clues about common shortcomings of interpretations. In this particular case, it is difficult to determine which interpreter produced the target text. There were several interpreters working together to create the interpretations. The Deaf interpreter offered a rationale of why the work products differed: there was no time to understand what specific signs meant and interpreters cannot show they are lost on the platform.

The responsibility does not lie with individual interpreters alone. It takes a team to create effective, accurate interpretations. The responsibility lies with the institution hosting the conference to ensure that interpreters have a clear understanding of logistics and all the tools they need to provide effective interpretations. Interpreters should be given the opportunity to discuss with the whole team how the interpreting sequences should occur rather than being forced to delve in and figure things out as they go. Ample preparation of the information being presented at the conference is essential including interaction with the presenters. The Deaf interpreter respondent stated that having background information helps her "survive" the interpreting process.

The review of the work products and reflections from those who worked the conference brought to light two important elements in ensuring optimal interpreting services: preparation and utilization of Deaf interpreters. Based on our textual analysis, when Deaf interpreters were actively involved in monologic interpreting rather than in supporting roles, deletions were less obvious. The first two monologic texts were similar because there was more ASL used in those texts. The third monologic and the dialogic text were a mix of more sign languages and thus more IS. It appears that as more IS or other sign languages are used, the simultaneous interpretation products become weaker.

It is common for conference interpreters to be held responsible for the success of the interpreting process (International Association of Conference Interpreters, 2013) but this case study has demonstrated that it should not be so. First, being put in a multilingual and multicultural setting without having an optimal toolkit can be cognitively taxing on the interpreter (de Wit, 2010). As Pöchhacker (2004) points out, further research on cognitive processing demands on interpreters is needed. Once some benchmarks are established, steps can be taken to investigate the cognitive demands on interpreters who work in multicultural and multilingual settings. It is recommended that interpreters working with several sign languages analyze the concepts before articulating the target text through the free interpretation strategy (McKee & Napier, 2002). Finally, results reveal that the underlying problem was not the interpreters but the logistics and the interpreting process.

Second, the responsibility lies with all key players involved in international conference events. Effective communication and coordination of logistics and interpretation could remove added layers of complication for interpreters if they were offered the optimal work environment to focus on getting the message across accurately. Timely planning is essential. Interpreting services at this conference was requested at the last minute. The successful implementation of the protocol at the TISLR9 was not followed at this conference, which complicated matters. Sufficient preparation and thorough discussions about logistics could have prevented or reduced substitutions and omissions in the simultaneous interpretation product. We believe this particular event to be representative of how conferences are coordinated across the country. Preparation is even more crucial because of the use of IS. One of the respondents in this case study reported that she had a chance to converse with one of the Deaf presenters for more than an hour to prepare. This was also the time for her to develop a feeling of the Deaf presenter's ASL fluency and determine what the presenter's use of IS would look like and how much ASL would be used in the presentation.

Practical limitations do exist such as availability of interpreters, budget constraints, and effective logistics. In our experience, these oftentimes have to trump qualifications. However, the results of this case study confirm the importance of having a successful protocol like the one for TISLR conferences in place. Rather than only focusing on ensuring the right interpreters are in place and giving preparation materials, there is a need for an advisory committee and ongoing collaboration with all the key players as well as staying current with the AIIC's guidelines to help strengthen the interpreting experience at international events. Coordinators might want to disregard the interpreters' motivation and desire to work at such prestigious events and conduct honest assessments of the interpreters' knowledge, training, and experience to determine the appropriate assignments.

In the first two texts and the dialogic text, there seemed to be no standard in how Deaf-hearing teams worked together (i.e., who was feeding when and how they were maintaining sight lines). It was a "do whatever is necessary in the moment" situation. To counter these ad hoc decisions, coordinators could confirm that the Deaf-hearing teams have previously worked together at conferences and are able to communicate and work together effectively before assigning them to international events (Stone & Russell, 2013), possibly letting the Deaf interpreters select their hearing interpreter team (Stone & Russell, 2014).Advance preparations are needed between Deaf-hearing teams (Stone & Russell, 2014). As evident in the deconstruction of simultaneous interpretation and translation products, inclusion of Deaf interpreters who know several sign languages and IS ensures a more successful simultaneous interpretation product.

Training is clearly necessary for interpreters to be prepared for working in such settings. This type of training is not available in traditional curricula. Our training recommendations are twofold: first, train Deaf-hearing interpreter teams how to effectively work together in conferences, including international events that deal with more than two cultures and two languages. Quality assessment and/or training for Deaf-hearing teams working in conference settings needs to be developed. Second, interpreters should receive training in how to manage interpretations with IS. Ensuring interpreters are trained and competent in IS is an ongoing challenge. "The ideal situation is for all Deaf people to have interpreters in their own languages at every meeting and every conference" (Aquiline, 2006, p. 146). Sadly, this is not possible due to fiscal limitations. IS is a mode of communication that allows multilingual and multicultural attendees at an international conference to convene. It is the attendees and their sign languages that define the IS at a specific event. The Deaf interpreter expressed that interpreting with IS is frustrating because IS usage differs based on the consumers being served. As we have previously stated, IS is a continuous, dynamic process. Interpreters must work with the consumer(s) to find the right fit, and thus interpreters need to be trained to expand their range and be flexible according to the languages exhibited in IS. IS has been recognized to be "systematic and rule-governed" (Supalla & Webb, 1995, p. 347), and thus a training curriculum for interpreters to learn about the structure and rules of using IS could be developed. However, as Supalla and Webb (1995) discovered, morphological and syntactic devices are being derived from the native sign languages to express in IS. Consequently, properties of IS change from one international conference to another depending on participants and location. An additional layer of complexity lies with the fact that IS has a "continuously varying look" (Supalla et al., 2010, p. 212). Based on our observations in this case study, each Deaf African speaker had varying fluency of ASL, and thus their uses of IS at this conference were different, which forced the interpreters to continue to find working synergy. Creating one universal training protocol for interpreting in IS would be challenging as Moody (2008) states, "Because IS is evolving so fast, it would be very difficult to develop a curriculum for instruction" (p. 27).

CONCLUSION

Through this study the researchers intended to offer insight into interpreted work products, coordination of services, and teamwork at an international conference with a mixture of sign languages in Deaf and hearing interpreting teams from perspectives of different members of the whole team. This was a case study of one conference, which is a potential weakness. Another weakness is conducting interviews long after the conference was over; hence, the information was not as fresh in the interpreters' minds. However, the implications from this study are important and require further exploration of interpreting at multilingual and multicultural events from different angles. The approach used in the researchers' internship work presented a new idea for reflective practice as interpreters. This approach could be used as an assessment tool to provide further support to interpreters as they work toward being better prepared for interpreting in such settings. Essentially, by recording their own simultaneous interpretation work, they could reflect on their process and product by doing a translation of the source text to compare with their simultaneous interpretation product. This would lead them to come up with areas they need to work on further and tailor their professional development plans to address those specific areas, better preparing them for future international conference work.

REFERENCES

Aquiline, C. (2006). Interpreting: A global responsibility. In R. L. McKee (Ed.), *Proceedings of the inaugural conference of the World Association of Sign Language Interpreters* (pp. 141–148). Coleford, UK: Douglas McLean.

Bentley-Sassaman, J. (2010). *Experiences and training needs of Deaf and hearing interpreter teams* (Unpublished doctoral dissertation). Walden

University, Naples, FL. Retrieved from http://diinstitute.org/wp-content/uploads/2011/09/Bentley-Sassaman_DoctoralStudy.pdf

Christoffels, I. K., & De Groot, A. M. (2005). Simultaneous interpreting: A cognitive perspective. In J. Kroll & A. M. De Groot (Eds.), *Handbook of bilingualism: A psycholinguistic approach* (pp. 454–479). New York, NY: Oxford University Press.

Collins, J. M., & Walker, J. (2006). What is a Deaf interpreter? In R. L. McKee (Ed.), *Proceedings of the inaugural conference of the World Association of Sign Language Interpreters* (pp. 79–90). Coleford, UK: Douglas McLean.

Creswell, J. W. (2007). *Qualitative inquiry and research design: Choosing among five approaches* (2nd ed.). Thousand Oaks, CA: Sage.

Edwards, J. (2010). The treason of translation? Bingualism, linguistic borders, and identity. In H. Tonkin & M. E. Frank (Eds.), *The translator as mediator of cultures* (pp. 89–105). Amsterdam, the Netherlands: John Benjamins.

Forestal, E., Ressler, C., Morales, M., White, S., Jimenez, A., Fedorov, A., Price, S., & James, S. (2012). *Examples of a Deaf interpreter's work*. Retrieved from http://digitalcommons.unf.edu/asleimats/50

Gile, D. (1997). Conference interpreting as a cognitive management problem. In J. E. Danks, G. M. Shreve, S. B. Fountain, & M. K. McBeath (Eds.), *Cognitive processes in translation and interpreting* (pp. 196–214). Thousand Oaks, CA: Sage.

Glesne, C. (1999). *Becoming qualitative researchers: An introduction* (4th ed.). New York, NY: Longman.

Hiddinga, A., & Crasborn, O. (2011). Sign language and globalization. *Language in Society*, 40, 483–505.

Hoza, J. (2010). *Team interpreting as collaboration and interdependence*. Alexandria, VA: Registry of Interpreters for the Deaf.

International Association of Conference Interpreters. (2013). *Practical guide for professional conference interpreters*. Retreived from http://aiic.net/page/628/practical-guide-for-professional-conference-interpreters/lang/1

Kent, S. J. (2004). "Why bother?" Institutionalization, interpreter decisions, and power relations. In C. Wadensjö, B. E. Dimitrova, & A. Nilsson (Eds.), *The critical link 4: Professionalisation of interpreting in the community: International Conference on Interpreting in Legal, Health, and Social Service Settings* (pp. 193–204). Amsterdam, the Netherlands: John Benjamins.

Maxwell, J. A. (2005). *Qualitative research design: An interactive approach* (2nd ed.). Thousand Oaks, CA: Sage.

McKee, R. L., & Napier, J. (2002). Interpreting into international sign pidgin: An analysis. *Sign Language and Linguistics*, 5(1), 27–54.

Mindess, A. (1999). *Reading between the signs: Intercultural communication for sign language interpreters*. Yarmouth, ME: Intercultural Press.

Moody, B. (2008). The role of International Sign interpreting in today's world. In C. Roy (Ed.), *Diversity and community in the worldwide sign language interpreting profession* (pp. 19–33). Coleford, UK: Douglas McLean.

Nicodemus, B., & Taylor, M. M. (2014). Deaf and hearing interpreting team preparation: A study using conversation analysis. In R. Adam, C. Stone, S. D. Collins, & M. Metzger (Eds.), *Deaf interpreters at work: International insights* (pp. 90–116). Washington, DC: Gallaudet University Press.

Pöchhaker, F. (2004). *Introducing interpreting studies*. London, UK: Routledge.

Reagan, T. (2010). Translating and interpreting sign language: Mediating the DEAF-WORLD. In H. Tonkin & M. E. Frank (Eds.), *The translator as mediator of cultures* (pp. 53–72). Amsterdam, the Netherlands: John Benjamins.

Ressler, C. I. (1999). A comparative analysis of a direct interpretation and an intermediary interpretation in American Sign Language. *Journal of Interpretation*, 71–102.

Rosenstock, R. (2004). *An investigation of International Sign: Analyzing structure and comprehension* (Unpublished doctoral dissertation). Gallaudet University, Washington, DC.

Rosenstock, R. (2008). The role of iconicity in International Sign. *Sign Language Studies, 8*(2), 131–159.

Seleskovitch, D. (1978). *Interpreting for international conferences*. Washington, DC: Pen and Booth.

Sheneman, N. (2015). *Deaf interpreters' ethics: Reflections on training and decision making* (Unpublished manuscript).

Stone, C., & Russell, D. (2013). Interpreting in International Sign: Decisions of Deaf and non-Deaf interpreters. In B. Costello, M. Thumann, & R. Shaw (Eds.), *Proceedings of the Conference of the World Association of Sign Language Interpreters* (pp. 100–118). Coleford, UK: Douglas McLean.

Stone, C., & Russell, D. (2014). Conference interpreting and interpreting teams. In R. Adam, C. Stone, S. Collins, & M. Metzger (Eds.), *Deaf interpreters at work: International insights* (pp. 140–165). Washington, DC: Gallaudet University Press.

Supalla, T., Clark, P., Solow, S. N., & Muller de Quadros, R. (2010). Developing protocols for interpreting in multilingual international conferences. In R. L. McKee & J. E. Davis (Eds.), *Interpreting in multilingual, multicultural contexts* (pp. 197–225). Washington, DC: Gallaudet University Press.

Supalla, T., & Webb, R. (1995). The grammar of International Sign: A new look at pidgin languages. In K. Emmorey & J. Reilly (Eds.), *Language, gesture, and space* (pp. 333–351). Hillsdale, NJ: Lawrence Erlbaum.

Turner, G. H., & Napier, J. (2014). On the importance of professional sign language interpreting to political participation. In A. Pabsch (Ed.), *UNCRPD implementation in Europe: A deaf perspective—Article 29: Participation in political and public life* (pp. 54–71). Brussels, Belgium: EUD.

Wit, M. de. (2010). Sign language interpreting in multilingual international settings. In R. L. McKee & J. E. Davis (Eds.), *Interpreting in multilingual, multicultural contexts* (pp. 226–242). Washington, DC: Gallaudet University Press.

Yin, R. K. (2003). *Case study research: Design and methods* (3rd ed.). Thousand Oaks, CA: Sage.

Complexity of International Sign for Inexperienced Interpreters: Insights From a Deaf IS Instructor

Joni Oyserman

In this chapter, I focus on how inexperienced interpreters view, acquire, and use International Sign (IS). A profile of this group is developed on the basis of empirical observations and insights concerning linguistic aspects, which draws on IS training courses, the author's years of international experience, and interviews with individual interpreters. I discuss some IS teaching methods, highlighting specific effective techniques, and whether IS can be acquired through formalized training. In particular, I examine the notion of an "IS designation" and question which skills ("I know, I can, and I have knowledge of") an interpreter would need to acquire to earn this label. Those skills are explored to provide inexperienced IS interpreters with guidelines for becoming competent in the eyes of the international Deaf community.

Using my own perspective and based on my personal experiences, I follow the definition of IS as a lingua franca, as stated by Rosenstock (2004), and focus on my experiences as an instructor of "inexperienced" interpreters, by which I mean interpreters who have been doing interpreting work in their own national sign language for some time but have no experience with IS. This group of inexperienced interpreters is large, because many interpreters either have not worked abroad or have never had the opportunity to work in an international setting. For this reason, they are proficient in only a single sign language. Being multilingual is a prerequisite for being able to interpret in IS, as noted by Moody (2002) and Mesch (2010). To use the situation in the Netherlands as an example, out of a pool of around 480[1] registered interpreters, there are only a few who can translate to and from IS, as indicated in their profile on the

1. Stichting Register Tolken Gebarentaal, http://www.stichtingrtg.nl

Register Tolken Gebarentaal (RTG, a Dutch register database for certified sign language interpreters only) list and based on my personal experience. Those interpreters have all studied multiple sign languages and have more than two spoken languages at their command. It is remarkable that this group is not expanding with the addition of new interpreters. This seems to be related to the way inexperienced interpreters view IS, and this is what I focus on in this article.

Instinctively, learning IS poses quite a challenge because interpreters think that their skills will never be able to match those of deaf IS users who conduct smooth conversations with each other (Hiddinga & Crasborn, 2011; Green, 2014). That smoothness makes interpreters wonder what strategies, tools, and skills are used by the Deaf and whether they as interpreters can acquire them—and if so, how—in spite of the fact that they are L2 signers and that they have only partially acquired the inherent cultural aspect. McKee and Napier (2002, p. 51) cite this issue:

> IS interpreters clearly need a depth of automatic proficiency in manipulating all these grammatical structures of sign language. They must also possess the linguistic flexibility and imagination to think beyond known lexicon and improvise with productive sign and gesture resources to express meaning in unconventionalized, yet characteristically "Deaf" ways.

In his article, Moody (2002) offers a number of pointers for new interpreters, suggesting that they "make it representational" and "act it out," and that they ask to be accompanied by experienced interpreters. In short, the standard advice for expanding one's knowledge of IS is to travel a lot, make contacts at international Deaf events, and regularly visit Deaf foreigners in one's own country (Mesch, 2010; Moody, 2002). However, the barriers to actually implementing this advice are high. Many interpreters prefer to first attend workshops or training courses in IS prior to going to an European Forum of Sign Language Interpreters (efsli) conference, a World Association of Sign Language Interpreters (WASLI) conference, or some other conference where interpreting is done from the source language to IS and vice versa.

Interpreters often explain that they want to know beforehand what aspects they should study when observing IS situations, so that in this way they can explore IS more methodically. However, Rosenstock (2004, p. 255) remarks, "Clearly, the experience gained from work with IS cannot be replaced by formalized training."

Second, when doing interpreting work, people want to apply layers (grids with length, width, height, and depth coordination points in three dimensions) in their own interpretative space.[2] Prior to one's first experiences, the expectation is often that IS entails more visual thinking, broader insight into information processing and stimulation of creative thinking. One often experiences one's own national sign language in a way that is limiting in certain situations and views IS as something that stretches one's interpreting skills. After their first IS experiences, people indicate that these preconceptions were, in fact, correct, and they still find this striking in spite of their prior expectations.[3]

Here I first discuss my empirical observations and insights concerning linguistic aspects exhibited by inexperienced interpreters, from the perspective of an instructor. I derive these insights from IS training courses and interviews with individual interpreters, and I focus on a few linguistic aspects. Then I discuss teaching methods for IS in further detail, before bringing the article to a close with a short conclusion.

THE IS DESIGNATION

IS designation is a term I use to refer to a sort of standard by which to measure whether or not an interpreter is qualified to work as an IS interpreter. As for the character of IS, during training courses, the inexperienced interpreters constantly ask whether the ultimate framework for IS is actually ASL/English. This is expected because of the ease with which vocabulary items can be borrowed. However, the question can be answered in the negative. In fact, Deaf people outside the United States have long believed that ASL has had an excessively "colonizing" influence (Mesch, 2010).

The Deaf authors of the Amsterdam Manifesto (Rathmann et al., 2000) thought that ASL and BSL could be used as a lingua franca in countries outside of North America and stated that this would be standard practice at conferences by 2010. This notion has since become outdated, and there is continuing evidence for community support for IS. In the first place, the lingua franca most non-American Deaf people know is not ASL, but IS. Secondly, in most countries no courses are offered in BSL or ASL, giving

2. Personal communication with various interpreters in workshops and training sessions.

3. Results from evaluation interviews at the end of workshops attended.

Deaf people no opportunity to acquire these languages. Thirdly, there are practically no ASL interpreters living and working in countries outside of North America. And finally, finances also play a role. A conference budget is usually insufficient to pay for non-domestic interpreters for all conference talks, whereas enough funding is usually available to cover expenses for domestic interpreters.[4] And yet, the status of IS goes unmentioned in the manifesto. Furthermore, the document has not been updated, in spite of the fact that IS has a clearer position now in 2015 and is developing independently of ASL and BSL.

The friction between ASL and IS came to the fore during the 2013 Theoretical Issues in Sign Language Research (TISLR) conference in London. Many of the Deaf attendees were not British or American, and for them it was very difficult or impossible to follow the interpreters because they were interpreting to and from American Sign Language (ASL). The British Sign Language (BSL) interpreters on the other side of the podium offered no alternative, and attendees missed a great deal of information. After discussion, many people publicly asked the Sign Language Linguistics Society (SLLS)[5] at subsequent TISLR conferences to employ only interpreters who were considered IS interpreters by Deaf people themselves.[6] That means that more IS interpreters are needed. Would an IS designation be something an official institution, such as the World Federation of the Deaf (WFD), give for IS work? Or something interpreters gain through experience from the Deaf community? For this reason, interpreters must get away from the idea that ASL is the ultimate framework, so that they can position themselves more broadly if they want to acquire IS. Further exploration of the notion of an IS designation is necessary to expand the pool of interpreters having the right qualifications.

What would this IS designation entail? This question raises issues concerning the layered nature of IS. Who can determine what standard needs to be met to warrant the IS designation at a conference? This is a difficult question because IS interpreters have a great deal of freedom in the way they interpret, which has certain implications for the ability to safeguard the transfer of information (McKee & Napier, 2002).

4. Personal knowledge and communication with several conference organizations since 1998, e.g., the TISLR 2000 conference, for which I was assistant interpreter coordinator.

5. Sign Language Linguistics Society, www.slls.eu.

6. Dawei Ni, question during the floor discussion on the last day of the 2013 TISLR Conference on behalf of Deaf participants.

ASL/English does not play the dominant role when conferences are organized by Deaf people, who are free to determine the language of communication. This is what we saw, for example, with the 2013 Lecturer Sign Language Conference (LESICO) conference for Deaf instructors of sign language in Prague. The attendees at this conference were Deaf and came from all over Europe. The PowerPoint slides during the presentations were in English, but that should not affect IS; one must not switch to ASL or use too many English mouthings because that can facilitate a switch to ASL. The same holds for Deaf Academics[7] conferences.

We also see this problematic use of mouthings in workshops where attendees are not predominantly English speaking. In 2014, I gave a workshop on IS to French-Swiss interpreters, where participants had only a minimal command of English or none at all. Variation occurred in the French-based mouthings. Additionally, two participants came from German-speaking regions, and they used French mouthings half the time and German mouthings the other half. These examples also illustrate the fact that IS has its roots spread across Western Europe (Green, 2014), making it difficult to view it as a single, unified system in the same way as English.

It is important to take inventory of the various IS tools to get a clear idea about the structure of the language. IS can then be further stabilized. This will lead to more coordination and unity concerning interpreting in IS. Rosenstock (2004, p. 255) gives the following advice with implications for interpreter training:

> Knowledge about structures that are helpful to the audience in understanding IS can be passed on to new IS interpreters, leading to an advantage in overall comprehension. The comprehensive description of IS will provide IS trainers with the means to develop a curriculum and better the education for IS interpreters. Ultimately this will lead to improved service for the consumers of IS.

It is customary to develop a curriculum for teaching language skills, but to do this the linguistic structure of the language must first be clear. In this connection, it must be borne in mind that IS does not have the same degree of linguistic structure that national sign languages have. In fact, linguists consider it to be a pidgin (Green, 2014; McKee & Napier,

7. "The Deaf Academics conferences are held in International Sign only to provide direct access to academic discourse instead of through sign language interpreters," http://deafacademics2015.com.

2002; Moody, 2002). However, in her report for the World Federation of the Deaf (WFD), Mesch (2010) described how Deaf users of sign language themselves do not view IS as either a pidgin or a creole, but more as a mixed form. IS does not have a full-fledged grammatical system in the way that other sign languages have. It is a mix of sign languages used in conversations between two or more deaf people from different countries. Specifically, IS uses a mix of lexical items from different sign languages with a mixture of grammatical features from those languages, depending on the interpreter's knowledge of sign languages and the audience (Mesch, 2010). According to Rosenstock: "Although a definition of IS based on structural features might be premature, we can define it by its use as a lingua franca"(2004, pp. 50ff.). In many cases, though, as Rosenstock (2004, p. 51) suggests, a lingua franca does not necessarily have to be a full-fledged language. I agree with her that it is safe to call IS a lingua franca among the international Deaf Community, even though its linguistic status remains unclear.

So, what should a curriculum with modules be based on? An interesting option is to look at the Common European Framework of References for Languages: Learning, Teaching, Assessment (CEFR).[8] The CEFR objectives are described by the Council of Europe as follows:

> The Common European Framework provides a common basis for the elaboration of language syllabuses, curriculum guidelines, examinations, textbooks, etc., across Europe. It describes in a comprehensive way what language learners have to learn to do in order to use a language for communication and what knowledge and skills they have to develop so as to be able to act effectively. The description also covers the cultural context in which language is set. The Framework also defines levels of proficiency which allow learners' progress to be measured at each stage of learning and on a life-long basis.
>
> The Common European Framework is intended to overcome the barriers to communication among professionals working in the field of modern languages arising from the different educational systems in Europe. (Council of Europe, 2001, p. 1)

The CEFR contains descriptors for acquiring language skills: the so-called "can do" statements for sign languages as described in ATERK

8. Retrieved from http://www.coe.int/t/dg4/linguistic/Source/Framework_EN.pdf

(2013). The overviews of the "can do" statements give step-by-step descriptions of what a language learner is supposed to have mastered after having undergone language training for a certain period of time. Provided this framework is selected, the three-pronged regime of "I know, I can, and I have knowledge of" can be nicely applied to IS training for interpreters. In my view, if a number of "can do" statements can be assembled, independently of the CEFR skill levels A1 through C2 (which only apply to national languages), one will come closer to achieving homogeneity in IS. Interpreters can also gain insight into the skills required by IS and to reflect upon the question: Am I well suited for IS work? If so, what skills have I already developed to a considerable extent? What skills do I still need to develop? To be eligible for the IS designation, there are a number of necessary skills that inexperienced interpreters first need to further develop.

SKILLS: WHAT THE INTERPRETERS THINK

An interesting question is what skills need to be acquired to be able to interpret to and from IS. No clear description exists of what one should know and be able to do, and what knowledge one needs to have in such a way that items can be checked off a list one by one, or that a certificate can be earned by taking a test in a simulated situation. A citation from McKee, et al. (2014, p. 1) also makes this clear:

> Most learners of sign language aim to make use of their language skills to interact with members of the local target community, thus giving sign language teachers a responsibility for preparing learners not only with language competencies but also with the pragmatic and cultural knowledge needed to engage with Deaf sign language users in a visual modality, in real contexts.

In interviews with a few inexperienced interpreters (with zero to minimal experience with IS, but with a few years of experience with national sign languages) I posed a number of questions, two of which I elaborate on here. Question 1: "Suppose that you had the choice of taking a seven-week course, a two-day workshop, or a training program in IS. What would you choose?" One of the inexperienced interpreters (who first came into contact with IS in 2011) answered that one cannot learn IS through formal instruction. The only optimal way to learn IS is by travelling a lot and attending international events, as also advised by Moody (2002). Another interpreter, who first came into contact with IS in 2008, indicates that she is open to the idea of further training. What she would most like is to take a workshop lasting several days together with Deaf people from Western countries as well as from Asia and Africa. In her view, in that way she could learn firsthand what IS means for Deaf people from different continents. Then she could also be at her ease to ask questions and learn before she attends international events and gains experience for actual interpreting work later. Her view is that the IS interpreter designation should not be used indiscriminately. In spite of the fact that she has been familiar with IS since 2008, she absolutely does not label herself an IS interpreter because she thinks that one must first learn what IS entails. In her mind, this requires guidelines, and hence actual training.

As regards question 2, "Is being multilingual a requirement to being a good IS interpreter?" the answer was affirmative. The reasoning is that an interpreter can draw on a much richer vocabulary and grammatical differences. Furthermore, a multilingual interpreter is more accustomed to bridging language barriers because he or she is more adept at switching, has a higher standard of thinking creatively, and can create signs on the fly. Being multilingual stimulates creativity and hence also visual thinking and learning. Here I discuss three components (visual thinking, use of space, influence of oral components), although there certainly are more.

VISUAL THINKING

At the core of IS for Deaf signers is the high degree of visual (pictorial) thinking that is used. The cause of this lies in the fact they employ the visual channel—the eyes—to a greater extent than is customary (Watanabe, Matsuda, Nishioka, & Namatame, 2011; Emmorey & McCullough, 2009).

Through the eyes, information is taken in, processed, and set aside, all at lightning speed. A Deaf person—L1 or L2, it does not make much of a difference—can use this to analyze structures in his or her own sign language. For this reason, the Deaf person needs to have at least near-native command of the first sign language in all grammatical aspects. The same holds for prosody, both in production and in interaction. The analytical process allows an increasingly accurate use of the abovementioned combinations.

How powerful the resulting combinations are depends heavily on the interaction between conversation participants. It can happen that one signer assumes a more dominant role than the other, who mainly copies the signs in the input. That may sound like a complicated process, but IS conversation participants have often settled on what tools (lexicon, use of space, use of hand shape, nonmanual structures, prosody, etc.) should be used for a smooth conversation within 10 or 15 min.

The fact that the conversation proceeds so smoothly seems to point to the presence of an internal trigger. A sign language user can turn this trigger on and off, so to speak, when making contact with a Deaf person from another country. Not knowing the other person's lexicon does not play an all-important role here. A sign can be copied back and be communicatively confirmed, such as by nodding one's head in confirmation and making the sign back. Signs can also be agreed upon that are not derived from the national sign languages of the conversation participants, which requires a certain amount of visual creativity. In this way a lexical database is built up over the course of the conversation. In this case, students of IS would have to understand and practice cross-signing as a first step before moving into the more formal setting of interpreting IS at conferences, which is largely unilateral in nature (i.e., interpreting a presentation).

Another important factor is that IS conversation partners generally produce a great number of highly iconic signs. As Rosenstock (2008, p. 154) states, "iconicity plays an important role on all levels of this communication system." Schermer and Pfau (2008, p. 51) describe an iconic sign as "a sign with a direct relation between the form and meaning and has multiple gradations from highly iconic to arbitrary." These signs are conceptually visual and are easy to understand and adopt. Signers who commit themselves to IS for a longer period can use this to employ abstract signs with increasing frequency. These signs need not be highly iconic to be interpretable.

Going back to the standard of interpreters: In the Netherlands, for example, on average, interpreters achieve a final level of B2 (Nederlandse Gebarentaal Functional Assessment [NFA]; Van den Broek-Laven, Boers-Visker, & van den Bogaerde, 2014), which is not near native, after a four-year degree program in interpreting. After that, it is the new interpreter's task to gain further mastery in the work field, meaning that it takes additional time to understand or analyze the linguistic and cultural structures of their own sign language. The adjustment processes during sign language conversations that results from this is a longer process. Here the assumption is that an interpreter's first language is a spoken language. So, the thinking process involved in translating words into sign language will proceed sequentially, whereas a Deaf person uses a simultaneous thinking process in which the transition to visual images is made quickly. If an interpreter knows another sign language or knows foreign Deaf people, this will occur more quickly, but this is often not the case.

For these reasons, interpreters need to be thoroughly trained in the visual thought process. First, the auditory channel must be minimized to free up space for the visual channel. Visual "layers" can be constructed in this way so that images are created during a story and conversation, which can be easily translated into IS. Second, the interpreter should have directed practice in mentioning details. Interpreters often appear to only see the main narrative line and to neglect details, a phenomenon that can in part be traced to the importance of summarizing while interpreting. Third, it is important to not become dependent on mouthings (often English), while at the same time one must avoid reverting to pantomime. Fourth, it is important that interpreters do not "lock up" their body but have the courage to employ role-shifting, body lean, and nonmanual markers. Fifth, work must be done to expand the use of facial expressions. Sixth, the way one consciously positions the direction of one's glance determines either completely or partially how the information is seen. Visual thinking is inextricably bound to the space in which signed sentences are placed and produced. Signed sentences are produced or placed in this space. Here I discuss how the space is organized to increase the density of information in IS as much as possible and thus gain time in translation.

USE OF SPACE

McKee and Napier (2002) state that IS interpreters tend to employ a larger space and consequently use larger sign movements as compared with interpreters of national sign languages. The cause of this is assumed to derive from the fact that IS interpreters often work with larger audiences. In contrast, interpreters working in national languages interpret with less "volume" because they are interpreting for a smaller audience. The aforementioned authors suggest that the farther away that the audience is sitting, the greater the volume.

They also argue that the increased volume goes hand in hand with the longer and more deliberate articulation of signs. This is done to make the translation as clear as possible for the entire audience. In contrast to these authors, Rosenstock (2004) described how an ASL sign is produced with more volume than its IS counterpart. She uses the READ sign as an example. This is an interesting fact. However, this research was conducted in a setting where the majority of the audience used ASL. It is still a question as to whether the size of the audience influences the volume, the speed of articulation of a sign, and the space and whether IS is always signed using greater volumes.

I believe that the volume of the signing space is certainly dependent on the size of the room. This can be compared with screaming: to make yourself understood, your voice needs to carry farther. Over the years, I myself have given various presentations both in various sign languages and in IS for different types of audiences. I use the size of the room and the audience to determine how large my signing space should be without losing speed. This is a natural technique for communicating your message as efficiently and effectively as possible in any sign language. Looking exclusively at my IS presentations, I can say with certainty that IS uses an entire range of volumes. In other words, I would not be doing either my message or myself justice by slowing down the speed of my presentation to always articulate at a large volume. In this respect, interpreters actually gain translation time by focusing on making the most efficient use possible of the signing space, and this entails making greater use of one's creative capacity to make productive signs.

An important tool for making constructive use of the signing space is "wiping clear." There are a number of conventional signs for doing this: (a) forming a B-hand with both hands making a sideward motion, (b) clasping one's hands together as a rest position, (c) letting one's arms drop loosely after the end of a sentence, and (d) putting one hand atop the other with the palms resting on the stomach, with the fingers of the left hand pointing right and those of the right hand pointing left. By wiping clear, one lets the audience see how the information in the space is being structured and used.

The density of the information being interpreted is significant. In my personal observation experiences I have seen that the greater the information density, the higher the quality and the more closely the interpreter stays to the presenter in terms of the original message. The biggest bottleneck in this respect is the frequent duplication of signs. This implies that both hand articulators produce exactly the same sign symmetrically with the same meaning. In other words, a given sign is simultaneously performed using both hands. This can be seen, for example, in the hand-doubling of the THANK-YOU sign as described by McKee & Napier (2002, p. 34). The interpreters need to use hand articulators independently from each other to attain higher information output. For the interpreters, this habit actually impedes high information density and leads to a strong tendency to summarize because of the many details that get omitted. The audience notices quickly that the information is being summarized and has the constant impression that information is being missed.

Another aspect is that inexperienced interpreters often have difficulty using the signing space efficiently. They particularly experience problems with the organization of the grid space. The left–right and up–down organization does not get used in an optimal way, leading to a loss of information due to the flat way in which the space is used, as a horizontal plane. As a consequence, there is often a tendency to produce a lot of information in a particular location in the space with the arms stretched out and hands mirroring each other, which locks the interpreter up, so to speak. In this way, it takes too long to bring one's hands back to the body, slowing down the speed of translation. Morphologically, this production of signs in a flat space proceeds sequentially, slowing down the interpretation.

Another problem is that interpreters sign information with one of their hands while the other hand hangs loosely. The information to the right and left in the way the signing space is consciously arranged needs to be kept distinct. As a matter of fact, it needs to be organized in layers and sections to avoid the overlapping of signs and so that each uttering is clearly and neatly brought to an end. In national sign languages, not much attention needs to be paid to separating signed utterances, and there is more overlapping in transition between utterances without any loss of meaning. In short, to achieve the highest possible information density in the signing space, interpreters need to learn that each hand has its own "information browser" that can operate independently. One way to achieve this is by training one's brain by taking piano, guitar, saxophone, or drum lessons. This is because when you play an instrument you learn to make your hands function independently of each other in order to achieve an informational whole. Inexperienced interpreters who have used this technique were asked about their experiences, and they confirmed that it is helpful. Deaf IS interpreters also function as model signers, much as L1 signers. In this context it is interesting to note that after studying various sources they use a smaller signing space compared to hearing IS interpreters.

THE INFLUENCE OF ORAL COMPONENTS

From a historical standpoint, IS signs have their roots in Western sign language families. One influential factor in this regard is the fact the WFD[9] is based in Helsinki (formerly in Rome). All WFD conference presentations, reports, and meeting documents are produced in English. For this reason, English is the preferred language at most meetings with respect to the spoken components. If a Deaf person prefers not to use a spoken component, the reason is practically always that he/she is not proficient in English. In that case, the Deaf person will sign with his mouth closed and will make more intensive use of his shoulders, upper body, and facial expressions. Inexperienced interpreters (especially those from countries where spoken components are dominant in sign languages) have a lot of trouble in this respect. The effect is that they are not able to include as much information, leading them to produce incomplete translations and making them feel insecure about their own skills. As an instructor, I have shown a few video clips in which Deaf people sign with their mouths closed and others in which more spoken components are used. In the latter case, the interpreters translate with much more confidence and efficiency and with greater information density. This suggests that interpreters are strongly predisposed to English with respect to spoken components.

It is also important to realize that interpreting work in 2015 is what it was in 2000 (or earlier). In recent decades English has strongly taken root globally due to the rise of the Internet and other technologies. This also has an impact on interpreters who are hearing and who receive a great deal of English through the educational system. We see this tendency with Deaf people as well: All around the world, Deaf people are becoming increasingly better educated and they are exposed to increasing amounts of English through the Internet, international exchanges through chat programs, contacts and camps offered by the European Union of

9. The World Federation of the Deaf is an international, nongovernmental central organization of national associations of Deaf people, with a current membership of associations in 133 countries worldwide. Retrieved from http://wfdeaf.org/whoarewe/mission-and-objectives.

Deaf Youth (EUDY)[10] and Frontrunners,[11] subtitled films, and so forth. It is especially this well-educated segment of the Deaf community that is important for IS interpreters. This segment is much more accustomed to going to conferences and also acquires more English to be able to participate during them.

But the less educated members of the Deaf community (i.e., those without a university education) are also starting to use more English through chat programs and international forums concerning topics related to deafness. They enjoy watching videos on YouTube and consider Skype and Oovoo as a solution for coming into contact with Deaf people from other countries without having to type and read in English when they are not fluent enough in that language. Young people are particularly active because they find the news, information, and clips by stand-up comics from other countries interesting. These young people also boost each other by referring one another to international videos at gatherings and because they think it is cool to be the first one to take notice of a certain video and to use all sorts of English words. Being able to understand these videos and words upgrades their status within the group.[12] They do their best to acquire a basic knowledge of English, especially in terms of lexical items. This actually contrasts with what is claimed by Hiddinga and Crasborn (2011): that IS interpreters play an important role in bridging the linguistic channels between various Deaf people from different countries, precisely because these Deaf people are so reliant on their national sign languages. IS with English mouthings is probably primarily accessible only for the better educated because they are the one who gain access to English.

This suggests that the work situation of IS interpreters will probably change within the next decade or two due to globalization of sign language users. I suspect the broad character of IS will disappear because more conventions will be established in IS usage, leading IS, as a lingua franca, to become more conventionalized. It is nice to philosophize that

10. European Union of the Deaf Youth is an organization of and for young Deaf people in the European Union between the ages of 18 and 30; http://eudy.info.

11. Frontrunners is an international educational program for young deaf people. During the past 10 years they have educated more than 110 Frontrunners; http://frontrunners.dk.

12. Personal communication from M. de Geus, a counselor for Deaf young people in mainstream education.

IS will continue to acquire lexical and grammatical features in tandem with fully fledged, officially recognized sign languages.

TEACHING METHODS

Because English is still not as widely known among Deaf people as among the hearing, in some IS situations—certainly when non-Western Deaf people are involved—an interpreter will not be able to fall back on either the spoken component, his own national sign language, or finger-spelling. For these situations it is important that interpreters be extensively trained to develop their creative capacity. This increases one's ability to think visually so that a way can be created more quickly to translate a given concept from word into image and vice versa, and to "keep heading forward" during the process of interpreting. Otherwise the interpreter falls too far behind in the translation and becomes too encumbered to interpret smoothly. This training can be done using a variety of methods. Here are seven examples of effective techniques I use during IS workshops for inexperienced interpreters:

1. Watching an animated film (e.g., *Simon's Cat*) without audio and retelling the story afterward.
2. Observing in pairs what the instructor signs and discussing with each other which iconic signs could be recognized and which signs were more difficult to recognize.
3. Consulting an online dictionary[13] of IS, exploring which signs are similar and dissimilar to those in their national sign language, and practicing this vocabulary.
4. The following arrangement is used for group exercises: one interpreter sits right behind a row of four or five interpreters, who are either sitting or standing, and reads a simple text aloud at a leisurely pace. (Various collections of texts are available arranged in increasing difficulty in their national written language and in English.) The row of interpreters listens and translates into IS to the best of their ability, and this is recorded on video. The recordings are viewed, analyzed, and discussed together in the group. This exercise is then repeated twice.
5. In groups of three, the interpreters use a laptop together to

13. http://www.handspeak.com/world/isl/

watch an IS video by Deaf people (enough of these can be found online, such as on the ProSign, EUD, LESICO, WFD, Eurovision, and TedEx websites). The videos are selected beforehand by the instructor, and progress from short, simple fragments to longer, more complex films. First we discuss the IS film together in terms of context and on the conceptual level. Then one of the participants in the group proceeds to translate what is signed into English or his own national language, while the other two people listen to see whether it is being translated correctly. At the same time, one of the others translates it back into IS. In this way, one can compare on the spot the interpreter's own IS with that in the film. The instructor provides feedback.

6. The instructor discusses a number of IS films for the whole group and explains what the context is. By playing the film in slow motion the interpreters can easily parse the signed utterances, analyze the way the space is organized, and recognize the lexical items.
7. With respect to using one's shoulders, body shift, and body lean, the instructor shows a number of examples of how these can be executed simultaneously with facial expressions.

These exercises have a striking effect. The interpreters' utterances at the beginning of the course are different in character from those they produce at the end. I watch the interpreters grow in their ability and courage to use iconic signs and make more conscious use of the space. The result yielded by the exercises on visual thinking is that the interpreters recognize more quickly and easily how they can work visually. The teaching methods listed here make the interpreters work on their skills in a very active way, whether alone or in a group. Looking back at the recordings helps identify bottlenecks and areas for improvement.

CONCLUSION

The article has discussed several IS skills, namely (1) visual thinking, (2) use of space, and (3) nonmanual features. To earn the IS designation, inexperienced interpreters first need to continue developing or refining these skills. In addition, being multilingual in spoken languages and sign languages is a requirement for having access to a larger stock of vocabulary items, intertwined with a broader knowledge of the grammatical aspects. The acquisition of IS skills can take a number of different paths: (1) traveling a lot, making contacts at international events with Deaf people, and regularly visiting foreign Deaf people in one's own country, (2) taking workshops or courses offered in IS, and (3) learning a second sign language. There is a great need for a pool of interpreters, especially for Deaf people with hands-on experience as L1 signers and instructors. When there is a broad and diverse pool, the group of inexperienced interpreters will be less wary of being designated as IS interpreters without knowing, perceiving, or being able to ascertain whether they are sufficiently skilled in IS in the eyes of the international Deaf community. Only then will we see a significant influx of new, good IS interpreters.

REFERENCES

Allsop, L., Woll, B., & Brauti, J. M. (1994). International Sign: The creation of an international deaf community and sign language. In H. Bos & T. Schermer (Eds.), *Sign Language Research 1994: Proceedings of the Fourth European Congress on Sign Language Research* (pp. 171–188). Hamburg, Germany: Signum Press.

ATERK. (2013). *Europees Referentie Kader voor talen: Gebarentalen.* Hogeschool Utrecht. Retrieved from https://www.academia.edu/3748474/ATERK_NGT_2013_Europees_Referentiekader_voor_Talen_Gebarentalen_CEFR_CEFR_for_Sign_Languages_Dutch_version

British Deaf Association. (1975). *Gestuno: International sign language of the Deaf.* Carlisle, UK: BDA.

Council of Europe. (2001). *Common European framework of reference for languages: Learning, teaching, assessment (CEFR).* Retrieved from http://www.coe.int/t/dg4/linguistic/Source/Framework_EN.pdf

Emmorey, K., & McCullough, S. (2009). The bimodal bilingual brain: Effects of sign language experience. *Brain and Language, 109*, 124–132.

Green, E. M. (2014). Building the tower of Babel: International Sign, linguistic commensuration, and moral orientation. *Language in Society, 43*(4), 445–465.

Hiddinga, A., & Crasborn, O. (2011). Signed languages and globalization. *Language in Society, 40*(4), 483–505.

Lesico. (2013). *International Conference of Sign Language Teachers.* Retrieved from http://www.lesico-conference.com.

McKee, D., Rosen, R. S., & McKee, R. (2014). *Teaching and learning signed languages: International perspectives and practices.* Basingstoke, UK: Palgrave MacMillan.

McKee, R., & Napier, J. (2002). Interpreting into International Sign pidgin: An analysis. *Sign Language and Linguistics, 5*(1), 27–54.

Mesch, J. (2010). *Perspectives on the concept and definition of International Sign* (Unpublished report, World Federation of the Deaf). Retrieved from http://www.wfdeaf.org/wp-content/uploads/2012/03/Perspectives-on-the-Concept-and-Definition-of-IS_Mesch-FINAL.pdf

Moody, B. (2002). International Sign: A practitioner's perspective. *Journal of Interpretation,* 1–47.

Oyserman, J. (2003). International Sign. *Interpres, 6,* 13.

Oyserman, J., & De Geus, M. D. (2014). *International Sign for Sign Language Interpreters: Workshop A: Basic reader*. Amsterdam, the Netherlands: Signhands.

Rathmann, C., Mathur, G., & Boudreault, P. (2000). *Amsterdam manifesto.* Retrieved from http://www.deafacademics.org/conferences/amsterdam_manifesto.pdf

Rosenstock, R. (2004). *An investigation of International Sign: Analyzing structure and comprehension* (Unpublished doctoral dissertation). Gallaudet University, Washington, DC.

Rosenstock, R. (2008). The role of iconicity in International Sign. *Sign Language Studies*, *8*(2), 131–159.

Schermer, T., & Pfau, R. (2008). *Psycholinguïstiek*. In A. Baker, B. van den Bogaerde, R. Pfau, & T. Schermer (Eds.), *Gebarentaalwetenschap: Een Inleiding* (pp. 43–62). Deventer, the Netherlands: Van Tricht.

Van den Broek-Laven, A., Boers-Visker, E., & van den Bogaerde, B. (2014). Determining aspects of text difficulty for the Sign Language of the Netherlands (NGT) Functional Assessment instrument. *Papers in Language Testing and Assessment, 3*(2), 53–75.

Watanabe, K., Matsuda, T., Nishioka, T., & Namatame, M. (2011). Eye gaze during observation of static faces in deaf people. *PLOS ONE, 6*(2). Retrieved from http://journals.plos.org/plosone/article?id=10.1371/journal.pone.0016919.

Webb, R., & Supalla, T. (1994). Negation in International Sign. In I. Ahlen, B. Bergman, M. Brennan, & M. Durham (Eds.), *Perspectives on sign language structure: Papers from the Fifth International Symposium on Sign Language Research* (pp. 173–186). Durham, UK: ISLA.

Index

Figures and tables are indicated by "f" and "t" following the page numbers.